IPv6 Clearly Explained

IPv6 Clearly Explained

Pete Loshin

Morgan Kaufmann Publishers, Inc.
San Francisco, California

Cover photo © by Archive Photos/Image Bank.

This book is printed on acid-free paper. ∞

Morgan Kaufmann Publishers, Inc.
340 Pine Street
San Francisco, CA 94104

Library of Congress Cataloging-in-Publication Data
Loshin, Peter
    IPv6 clearly explained / Peter Loshin.
      p. cm.
    Includes bibliographical references and index.
    ISBN 0-12-455838-0 (alk. paper)
    1. TCP/IP (Computer network protocol) I. Title.
TK5105.585.L66 1999
004.6'2--dc21
                                  98-38741
                                    CIP

Printed in the United States of America
98 99 00 01 02 IP 9 8 7 6 5 4 3 2 1

Contents

Acknowledgments

It takes a lot of great people to put together a book like this, even though it doesn't always seem that way when the writer is up past midnight, again, trying to finish a manuscript before a deadline (or not too long after the deadline has passed). And this book is no exception. At the top of the list are Ken Morton at AP Professional, whose vision and foresight helped make it possible. Thanks also go to Jennifer Vilaga and Samantha Libby, both editorial assistants at AP Professional, whose attention to detail helped ease the writing process. Special thanks, as usual, to the rest of the APP production team who helped make this book look and read as well as it does, in particular senior production editor Linda Hamilton-Korey.

Of particular importance are the people who read my early manuscripts and pointed out the technical errors, flaws, and infelicitous turns of phrase. My gratitude goes out particularly to Bob Fink, of the Lawrence Berkeley Lab, and to David C. Lee, Ph.D., Visiting

Assistant Professor at Virginia Tech. Other early readers include Jason Scott McDaniel, Eduardo Tejedor Sanchez, Richard Nicholls, Francis Silva, Gianluca Capitani, John Kristoff, Andri Yoga, Girish Chiruvolu, and Brian Haberman.

As always, finally but most importantly I must thank my family: Lisa Loshin and Jacy Moses Loshin, who gave me good reasons to finish this book.

Introduction

Do you remember record albums? How about eight-track tapes? Betamax videotapes? Old-timers who remember the Victrola may also remember not only hand cranking the record player but also that the original Edison records were recorded on wax-covered cylinders. Old-timers in the computer business can recite a long list of technologies that were once standards and have now been bypassed: floppy diskettes that were actually floppy and as big as eight inches wide; mag tape; paper tape; and even Hollerith cards (those so-called "IBM cards" that you weren't supposed to fold, spindle, or mutilate). Anyone who has ever been through a major upgrade of a technology knows it can be a difficult process—not just trying to choose the right technology upgrade path but also making provision for the transition.

A very important technology upgrade is coming. This one may affect as many as 100 million users: anyone who uses the Internet.

Although many people think of the Internet as a relatively new technology, its underlying standards and specifications were largely set by the late 1970s and early 1980s. The Internet Protocol, or IP, is the foundation of TCP/IP, the suite of networking protocols that define the Internet (and all intranets and extranets, as well). As the size of the edifice built on top of IP increases, the foundation is developing serious cracks and will not be able to support continued growth for very much longer. An upgrade to the current version of IP (version 4) has been largely defined and specified, and vendors and implementers are in the process of rolling it out.

IP version 6, or IPv6 for short, is probably the most significant network upgrade in the history of technology. It will require every company in the world selling TCP/IP-enabled software, hardware, or services to evaluate the need to upgrade or modify their products; it will require the users or administrators of virtually every networked computer system on the planet to consider how best to migrate to the next generation of internetworking protocol.

The effort to come up with an acceptable alternative to the current version of IP is no less than a race against time: If IP network addresses could be assigned with perfect efficiency, there is still an absolute maximum of slightly more than four billion hosts possible. IPv4 uses a less efficient, hierarchical addressing scheme that allows much more efficient routing while at the same restricting the gross number of networks and hosts that can be connected to the global Internet. Anyone with any interest in the continued viability and growth of the Internet or TCP/IP networking needs to read this book to better understand how IP works, why IPv6 will work better, and what they must do to be prepared for the change.

Building on discussion of how the current versions of IP and other protocols in the TCP/IP suite work and behave, in the first part I discuss the problems that arose over the past 20 years, as well as the various solutions proposed to solve them. Also included are an introduction of the new features, functions, and operation of the new IPv6 and related protocols like the Internet Control Message Protocol (ICMP), Domain Name System (DNS), and routing protocols.

The second part delves in detail into the workings of the new protocols, with particular attention to handling IPv6 addresses, IPv6 extensions, IPv6 support for authentication and security, IPv6 anycast and multicast support, and support for mobile hosts in IPv6. Also included here are discussions of IPv6 routing issues and solutions, as well as other protocols, like DNS and ICMP, that will change to accommodate the new version of IP.

The final part examines the issues of deployment. Discussed here are strategies that network product vendors are taking with their products as well as strategies for transition appropriate for individual users and smaller organizations as well as for larger organizations with correspondingly larger networks. Options include tunneling approaches, dual-stack approaches, and development of an Internet backbone structure supporting IPv6.

Rounding out the book are appendices that include a list of relevant RFCs as well as the complete text of several of the most important and interesting IPv6 RFCs, and an index.

Who Should Read This Book?

If your work involves the Internet or any other TCP/IP network, you should read this book. Whether you build networks, support networks, manage or administer networks, manage a business that uses TCP/IP networks, or work for an organization that sells products or services that use TCP/IP networks, you must prepare yourself for what comes next. This book will help you prepare for the change that is almost upon us.

What Is in This Book

This book is organized in three parts. Part One provides a basic introduction not only to IPv6 itself, but also to IP version 4 and related protocols that need updating. After reading Part One, not only will you get an introduction to the IPv6 protocol itself, but you will also understand why the IPv6 update is necessary, how IPv6 evolved over several years to take its current shape, and what related protocols will be affected.

Part Two delves in detail into the workings of the new protocols, with particular attention to how IPv6 works: IPv6 addresses, IPv6 extensions, IPv6 support for authentication and security, IPv6 any-cast and multicast support, and support for mobile hosts in IPv6. Also included here are discussions of IPv6 routing issues and solutions, as well as other protocols, like DNS and ICMP, that will change to accommodate the new version of IP.

Building on the first two parts of the book, Part Three examines the issues of transition and deployment. Discussed here are strategies that network product vendors are taking with their products as well as strategies for transition appropriate for individual users and smaller organizations as well as for larger organizations with correspondingly larger networks. Options include tunneling approaches, dual-stack approaches, and development of an Internet backbone structure supporting IPv6.

Chapter 1: Why Upgrade the Internet Protocol?

This chapter explains why the Internet Protocol is in need of an upgrade, why this need is urgent, and what ramifications the upgrade will have on users, administrators, and architects and designers of IP-based networks.

Chapter 2: A Brief Introduction to TCP/IP Internetworking

This chapter provides a brief introduction to TCP/IP internetworking, summarizing the basic theoretical and practical underpinnings of TCP/IP. Paying particular attention to the current version of IP, IPv4, and how it works (from IP addressing to IP routing issues), this chapter represents a refresher course for readers who have not recently studied TCP/IP networking while providing a compressed introduction for readers without previous exposure to TCP/IP.

Chapter 3: What's Wrong with IPv4?

This chapter examines the problems with IPv4. Despite its incredible success, IPv4 can stand some improvement. The most notable and visible improvement is in the size of its address space; other issues relate to performance and the way the IP headers are designed and used. Security, performance, and administrative control issues are all discussed in this chapter.

Chapter 4: The Roads to IPng

IPng, or IP the Next Generation, did not spring into being fully formed but rather evolved over time, with several antecedent proposals. This chapter examines the different approaches proposed to upgrade IPv4 and discusses how those proposals contributed to the ultimate form of IPv6.

Chapter 5: The Shape of IPv6

This chapter introduces the update to IPv4, examining the fields of the new protocol header and the IPv6 address space and highlighting the changes and new features of IPv6. Also introduced here are the various control and routing protocols that must also be updated, as well as discussion of the impact IPv6 will have on existing transport and application protocols.

Chapter 6: IPv6 Addressing

This chapter examines the IPv6 address space in detail, including discussion of IPv6 address formats and nomenclature, hierarchical network addressing, introduction to mobile networking requirements, IPv6 address classes, and unicast, anycast, and multicast addressing.

Chapter 7: IPv6 Extension Headers

This chapter discusses the implications of the IPv6 header fields, how they work, and how they differ from IPv4. Particular attention will be paid to the use of header extensions, as well as discussion of the use of jumbograms, source routing, and security.

Chapter 8: IPv6 Routing

This chapter explains how IPv6 routing works, as well as examining the routing issues that IPv6 was intended to resolve and new or modified routing protocols for IPv6. The different transmission types (unicast, anycast, and multicast) are also discussed here as they relate to routing.

Chapter 9: IPv6 Authentication and Security

The desirability and utility of authentication and security features at the IP layer have been debated for years. This chapter discusses how authentication and security, including secure password transmission, encryption, and digital signatures on datagrams, are implemented under IPv6.

Chapter 10: Related Next-Generation Protocols

Protocols within the TCP/IP suite that interoperate directly with the Internet Protocol include various routing protocols as well as the Internet Control Message Protocol (ICMP), the Transport Control Protocol (TCP), and the User Datagram Protocol (UDP). This chapter examines how these protocols must be modified, or whether they must be modified at all, to accommodate IPv6.

Chapter 11: Autoconfiguration and Mobile IP

One of the design goals for IPv6 was to facilitate "plug and play"—the ability to plug a computer (or other device) into an IPv6 network and have it work without any need for a network administrator to fiddle with network configurations. Mobile IP, or the ability for a node or a network to seamlessly pass from one network or network provider to another, is another design goal for IPv6 and is also closely linked to the autoconfiguration problem. This chapter examines how IPv6 autoconfiguration and mobile IP are accomplished.

Chapter 12: IPv6 Transition Strategies

If IPv6 required a global cutover from IPv4, it would never fly. For IPv6 to work, the transition from IPv4 must be smooth—and allow an easy migration path with backward and forward compatibility. Updating existing networks to IPv6 is possible with relatively low impact as long as the upgrade is done methodically and intelligently. This chapter discusses the dual-stack and IPv6 tunneling strategies being proposed for a smooth transition.

Chapter 13: IPv6 Solutions

Networking products supporting IPv6 have slowly but surely been making their way to market. This chapter highlights some of the products currently or soon to be available that incorporate IPv6 support and explains how they are used and how they may be useful to network professionals.

Appendices

Appendix A provides an index to all RFCs relating to IPv6 as of the fall of 1998. Appendix B includes a handful of the most important and interesting RFCs relating to IPv6. Although some parts of some RFCs can be dry reading, most are models of technical writing, presenting a wealth of technical information in tight, elegant prose. Most readers with a relatively modest technical education will be able to profit from reading most RFCs. Those selected for inclusion here represent some of the most important and interesting RFCs relating to IPv6.

Using This Book

Readers with different levels of networking experience will use this book in different ways.

Those with significant TCP/IP networking experience may find it most useful as a technical reference. They may find it most beneficial to either skip or skim most Chapters 1 through 4, and continue on with Chapter 5, the introduction to IPv6. They may then either read the rest of the book straight through or skip directly to the topics of greatest interest.

Network-savvy readers who are relatively new to TCP/IP should read all of the first five chapters, but at the least Chapter 2 for a quick introduction to TCP/IP and Chapter 5 to get the basics before moving on to the rest of the book. Network novices will benefit from reading the entire book and may even want to take a look at an introductory TCP/IP text. A good one is *TCP/IP Clearly Explained* (AP Professional, 1997) by Pete Loshin.

If you will be programming IPv6-enabled network applications or building any other type of IPv6-enabled products, this book will give you a basic understanding of the new protocols and may be a helpful companion text when reading the IPv6 RFCs.

Tell Me What You Think

This is your book; I wrote it to help you understand this exciting new technology. If there was some part you didn't understand, or didn't like, or think is wrong, please let me know. If there was some part you found particularly useful, interesting, or well-written, let me know about that, too. Feedback from readers is one of the most important tools available to improve a book, and it is one of the most gratifying moments in my day when I receive e-mail from a reader. You can reach me at:

`pete@loshin.com`

Alternatively, you can send postal mail to me, in care of the publisher, at:

Pete Loshin
c/o Morgan Kaufmann
200 Wheeler Road
Burlington, MA 01803

1

Why Upgrade the Internet Protocol?

Age alone is no reason to replace something that is perfectly good as it is. Unfortunately, just because something is pretty good as it is doesn't mean that you can keep using it forever—no matter how great it is now, newer things may eclipse it, or it may just wear out or get used up. Maintaining what you've got is even more important when you consider parts of an infrastructure; and knowing when to upgrade and how to upgrade with the minimum of confusion, disruption, and expense are even more important.

The Internet and untold numbers of smaller, private networks use as their basic network infrastructure the Internet Protocol version 4, also known as IPv4. IPv4 has been an incredibly successful protocol, able to scale from connecting hundreds or thousands of hosts on dozens or hundreds of separate networks all the way up to linking the tens of millions of hosts estimated to be part of the global Internet. First designed in the mid-1970s, IP is showing its age in several ways, to be introduced later in this chapter and examined in greater detail throughout this book. Like a heavily used highway or bridge, IPv4 is reaching the end of its useful lifespan and must be upgraded soon.

This chapter takes a look at the following topics:

- What is IPv4, and why it is so important?
- What is wrong with IPv4, and why does it need to be upgraded?
- Why is it important that we fix IP sooner rather than later?
- What impact will the IP upgrade have on users, administrators, managers, and vendors?

In this book, I use *IP* to refer to any version of the Internet Protocol; *IPv4* to refer to the version of IP current as of 1998 and earlier. *IPv6* refers to the version of IP that the Internet Engineering Task Force (IETF) has determined will replace IPv4 and that is documented in the most recent IETF Request for Comment (RFC) documents.

Impact of the Internet Protocol

Unlike elements, compounds, and services that have been woven into our (and our parents' and grandparents') daily life, IP has not quite yet achieved the ubiquity and familiarity that would allow us to take it for granted in the same way we take for granted easy access to electricity or the use of an extensive network of paved roads. Even so, support for IP is one of the most common features of virtually any new computer hardware, software, or network product, regardless of whether the product is intended for personal computers or for mainframes. The Internet Protocol (with its related protocols) is the one thing upon which IBM and Apple,

Microsoft, Netscape, Sun, Novell, Compaq, Lotus, and virtually every other major computer vendor can agree. This section introduces these issues:

♦ What exactly is IP?
♦ Where can IP be used?
♦ How many people, computers, networks use IP?
♦ What can we expect to happen when IP changes?

What Is the Internet Protocol?

The root problem that IP solves is how to link networks, which in turn link computers, in such a way that none of the participating computers need to know any details about any of the other computers except for an address. This requires three things: first, that each computer in the network of networks must be uniquely identifiable; second, that all computers must be able to send and receive data to and from all other computers in a format that any computer can understand; finally, that it must be possible for a computer to reliably transmit data to another computer without having any knowledge about that computer and its network other than the computer's network address. IP achieves these goals. For more details, see Chapter 2; but here is an abbreviated (and perhaps overly simplified) introduction.

A network of networks is also known as an *internetwork*, or *internet* for short—the global *Internet* was originally differentiated from other, smaller, internets by the use of the capital "I". More recently, the term *intranet* has replaced internet and refers to organizational networks that use TCP/IP.

The TCP/IP networking protocol suite is based on a model of internetworking that uses four layers to communicate between any two systems. At the bottom, just above the level of the physical network medium, is the data link layer, where computers format data for transmission along their network media, such as Ethernet cables or wireless transmitters. This layer provides the mechanism by which two systems connected to the same medium can communicate, but it does not provide any mechanism for communicating with systems not connected to that medium. In other words, all the PCs connected to an office Ethernet hub can communicate directly with each other using the data link layer, but only those computers connected to that hub can communicate with each other.

At the data link layer, data is sent to addresses that are associated with a computer's network interface. This means every device that connects a computer to a network has an address that is similar to a serial number: It is usually unique to that connectivity device, and each device "listens" for data packages that are addressed to its own address. If a system doesn't have a device to connect to a particular network, it cannot communicate directly at the data link layer with any other system that is on the network.

Part of the reason systems not on the same physical network can't communicate directly through the data link layer is that computers connected to different networks often use different protocols. For example, data transmitted to an Ethernet network would not be understood by a computer using a Token Ring network. Another reason is that you need special types of systems, often called *gateways*, to link networks running different link layer protocols. The gateway is a computer connected to two or more networks running different protocols that is able to translate data transmitted from one network data link layer protocol to another. But even with a gateway, you need more to communicate in a heterogeneous internetwork.

The next layer up is called the Internet layer, and it is at this layer that communication is enabled between devices not on the same physical network. Each interface is given an Internet layer address, which is unique among all systems connected to the internetwork (a system using IP to connect to a network is usually called a *host*). All hosts connected to the same internetwork are able to interpret these addresses and use assorted mechanisms to correlate these addresses with data link layer addresses when necessary. It is at the Internet layer that devices called *routers* become useful: These systems (which may also be network protocol gateways) are connected to two or more networks and are used by hosts connected to all of these networks to forward data packets that are intended for remote networks.

An example of a network requiring globally unique addressesis the telephone system: Each telephone subscriber must have a unique telephone number. As telephone networks expand and the numbers of subscribers increases, it is not unusual for telephone companies to expand the length of telephone numbers by adding exchanges and area codes. Unlike telephone numbers, Internet addresses, which are also numbers, must be no more and no less than 32 bits long. Just as a ten-digit telephone number, as used in the United States, limits the number of distinct phone numbers to a maximum of no more than 10^{10}, so a 32-bit address limits the number of distinct Internet addresses to no more than an absolute maximum of 2^{32}, or about four billion. As with telephone numbers, the actual number of possible addresses is less (in the case of Internet addresses, considerably less) because certain numbers are reserved or have some special significance. This address space limitation is at the root of the problem with IPv4 and will be discussed at much greater length throughout this book.

When an individual host needs to send data to another host, it checks on the destination host's Internet address. If the address turns out to be connected to the same physical network that the originating host is connected to, then the originating host simply sends a data package to the destination at the data link layer. In this case, the originating host on an Ethernet LAN would generate an Ethernet transmission addressed directly to the destination host.

However, when the originating host determines that the destination host is not connected to the same physical network, then the originating host sends the data to a router connected to the same physical network as the originating host. The router, in its turn, determines if the data is addressed to any hosts physically connected to any of the same networks that the router is connected to; if so, the router then simply forwards the data to the destination host. If the destination is not local to the router, however, the router will forward the data to some other router that may be connected to other networks. This continues until the data is finally handed off to a router connected to the same physical network as the destination host (if everything goes well).

The rest of TCP/IP networking operates at the transport layer, where data moves between actual processes on communicating systems, and the application layer, where data is moving between the applications themselves. These layers, along with the Internet layer in particular, will be discussed at more length in Chapter 2.

Where Is IP Used?

For many years, IP could be found almost exclusively implemented in networks at universities and research institutions. Commercial offerings incorporating IP did not start becoming common until the late 1980s and early 1990s; even then, these products were largely marketed as specialties. It is only since about 1995 that TCP/IP has been incorporated in personal computer products as a matter of course; since then both Novell and Microsoft have accepted IP as the networking protocol of choice to carry their print and file services network transmissions.

This means that not only is every computer connected to the Internet using IP, but also any computer using these network operating systems to communicate with organizational resources, whether connected to the Internet or not.

IP support is available for virtually any computer in current use, from handheld personal computers through the most powerful supercomputers; it is also increasingly being used to communicate with other types of devices to allow remote control of household appliances and security systems through embedded web servers accessed from anywhere with a web browser client.

Networks using IP include the Internet as well as corporate networks, called intranets, that may range from just a few hosts connected together at a single office to tens of thousands of hosts in branch offices located around the world. Another special type of IP network, the extranet, can be a private IP network that securely links entities with a common goal. For example, extranets may be built to support work groups whose members may cross organizational boundaries or to link trading partners wishing to use the extranet to carry ordering and fulfillment information. (To find out more about extranets, see my book, *Extranet Design and Implementation*, SYBEX, 1997.)

The number of products that incorporate IP, from computer hardware and software to home entertainment products, cellular telephones, and even automobiles with wireless Internet connectivity, demonstrates how important IP is to the world's communication infrastructure.

How Many People Use IP?

The question of how many people use systems connected to IP networks is a complex one. There was a time when it was a relatively easy matter to determine the number of networks running IP and connected to the global Internet: One could simply count up the number of network addresses that had been assigned by the various network authorities. This would not necessarily be accurate as it neglects those networks running IP and not connected to the Internet.

Things are more complicated now, however, as a single network address may be *subnetted* to be shared by more than one organization using the same Internet service provider. Likewise, there are many organizations connected to the Internet using *network address translation* (this method uses a gateway that acts as an intermediary between internal and external hosts and networks, translating the internal network addresses, accessible only within the internal network, into different addresses that can be accessed by external hosts); these networks will not show up in any official counts either. Both these techniques, discussed at greater length later, make it possible for more networks to be connected but also make it more difficult to do an accurate Internet census.

Even when an accurate census of networks was possible, not all hosts within each network were countable. Today, with far greater use of network address translation and firewalls to hide corporate resources from prying eyes, the numbers and names of hosts connected to any given network are rarely discernable or available to anyone outside the organization.

Finally, attempting to figure out the number of individual users who are accessing IP networks through any of these systems is even more difficult to guess. Mainframes and supercomputers may have hundreds of users (or more), while there are other individuals who may use several different personal computers: The result is that you would need to divine some average number of users per computer, when the actual number of users per computer might routinely be as high as 300 users (or more) or as low as 1/3 users per computer (or less).

With dizzying growth rates over the past ten years, research analysts have come up with a variety of different estimates, but there is no question in anyone's mind that there are easily tens of millions of computers connected to the Internet, and the number of individuals using IP could easily be as high as 100 million or more.

What Happens if IP Changes?

As you can see, IP's upgrade will affect a lot of people and organizations. When the change from IPv4 to IPv6 actually occurs, several things might happen, and they all depend to some extent on what the network administrators do. First, nothing may change: no software/hardware upgrades, no changes in services, nothing—this might be the case if a network administrator chooses not to upgrade at all or to upgrade just the Internet connection. Alternatively, a lot could change, with the downside being a fair amount of disruption to distribute and configure the new network software and deal with installing/upgrading applications and handling the fallout from a major upgrade; on the plus side, there are going to be significant bonuses for users, organizations, and administrators.

Transition scenarios as well as different transition strategies are discussed at great length in Chapter 12.

IPv4 Limitations and Shortcomings

Given the breakneck pace of change in the computer industry, saying that IPv4 has limitations and shortcomings is very much like saying that the internal combustion engine is a flawed power source for cars and trucks. IP is a very strong protocol and has proved itself on countless hosts connected to networks ranging from a few nodes to the global Internet. Unlike with the choice of motive power for vehicles—there is nothing stopping anyone from putting on the road an electric-, solar-, or wind-powered vehicle that can do everything a gasoline- or diesel-powered vehicle can—upgrading IP will have significant impact on everyone using IP.

TCP/IP engineers and designers recognized the need for an upgrade as early as the late 1980s, when it became apparent that the existing IP address space would support continued Internet growth for only a relatively short time. This section introduces the reasons that IP must be upgraded, as well as some of the areas targeted for improvement at the same time. Included are

- ♦ *Address space limitations.* The IP address space crisis has been looming for years and is the prime motivating factor behind all the upgrade efforts.
- ♦ *Performance.* Although IP performs remarkably well, some of the design decisions made 20 and more years ago in retrospect could stand some improvement.
- ♦ *Security.* Long considered an issue to be addressed at the higher network layers, security has emerged as an area where the next version of IP could provide some useful functions.
- ♦ *Autoconfiguration.* Configuring IPv4 nodes has always been complex, but network administrators as well as users would prefer to be able to "plug and play": plug a computer into the network and start using it. Increased mobility of IP hosts also raises the issue of providing better support for configuring these hosts as they move across different networks and use different network access points.

The IP Address Space Crisis

The Internet has experienced astronomical growth, with the number of connected networks continuously doubling in less than a year for much of the past 10 to 15 years. Amazing as the growth is, it is not sufficient to cause the IP address crunch we are experiencing in the late 1990s.

IP addresses are 32 bits long, often represented as four two-digit hexadecimal numbers and more often expressed as four numbers from 0–255, separated by periods. Any individual IP host address consists of two parts: a network address, which specifies the network to which the host is connected (and which remains the same for all hosts connected to the same network), and a host address, which uniquely identifies the host within that network. This arrangement is at the same time both the source of IP's great strength as a network protocol and the source of the looming address space crisis.

With a total of over four billion possible addresses in the IPv4 address space, one might think that hundreds of millions of Internet hosts could easily be accommodated, and continued doubling could be supported for at least a few more years. However, this would only work if the addresses were distributed sequentially, with the first host getting address 1, the second host getting address 2, and so on. By using a hierarchical address format, in which a host is identified first by the network to which it is attached, IP enables very simple routing protocols that can move data from one host to another while requiring neither to know anything more than the other's IP addresses. Such hierarchical addressing distributes addressing responsibilities to the manager of each network, instead of requiring some central authority to assign individual IP addresses to each individual host connected to the Internet. Data is routed outside networks based on the network address—the host address is not relevant until the data is received at a router connected to the host's own network.

Assigning IP addresses sequentially to individual hosts through a central authority might make address assignment more efficient but would make almost any other network function impossible. For example, routing would be virtually impossible, requiring each intermediate router to check a centralized database to figure out where to send packets—and each router would need an up-to-date map of the Internet to know where to forward packets. Moving a host from one location to another would require constant updates of the central database, as would modifying or deleting host entries.

IP addresses are divided into five categories, only three of which are used for IP networks; these three categories were once thought to be sufficient for the future of internetworking. Class A addresses, of which there are only 126, would be used by only the very largest entities—like governments—because they support the greatest number of attached hosts: a theoretical maximum of over 16 million. Any one of the roughly 16,000 Class B addresses, intended for large organizations—like major universities and large corporations—can support a theoretical maximum of over 65,000 hosts. There are over two million Class C networks, each of which can support no more than 255 hosts, intended for any other organizations large enough to support an IP network.

While smaller organizations, some with only a handful of IP hosts, were using Class C addresses inefficiently, larger organizations seeking Class B addresses have increasingly found themselves having trouble finding one. And the few organizations lucky enough to have a Class A address have rarely come even close to using their 16 million addresses efficiently. The result is that over the past few years network address assignment procedures have been tightened, with greater attention to the preservation of existing, unassigned, addresses while attempting to distribute network address space more efficiently. At the same time, some methods for working around the address crunch have also become more common, including Classless Inter-Domain Routing (CIDR), network address translation, and use of nonrouting network addresses.

IP addressing will be explained in greater detail in Chapter 2, while problems, challenges, and stopgap solutions related to IPv4 addressing shortages will be discussed in Chapter 3, and the IPv6 address space will be explained in greater detail in Chapter 6.

IP Performance Issues

IP started out as an experiment in many ways, and its purpose was to find the optimal mechanisms for moving data reliably, robustly, and efficiently across internetworks linking dissimilar networks, which in turn allow dissimilar computers to interoperate. It has largely achieved that goal, but that doesn't mean it will be able to continue to do so, nor does it mean that it couldn't do better with some modifications. Over the years, it has become apparent not only that there is room for improvement in IP, but also that new developments make it desirable to modify IP as well. Issues like maximum transmission unit size and maximum packet size, design of the IP headers, use of checksums, deployment of IP options, and others have been addressed in this upgrade. All of these have been proposed and incorporated into IPv6 to improve performance and improve IPv6's ability to continue to serve as the basis of a network that continues to grow rapidly.

Problems and challenges related to IPv4 performance will be discussed in Chapter 3, while the solutions provided in IPv6 will be explained in greater detail in Chapter 7 and Chapter 8.

IP Security Issues

When the only organizations that could connect to the Internet were devoted to research and development, and most of those researchers knew each other at least by reputation, strong ties to the military and government helped insure that security was not a major issue. More importantly, the issue of security was long thought to be of less importance at the lower layers of the networking protocol stack, and responsibility for the security of an application was passed along to the application. In any case, IPv4 was designed with minimal security options, and the designers of IPv6 have added security options in response to strong support for them.

Improved IPv6 security implementations will definitely help improve interoperability through virtual private networks (VPNs). Security features introduced in IPv6 include encryption of data and authenticationof data being transmitted, whether it is encrypted or not. While these options may prove valuable, their value (and effi-cacy) may well hinge on politics rather than technology.

IPv4 security issues will be examined in Chapter 3, while the solu-tions to security and authentication provided in IPv6 will be explained in greater detail in Chapter 9.

Autoconfiguration

When IP was young, most computers lived in rooms with raised floors and cost more than most people made in a year (or longer). These systems weren't going anywhere: They stood in the same rooms and buildings from one year to the next, and their connec-tions to the Internet also remained fairly static, changing only rarely. There was no Internet service provider industry, and connec-tions were made through lines provided by the telephone company to link to someone else's network or to an Internet backbone.

Things are different now. With hundreds of Internet service provid-ers to choose from, customers could theoretically tune their connec-tions to switch among ISPs by the second to take advantage of rate differentials or other service differences—if only there were a way to do so without totally fouling up all network routing and for-warding to and from the customer's systems. Likewise, there is a growing population of users whose work styles require greater mobility of networking services. They may use one or more systems at their homes, a laptop or notebook system they carry around any-where in the world, or one of any number of available systems at their employer sites. Further complicating matters, these users may be working as consultants for more than one employer, or they may be working out of a number of different offices, or both. Finally, even when individuals remain at the same desks using a single computer, the computer they use may be upgraded or traded far more frequently than in the past.

Increasing mobility of the work force, as well as mobility of com-puters, means that adaptations in IP could make life easier for many. Some advances have been made already, under IPv4, in the form of Dynamic Host Configuration Protocol (DHCP), which allows systems to rely on servers to provide them with accurate and complete IP network configuration every time they boot up or just whenever they need it. For the time being, hosts—mobile and immobile—continue to depend on a single point of connection to the network. When you travel with a notebook system, you may be able to retain connectivity only by making a telephone call to your ISP. If that ISP doesn't offer a toll-free number to connect to when you are out of the area, you must make a toll call to the ISP's dial-up number.

However, more can be done, and IPv6 should make it possible to bypass the static connection to a single ISP and enable users' systems to detect the nearest network gateway and connect over that. It is still not entirely clear how this feature will be implemented, let alone accounted for, but with IPv6 it will be possible, and the technology is explained in Chapter 11.

A Sense of Urgency

Official recognition of the inadequacy of the IPv4 address architecture can be seen in RFC 1287, published in 1991, when the issues facing IP as it matured and grew were defined. Network addresses have been rationed closely since at least 1992, when the requirements for a new Class B address were raised and organizations not quite large enough to justify the midsize network address started receiving blocks of Class C addresses (RFCs 1366 and 1466).

Unlike many year 2000 efforts, begun at the last minute (or later), the IPv6 upgrade effort represents many years of work by many dedicated engineers and computer scientists. The work they have done should keep the Internet, as well as other IP networks, functioning efficiently and growing for many years.

2

A Brief Introduction to TCP/IP Internetworking

This chapter provides a brief introduction to TCP/IP internetworking, summarizing its basic theoretical and practical underpinnings. Paying particular attention to the current version of IP, IPv4, and how it works, including IP addressing and IP headers, this chapter can be considered both a compressed introduction to TCP/IP for those unfamiliar with it and a refresher course for more experienced readers.

Stating the Internetworking Problem

Simple networks link two or more computers with a single network medium; this could be a wire, a radio frequency, or any other medium of communication. Each system on this network must be uniquely identified, or else there is no way for one system to communicate with another system: All transmissions (with some exceptions explained in the box below) must be identifiably addressed to a particular system, and all transmissions (with no exceptions) must be bear an identifiable source so that responses (or error messages) can be properly addressed to the sender.

Broadcasting and Multicasting

Some transmissions can be addressed to more than one system at a time. These may be *broadcasts* that are intended to be received by every system connected to the network and are usually related to administrative tasks. Broadcast messages use special broadcast addresses as their destination, and all hosts on a network are designed to listen for messages directed at broadcast addresses.

Another type of address that can be received by more than one system is called a *multicast*. Particular systems may be listening for transmissions sent to a particular multicast address if they are subscribed to that address. These addresses are used as the destination address for information that more than one system may be interested in but that only those interested in want to receive. In other words, systems not subscribed to the multicast address do not pay any attention to those transmissions.

Setting up addresses for hosts on a simple network can be done in several ways:

- ♦ Start from 1 (or some other number), and number all hosts consecutively.
- ♦ Assign each host an address generated at random.
- ♦ Use a globally unique value for each host.

Each of these approaches has drawbacks. Numbering hosts consecutively works fine as long as the network never merges with any other network. In practice, departmental networks are often merged, as are entire organizations. Generating random addresses raises the issue of uniqueness, if not within a particular network, then across merged networks. Finally, using a globally unique value for each host solves the problem of duplicating addresses in any circumstance but requires that there be some central authority doling out addresses.

Hosts, Nodes, and Routers

IP refers to different types of hardware systems that can be connected to an IP network. These include

- *Node.* A node is any device that implements IP.
- *Router.* A router is any device that forwards data not explicitly addressed to itself. In other words, a router will accept a packet addressed to other nodes and forward it—usually because the router is connected to more than one physical network.
- *Host.* A host is any node that is not a router.

In fact, for most types of network interface devices there is such an authority making sure that each manufacturer of interface devices uses its own range of addresses, within which each device gets a unique number. This means that data on networks can be directed to the addresses associated with the network hardware interface used by each system connected to the network.

This essentially solves the problem for simple networks: If one system wants to send data to another system, it simply needs to associate its destination host with the destination host's network address and create a network transmission unit containing the data to be sent and transmit it over its own network interface. The destination host will receive it by whatever mechanism the network medium uses to deliver data.

Adding Complexity

The type of network, a *local area network* or *LAN*, just described works well as long as it remains a local network. In other words, it works well as long as all hosts are connected to the same network medium.

In practice, this means there is an upper limit to the number of hosts that can be connected to a single network. This upper limit is usually related to some physical aspect of the medium: the maximum volume of data that the network can carry (*bandwidth*), for example, or the maximum distance between the endpoints of a physical cable. In general, LANs are usually limited to linking no more than a few hundred different systems within a single building or small campus (wireless networks or those based on satellite technologies can be more widely dispersed but will still be limited by their bandwidth).

With the spread of personal computers to just about every desktop in many industries, organizations with more than a few hundred employees, or even smaller if they span more than one building or have multiple branches, are finding that LANs are not sufficient to solve all their networking problems. What becomes necessary is a method of linking networks—for example, departmental or branch office networks—together into an organizational internetwork.

If all networks within an organization are of the same type—for example, all Ethernet LANs—then there is the potential for a simple answer. One approach to connecting LANs is to use a bridge: The bridge listens to traffic on two networks, and when it hears on one network a transmission destined for the other network, it retransmits it onto the destination network. Ultimately, though, more complicated internetworks linking more than a few LANs get very hard to handle: It becomes necessary for the equipment linking the LANs to know the address and network location of each system. Even if systems stay in the same location and on the same network, as the number of systems increases the task of tracking and routing traffic becomes much more difficult.

Of course, such a scenario requires that all networks at a given location use the same media. In practice, organizations whose departments have been using networks for any length of time will find that they have more than one type of network medium in place, commonly including Ethernet, Token Ring, and others. The formats for sending data in any given medium are likely to differ in some form or another, meaning that for systems connected to disparate networks to interoperate it would be necessary for each system to know ahead of time what kind of network its destination is connected to and then create the data in the required format before sending. In addition, there would have to be some intermediate systems that could properly route that data and where necessary convert it to the appropriate physical format for transmission across a possibly very different network medium.

Consider what happens in a large corporation with many different divisions, branches, and departments. Each LAN would need to keep track of all structural changes, everywhere in the organization, in order to properly route data anywhere. Imagine the degree to which this kind of difficulty is magnified when the organization in question is not just a corporation but a government; the difficulty continues to grow when the internetwork in question spans organizations and becomes the global Internet we are familiar with today.

The solutions described above are simply not sufficient to solve the problem of routing data for an internetwork of any significant size, let alone the Internet. A different solution is necessary: It must make it possible for different systems, connected to different networks, to interoperate seamlessly without needing to know any more about each other than an internetwork address. Such a solution is described in the next section.

Layered Internetworking Models

The networking model described above assumes that all network communication is between systems connected to networks but does not specify how those systems communicate. In other words, it assumes that all data is simply formatted for the local network and transmitted over that interface; there is no discussion of how that data is formatted. By specifying more closely how data moves between the individuals or programs using it, we can break down the problem of seamless interoperability into more manageable parts.

Models that separate how data is treated as it passes from one system to another are often visualized as stacks of protocols to be used at different layers. The protocol implementations are also referred to as *protocol stacks*, and they represent the levels at which data can be manipulated and how that data is passed from one level up or down to the next.

The OSI Model

Often called the Open Systems Interconnection, or OSI, model of networking, the Basic Reference Model was devised originally to reflect an all-inclusive model for internetworking. Its seven layers, as shown in Figure 2.1, refer to different levels at which two inter-operating systems can communicate. Moving up from the bottom, the layers include the following:

- ◆ The *physical layer* refers to the actual medium over which the data moves; systems transmit raw electrical impulses (or other appropriate signals) to each other through the physical layer. Systems communicate at this layer through their physical connections to the medium.
- ◆ The *data link layer* adds protocols for actually interpreting data that has been transmitted over physical media, including reliability and retransmission functions, for example. Systems communicate at this layer through their actual network interfaces, which are connected directly to the network medium.
- ◆ The *network layer* provides the protocols that make it possible for one system to communicate with another system, linking systems together rather than just network interfaces. It is at this layer that communication can be considered to be happening between systems and not just between network interfaces. This is the layer concerned with delivery of data between two different nodes that may be on two different networks.
- ◆ The *transport layer* provides the protocols that make it possible for a process running on one system to connect to a process running on another system. In other words, this is the level at which it is possible to differentiate between two different programs running on a single host connecting to two other, different, programs running on a different host.

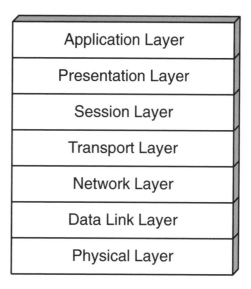

Figure 2.1. The OSI model for internetworking provides seven different levels at which systems can interoperate over networks.

- ♦ The *session layer* is where the flow and timing of a connection is handled; it is where the actual mechanics of a connection—whether or not the sender is transmitting and the receiver is receiving—are managed.

- ♦ The *presentation layer* provides a layer at which different systems translate their data into forms acceptable and understandable to each other. Programs on disparate systems must use standard formats that all systems can interpret, and this translation occurs at this level.

- ♦ The *application layer* protocols define how the actual programs using the network interact; for example, the application protocols for a network program might define the type of input required from the user or the type of output that the remote system responds with.

The Internet Model

As it turns out, however, internetworking researchers building actual networks found that they were able to produce a fully functional internetwork architecture using only four layers. The Internet model, shown in Figure 2.2, compresses network layering and makes internetworking somewhat simpler because fewer layers mean fewer interactions, which in turn mean more efficient networking implementation.

While the layers, in some cases, are similar to the OSI model layers, there are some differences. From the bottom, the main differences are, first, that in the Internet model the physical layer is dropped as a separate layer. This is probably because implementers can assume that data transmitted and received at the data link layer has been passed along the physical medium. Next, the network layer becomes the internet layer, making explicit the necessity of providing a way to link systems across networks. The transport layer absorbs most of the functions of the session layer, while the application layer absorbs most of the functions of the presentation layer.

Understanding how the layers work helps one understand how IP networking works, because in the Internet model it is much clearer at what levels communicating systems interact:

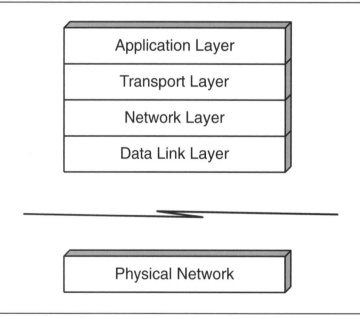

Figure 2.2. The Internet model does seamless, interoperable, internetworking with only four layers.

◆ At the data link layer (also known as the *network interface layer*) systems connected to the same network communicate with each other. The systems communicating at this layer may not necessarily be the same as those communicating at the other layers, because systems on two different networks cannot communicate directly at this layer.

◆ The internet layer (also called the network layer) is the layer at which systems communicate. Data transport units at this layer consist entirely of some payload data, preceded with addressing information. In other words, the data can be seen merely as being sent from the source system to the destination system. Two systems can be interacting in any number of different ways, but the data resulting from different application interactions—at least at this layer—is seen as merely having the same source and destination addresses and is not immediately differentiable.

◆ The transport layer is the layer at which processes communicate. This is the layer that makes it possible for two systems to have more than one stream of data flowing between them (see above).

◆ The application layer is the layer at which the user (whether an individual or a program) interacts with a network application.

In this book, we are mostly concerned with what happens at the internet layer and only with the other layers as they are affected by changes to the protocols defining the internet layer.

Encapsulation

To understand how the layers of the Internet model interact and enable seamless interoperability, it is necessary to understand the concept of *encapsulation*. Encapsulation in networking occurs when some chunk of data is, in a sense, wrapped up and packaged in some way to make it possible to transmit it. The best approach to understand how encapsulation works in the Internet model is to simply walk up and down the protocol stack.

For this example, consider an application that permits a client on one host to query a server on another host. Starting at the client application, the user enters in the query. The very first step in encapsulation at the application layer is to package that query in the application protocol's *protocol data unit* (see note). The PDU contains the data, and "wraps it up" with information about what to do with the data: a logical name, address, or some other pointer for the destination application on the remote host, for example, and anything else that is necessary for the next layer (the transport layer) to appropriately deal with the package.

Protocol data unit or *PDU* refers to the way a protocol packages a chunk of data. Different protocols refer to the chunks of data they work by different names. For example, Ethernet and other data link layer protocols refer to *frames*, IP refers to *IP datagrams* or sometimes *packets*, and so on. When speaking generally about protocols, or about unknown protocols, PDU is often used to refer to these data packages. PDUs usually consist of *headers* (usually at the start of the PDU, though sometimes added at the end as well) and some *payload* of data, to be used when the headers have been stripped off. PDU refers to the way the chunk is named but not to the actual chunk, which may also be called a message.

At the transport layer, the package passed along by the application is treated as simply a bunch of bits to be further processed by adding headers and passing along to the internet layer. Processes use *ports* to send and receive data, and in TCP/IP the transport layer adds the destination and source port numbers in the headers (among other items) and passes the newly packaged message on down the stack to the protocol operating at the internet layer.

The internet layer software accepts the message from the transport layer and, looking at the destination IP address, determines what to do with the data. In any case, internet layer headers are added with the actual network address of the source and destination hosts and the entire resulting package is passed on down the stack to the data link layer. This is where things get tricky: If the IP network software determines that the data is destined for a system on the same physical network as the source, the packet will be addressed at the data link layer to that destination. However, data destined for some other network must still be addressed to some system on the same physical network as the source: There is nowhere else for the data to go.

The one missing element is a system called a *router*. This is a *multi-homed host* that is connected to two or more physical networks at the same time and that is programmed to forward packets to remote networks. This means that when data is destined for a remote network, the IP software will cause the data link layer to address it to a router on the same physical network as the source host. The source and destination addresses at the internet layer remain the same; the destination address at the data link layer, however, will be different from the destination host's if the destination host is on a foreign network.

Now continue to follow the data back up the protocol stack. Once a data link layer message arrives at its destination, the receiving system strips off the data link layer headers and looks at the internet layer header. If that header has the same destination address as that of the host receiving it, those headers are stripped off in turn, and the payload is passed up to the transport layer. However, if the destination address is different from that of the host receiving the message, and if the receiving host is a router, that message will be repackaged and resent onto the appropriate network for forwarding.

When the transport layer gets the message, it strips off the headers and passes the payload on up to the appropriate application. Again, the application strips off the headers and processes the data. The protocols operating at the lower layers have no need to do anything with the payloads being carried after the data itself leaves the sender and until it arrives at the destination application. While there may be integrity checks of one sort or another, no lower-layer protocol ever needs to look at any part of the data being transmitted other than the headers provided by the upper layers. This is the mechanism by which it is possible to have dissimilar systems, connected to dissimilar networks, interoperate seamlessly. As long as the intervening systems all operate correctly (according to the standard protocols) and as long as both systems are using application software that can interoperate, the type of system, architecture of networks, or physical layout of either system is irrelevant.

The Internet Protocol

RFC 791, written in 1981, defines IP as it is currently being used. However, since then many RFCs have clarified and defined IPv4 addressing issues, running IP over particular network media, and the IPv4 type of service (TOS) bits. The interested reader is urged to look at RFC 791, if only to get an idea of how a protocol like IP was defined almost 20 years ago. However, the protocol works through the application of a few simple rules for manipulating data, a set of header fields that help determine how that data is manipulated, and an addressing scheme. These are explained briefly here.

IP Addressing

The IP address architecture depends on a highly structured address, space defined by its length: 32 bits. All IP addresses consist of 32 bits, or 4 bytes; the term *octet* (often used throughout the IP universe) is also common. These addresses are divided into different categories called *classes*, which define how they are treated; there are also certain addresses that have special meaning.

IP Address Structure

IP addresses are hierarchical and are usually read from left to right, with the high-order bits and bytes also the most significant bits and bytes. To illustrate, the first bits of an address signify what class the address belongs to; the first byte or bytes will signify the network that address belongs to. The least significant byte or bytes (or bits) will narrow down the address to a particular host. This structure means that routing outside networks can ignore individual hosts and needs only to track the locations of entire networks.

The 32-bit addresses are divided into two parts: The first part is the network address, the second part is the local address. Outside the local network, only the network address is important, while inside the local network, the local address is important while the network address is irrelevant (because of course all hosts are attached to the same local network).

IP network addresses are distributed to organizations, and the organizations themselves dole out the local addresses for hosts within the organization. This means that all possible local addresses within a particular network may not be assigned. This cuts down on the number of addresses available from the total of 2^{32} possible.

IP Address Classes

IP addresses were originally divided into three classes, A, B, and C, for numbering individual hosts within different classes of networks. A fourth class, D, was later added when IP multicast was accepted as a standard, but these addresses are not used for individual hosts nor are they identified with any particular network. Class A, B, and C addresses are used for what is increasingly being called *unicast*, meaning that the each of those addresses can identify only a single host, and that any data sent from or to a unicast address is being sent from a single host to another single host. Class D addresses are used for *multicast* transmissions, meaning that more than one host can receive data sent to a multicast address (multicast transmissions must still originate from a single host).

Examining the first few bits of an IP address will help classify the address. IP address classes are as follows:

- ◆ *Class A* addresses all begin with the first (high order) bit equal to zero. The network is specified by the next seven bits. This allows most of the first octet for network address and the remaining three octets for host addressing within each network. This means that there is an absolute maximum of 2^7 or 128 different possible combinations for network addresses, but the remaining 24 bits of the address can be used for host addressing. This means that there is an absolute maximum of 2^{24} or 16,777,216 unique host identifiers in each Class A address. (The real maximums are slightly less; see the following discussion.) It also means that Class A addresses can be identified by the value of the first octet. Any network address that starts with a number more than 0 and less than 128 would be a Class A network.

- *Class B* addresses all begin with the first two bits set to 10, with the next 14 bits available for network addressing. This allows most of the first two octets for network address and the remaining two octets for host addressing within each network. This means that there is an absolute maximum of 2^{14} (16,384) different Class B network addresses available and that each Class B network can have no more than 2^{16} (65,536) different unique host addresses. (The real maximum is slightly less; see the following discussion.) It also means that all Class B network addresses can be identified by the value of the first octet. Any network address that starts with 128 or higher, up to 191, refers to a Class B network.

- *Class C* addresses all begin with the first three bits set to 110, with the next 21 bits available for network addressing. This allows most of the first three octets for network address and the remaining octet for host addressing within each network. This means that there is an absolute maximum of 2^{21} (2,097,152) different Class C network addresses available, and that each Class C network can have no more than 2^{8} (256) different unique host addresses. (The real maximum is slightly less; see the following discussion.) It also means that all Class C network addresses can be identified by the value of the first octet. Any network address that starts with 192 or higher, up to 223, refers to a Class C network.

- *Class D* (multicast) addresses all begin with the first four bits set to 1110. Multicasts don't use the concept of network addresses, as hosts can receive multicasts anywhere on the internetwork, even if they are on different networks. There is an absolute maximum of 2^{28} (268,435,456) different multicast addresses, and all multicast addresses can be identified by the value of the first octet. Any IP address whose first octet is 224 or higher, up to 239, is a multicast address.

- *Class E* addresses all begin with the first five bits set to 11110. This portion of the IPv4 address space is currently reserved.

Special Cases

This total is further reduced by the use of some special network addresses that have special meanings. These addresses cannot be assigned to actual networks:

- ♦ Any address whose first octet is 127 (e.g., 127.0.0.1) is, by definition, treated as a loopback address. This is a required convention; all data addressed to the loopback address is treated by the network stack as data destined for actual transmission to itself, but while it is passed down the stack, the data is not actually transmitted on a network medium. This allows a host to communicate with itself through its own network interface (useful for testing purposes).
- ♦ Addresses that consist of all ones in the host part of the address are broadcast addresses. Data addressed to broadcast addresses are intended to be received by all hosts on a network. (See the following discussion for more details about broadcasting.)
- ♦ Addresses with all zeroes represent "this" network or host. In other words, a Class A address specifying a particular network but with the host portion of the network filled with 0s represents "this host" on that particular network. Likewise, a network address of all 0s (i.e., 0.0.121.1) refers to a particular host on "this" network.

These restrictions reduce the number of host and network addresses available. The loopback address takes away one Class A network address (127 would otherwise be the highest possible Class A network address value). Likewise, the reservation of the all zeroes address (0.0.0.0) eliminates another network address from Class A. So, instead of 0–127 being valid first octets for a Class A network, they are limited to 1–126: There are only 126 possible Class A addresses.

Reserved addresses also affect the total number of unique host addresses on each network. Instead of 2^n (where $n = 24$ for Class A, 16 for Class B, and 8 for Class C), the maximum number of hosts on a network is equal to $2^n - 2$. The all-zeroes and all-ones addresses are reserved, respectively, for "this host" and for the broadcast address. While this reduction is not terribly significant for Class A and Class B addresses, it does reduce available host addresses for Class C networks from 256 to 254. The loss of these addresses becomes even more significant as networks are subnetted. (Subnetting is discussed later.)

Broadcasts

In order to provide a mechanism by which all hosts on a network could receive a message, broadcasts were defined. Broadcasts can be useful. They allow a host to notify all other hosts on a network of a change. For example, a server may send a broadcast to advertise a change in status. Alternatively, broadcasts can be used by hosts when they do not yet know where they want to direct a transmission. For example, a workstation may broadcast a request when it is looking for a server but doesn't know the server's name or address.

As it happens, however, IPv6 will not implement broadcast addresses. The problem with broadcasts is that they tend to negatively affect performance of the network. Although they do not generate any more network traffic than unicasts on a baseband network like an Ethernet, they do pose problems in other configurations. Briefly, they can be cumbersome for networks that transmit over virtual circuit, like ATM, as well as problems in organizational internetworks where broadcasts must be passed across routers. The other problem with broadcast is that it adds traffic that every host must process, even though the messages are usually relevant only to a much smaller number of connected hosts. The retirement of broadcast is discussed at greater length in Chapter 6.

Subnets

The entire IP address space is organized hierarchically, with external routing based on the first part of the network address and internal routing the responsibility of the owner of the network address. This allows more compact and more efficient routing tables. However, the difference between handling routing for a 32-bit address space and for a 24-bit address space (for Class A networks) or even for a 16-bit address space (for Class B networks) is the difference between being way, way too huge to handle and being just too huge to handle. With most physical networks being capable of handling no more than a few hundred connected hosts, Class A and B holders need to devise their own internal hierarchies.

Subnetting is the answer. Subnets allow network managers to organize their network address space hierarchically. In an unsubnetted network, routers interpret network addresses strictly on the basis of network classes. If the first octet identifies a Class A address, the router ignores the other three octets (because they refer to the host address within the Class A). When you implement subnetting, however, you essentially tell the hosts on your network to mask out some portion of the host part of the address and treat that masked portion as a subnet. In other words, if you were to subnet the second octet of a Class A network, your routers will treat the Class A network address plus the first octet of the host portion of the address as if it were a two-octet network address.

Subnetting works for a couple of reasons. First, it allows system managers to organize their network address space to meet their needs. Second, it all happens invisibly to anyone outside the subnetted network. A datagram sent to a host address within a Class A network will always go to the same router to get into the organization; the sender does not need to know (or care) about what happens after it enters the destination organization's network.

You can subnet a network even if all hosts are connected to a single LAN, but if you have separate LANs (or segments) for your network, subnetting becomes more important. An unsubnetted internetwork that spans multiple segments is unwieldy and in some cases impossible. Repeaters, bridges, gateways, and routers all must be used in ways that may not result in optimal performance. This can cause some problems because most IP network addresses are now Class C addresses, which are much more difficult to subnet efficiently. The drawbacks of subnetting Class C addresses will be discussed at greater length in Chapter 3, but very simply, the reservation of all-ones and all-zeroes addresses within each subnet limits the number of hosts you can subnet within a Class C network.

The IP Header

IP datagrams are simply chunks of data (called the payload) preceded by a header. The data in IP datagrams, including data in the headers, is organized into 32-bit (four-byte or four-octet) words. Figure 2.3 shows how the IP header fields are arranged. As you can see, all IP datagram headers are at least five words (20 bytes) long, although with options, the headers can be longer.

IP Header Fields

IPv4 header fields include:

- *Version.* This four-bit field indicates which version of IP is in use. This is the first field processed, because the recipient must know how to interpret the rest of the header.
- *Header length.* IPv4 headers can be anywhere from 5 to 15 four-byte words. This field indicates the number of four-byte words that are in the header. The minimum acceptable value here is five; the maximum possible is 15 (which means the header is 60 bytes long and that options can take up to 40 bytes).
- *Type of service.* Only four bits of this eight-bit field are used to make type of service (TOS) requests of IP routers. One TOS bit may be chosen to signify preferences about how the datagram is to be processed: delay, throughput, reliability, or cost. Setting the delay bit on requests is intended to minimize delay; setting the throughput bit on requests high throughput; and setting the reliability bit on requests high reliability. TOS has not enjoyed great popularity in IPv4, for a number of reasons to be discussed in Chapter 3. Because there may often be no choice as to the route taken, these are considered suggestions, and the bits are set automatically to appropriate values by the higher level application protocol (for instance, remote network sessions request minimized delay, while file transfers request maximized throughput).
- *Datagram length.* The length, including the header, is of the entire datagram. At 16 bits, this limits IP datagrams

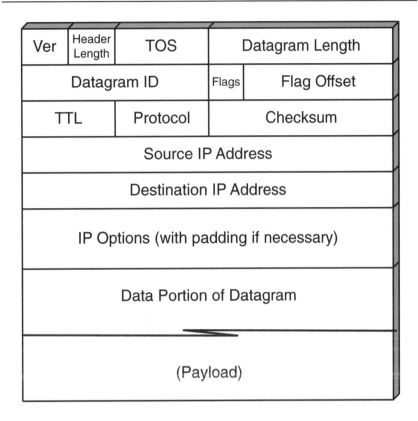

Figure 2.3. The IPv4 header includes a dozen different fields.

to a maximum size of 65,535 bytes long (2^{16}–1). This field is necessary because there is no "end of datagram" character or sequence for IP. Network hosts can use the datagram length to figure out where one datagram ends and other datagrams begin.

♦ *Datagram ID.* This unique 16-bit identifier is assigned to a datagram by the host that originates it. There is a single ID for each datagram when the originating host transmits, but these datagrams may be fragmented as they pass through different networks on their way to their destination. Fragmented datagrams all share the same datagram ID, which aids the receiving host in reassembling the fragments.

♦ *Flags.* The first of these three flag bits is unused, while the other two are used to control the way the datagram is fragmented. When set to 1, the "Don't Fragment" (DF) bit means that the datagram is not to be fragmented en route to its destination. If the datagram cannot be routed without fragmentation, the router attempting to fragment it throws it away instead and sends an error message back to the originating host. When the "More Fragments" (MF) bit is set to 1, it means the datagram is one of two or more fragments, but not the last of the fragments. If the MF bit is set to 0, it means either that there are no more fragments or that the datagram was not fragmented. Receiving hosts use this flag along with the fragment offset to reassemble fragmented datagrams.

♦ *Fragment offset.* The 13-bit value in this field specifies how many eight-byte units from the start of the original datagram the current datagram is. In other words, the first fragmented datagram would have a value of 0 for the offset; if the data in the second datagram starts 800 bytes from the beginning of the original datagram, the offset would be 100.

♦ *Time to live.* This eight-bit field indicates how long the datagram should be allowed to exist after entering the internetwork, measured in seconds. Time to live (TTL) was meant to measure of the number of seconds a datagram was to be allowed to exist in transit across an internetwork. The maximum value is 255; when TTL reaches 0 the datagram is discarded silently. The original intent was for each router to calculate how long it took to process each datagram and then decrement the TTL by that number of seconds. In practice, however, datagrams transit routers much more quickly than one second, so router vendors typically implement this as a simple decrement: As a datagram is forwarded, its TTL is decremented by one. In practice, TTL represents the maximum number of hops that a datagram can make before being discarded.

♦ *Protocol.* This field indicates what kind of payload is being carried by the datagram, typically identifying the transport layer protocol being used: usually a TCP connection or a UDP datagram.

♦ *Header checksum.* IPv4 does not provide any reliability services, but this checksum is done on the header only. It is calculating by treating the header as a series of 16-bit binary numbers (the checksum itself is set to 0 during the calculation) and adding them together. The result is then ones-complemented. This ensures that the datagram header is not corrupted but does not add any transmission reliability or error detection to IP.

♦ *Source/destination.* These are the actual 32-bit (four-octet) IPv4 addresses of the originating host and the destination host.

IP Options

IP options, as the name implies, are strictly optional and not often used—and the form they take in IPv6 is radically different. When used in IPv4, they are often used for network testing or debugging purposes.

Available options relate mostly to routing. For example, there are options that allow the sender to specify a required route the datagram must take—in other words, identifying the routers that the datagram should be handled by. Another option requires intervening routers to record their IP addresses or time-stamp the datagram. Some options, particularly those that indicate the IP addresses of routers the datagram must traverse, require additional data to be appended to the option.

Specifying routes adds length to the IP header, as do the options for recording routers or adding timestamps. When used, IP options are strung together without any delimiting characters, and if they do not end on a word boundary (number of bytes is not evenly divisible by four) padding characters are added. As noted in the description of the header length field, the options field can contain no more than 40 bytes of options and options data. IPv4 options are discussed at greater length in Chapter 3.

Moving Datagrams Around

Understanding how datagrams move around means understanding the IP addressing scheme and the IP datagram header fields. An IP host that originates a datagram creates an IP header for that datagram that includes its own address as the source and the IP address of the destination host. When this datagram is passed down the network protocol stack to the link layer, it must determine where the data must actually be sent *on the same local network*. In other words, the datagram has to be sent to a host connected to the same network that the sending host is connected to, even if the destination is on a different network.

The originating host checks the destination address. If it is on the same IP network and the same subnet, the host will use the Address Resolution Protocol (ARP) to send a broadcast to the local network and map the IP address to a link layer (for example, Ethernet) address. The datagram will then be encapsulated into a link layer frame and sent directly to its destination. However, if the destination address is on a different subnet or different IP network entirely, the sender must figure out where to send the datagram to be forwarded to the right network.

This is where routers come in handy. The sending host keeps track of local hosts as well as routers; usually, there are one or two routers on a subnet available to forward datagrams. The sending host encapsulates the IP datagram (addressed to its final destination and from the original sender) into a link layer frame that goes directly to the default router, which then opens up that frame and examines the IP datagram header. First, it looks at the version field. IPv4 implementations will accept only IP version 4 in this field. It continues processing the rest of the header fields. It decrements the time-to-live field and recalculates the header checksum.

The router also looks at the destination address to determine whether it is a local address on any network to which the router is directly connected. If the destination address is on a local network, the router then uses ARP to determine the destination's link layer address and then delivers the datagram encapsulated in a link layer frame. If the destination address is not local to any network to which the router is connected, then the router will continue to forward that datagram along to another router. This continues until the datagram reaches its destination network.

Figure 2.4 demonstrates how this works. This figure represents two different organizations, both connected to the Internet and both with three networks. Each network is connected to a single router, and each of these routers is connected to three networks as well as the Internet. When Host X originates a datagram intended for destination Host Y, the datagram is first sent on Network A to Router A. When Router A receives that datagram, the router unwraps the datagram and determines that the destination is not on any of the networks to which it is connected (A, B, or C). The router forwards the datagram to another router (which, in this example, is somewhere inside the Internet cloud), which continues to forward the datagram through the Internet

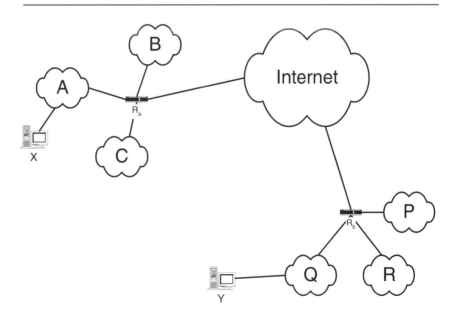

Figure 2.4. IP routing in action.

until it arrives at Router B. Once Router B receives the datagram, the router unwraps the datagram and discovers that the destination address is located on a local network, so this router queries the network using ARP to determine the proper link layer address to send the datagram to and then sends the datagram to that host.

Each router updates the time-to-live value as well as the header checksum; intermediate routers also modify values for the datagram ID and fragment offsets if a datagram must be fragmented between the sender and the recipient. This might occur if the original datagram is too large to pass across an intermediate network.

Internet Control Message Protocol (ICMP)

IP uses the Internet Control Message Protocol, or ICMP, to allow routers a mechanism to communicate path or route reachability status to other routers or to hosts requesting such information. ICMP has other functions, including providing responses to requests from other nodes for the current time or subnet masks in use. ICMP is most useful for providing information to other nodes, including:

♦ Notifying nodes of unreachable destinations.
♦ Sending error or status messages relating to particular routes or routers.
♦ Request/reply on the status of reachable nodes.
♦ Notification of timed-out (time to live has expired) datagrams.

ICMP is a very simple protocol, and it uses four fields to accomplish its functions. ICMPv6 is expanded to support an important new feature of IPv6, neighbor discovery, which is discussed in Chapter 10.

Routing, Transport, and Application Protocols

The details of routing, transport, and application protocols are best left to other texts, including the author's *TCP/IP Clearly Explained*

(AP Professional, 1997). In Chapter 8, routing protocols are discussed in greater detail relating to updates and modifications necessary so they will work with IPv6. Chapter 10 addresses modifications that will be necessary for transport and application protocols, among others. This section provides only the briefest of introductions to these topics.

Routing Protocols

Routing protocols help define the rules that routers use to determine where to forward packets and how to keep track of routing paths. Routers use a variety of protocols, including the Border Gateway Protocol (BGP), the Routing Information Protocol (RIP), and the Open Shortest Path First (OSPF) protocol, to communicate to other routers to which routes they are willing and able to forward packets. These protocols allow routers to respond to changes in network, link, and router status, and are key to IP's ability to support connectivity between any nodes in massively interconnected internetworks.

Transport Protocols

While the network layer Internet Protocol defines the rules for communication between specific nodes on an internetwork, the transport layer protocols define the rules for communication between specific processes running on hosts (or a single host, for that matter) on the same internetwork. Transport layer protocols commonly used with IP include the Transmission Control Protocol (TCP) and the User Datagram Protocol (UDP). Both these protocols are very important to IP networking, but they won't necessarily require significant modification to work with IPv6. Both will be discussed as they relate to IPv6 in Chapter 10, but this section provides a very brief introduction of these two transport protocols.

Transmission Control Protocol

TCP provides a mechanism for creating virtual circuits between two endpoint processes, which means that a TCP virtual connection behaves as if it were a full-duplex circuit carrying data between systems. TCP is called a reliable protocol because it provides guaranteed delivery of data between processes, and it provides mechanisms to optimize transmission performance depending on current network conditions. This means, for example, that transmission rates may gradually increase as long as all data is being received and acknowledged by the recipient. A delay will cause a sending host to slow down until further acknowledgment is received.

TCP is commonly used for interactive applications, particularly the web, where failure to receive some data may affect the ability of the application to perform correctly. TCP uses a *three-way handshake* to set up a circuit, as well as a formal termination of all circuits; in addition to various checksumming and other reliability functions, this adds to the overhead of using TCP and makes it less efficient than UDP.

User Datagram Protocol

UDP is a relatively simple protocol. It uses little more than source and destination information and is used mostly for applications with very simple request/reply architectures. It is unreliable, meaning there are no controls to determine whether a UDP datagram has been received. It is also connectionless, meaning that it does not require any kind of circuit to transmit data between hosts. UDP's connectionlessness makes it possible to use UDP to send data to a broadcast address, unlike TCP, which requires a specific source and destination address.

Application Protocols

Virtually all addressing issues are handled at the transport layer (for addresses or *ports* assigned to particular processes running on a node) and at the network layer (for IP addresses identifying a node on a particular network). Application protocols, such as the Hypertext Transport Protocol (HTTP), are largely removed from addressing considerations and thus should not require significant (if any) modifications to work with IPv6. How existing IP applications work with IPv6 network stacks will be discussed in Chapter 10.

3

What's Wrong with IPv4?

This chapter examines the problems with IPv4. Despite its incredible success, IPv4 can stand some improvement. The most notable and visible improvement is in the size of its address space; other issues relate to performance and the way the IP headers are designed and used. Security, performance, and administrative control issues are all discussed in this chapter.

Fix or Replace?

IPv4 works pretty well, particularly considering its age. Why replace it with something else? After all, if you do replace IPv4, every system in the universe that uses IPv4 will ultimately have to be upgraded—this makes the nightmare faced by large corporations investigating the latest Microsoft Windows upgrade look like a walk in the park. We're talking about perhaps 100 million or more systems, scattered across the globe, with untold numbers of different versions of TCP/IP networking software running on who knows how many different operating systems and hardware platforms. It would be unthinkable to require that all of these systems be upgraded at the same time.

Is there any way that we could avoid the chaos and misery an upgrade to IP would bring? Perhaps, perhaps not. It all depends on the degree to which a new protocol is necessary. In other words, if the only problem facing the protocol was a lack of addresses, it might be possible to work around that problem for quite some time with existing tools and techniques like subnetting, network address translation, or Classless Inter-Domain Routing (CIDR), as discussed below. However, such a stopgap approach can only work for so long—indeed, these techniques have been in use for years now and will ultimately hinder future growth of the Internet if an upgrade of IP is not implemented, simply because they limit the number of networks and hosts that can be connected.

Other problems with IPv4 are discussed later in this chapter, but they include issues relating not just to the shrinking address space but also to more general scalability issues, administrative problems, routing difficulties, improvement in services and the delivery of quality of service features, and security issues.

Ultimately, a good portion of the decision to replace the IPv4 protocol rather than just try to keep fixing it was made as a result of the many years of experience engineers have had with IPv4. We know what works well, what just works, and what could work much better. This is not a case of replacing a known quantity with an unknown quantity. The IPv6 designers built their new protocol on IPv4, taking what worked well, improving what worked, eliminating what detracted from performance and function—and adding some new features and functions that are clearly needed.

The rest of this section examines some of the measures currently being taken to address IPv4's shortcomings, followed by a discussion of the implications of a protocol transition like the proposed upgrade from IPv4 to IPv6.

Protocol Patches and Extensions

The most pressing issue facing IPv4 has been the size of the address space, and that is where a great deal of attention has been focused with efforts at reducing waste and improving efficiency of address allocation. Other issues, sometimes related to the address space, include routing, network administration and configuration, and IPv4 option extensions.

IPv4 Routing

One way or another, IPv4 packets traveling on the Internet or within an intranet must be routed from one network to another to reach their destinations. Routing protocols can use dynamic mechanisms for determining routes, but at some point all routing eventually depends on some router looking at a list of different routes and deciding which one is right. Routing lists comprise a list of networks and a list of interfaces connected to those networks; the router looks at a packet, determines what network it is on (or what network *that* network might be on), and then transmits the packet out the appropriate network interface.

The key here is that the more networks there are, the longer the routing list will be. And the longer the routing list, the longer (on average) it will take the router to figure out where to send the packet. This is not a problem if you have 10, or 100, or 1000 networks to keep track of. But when you get into the higher numbers as we have now with the Internet—with backbone routers routinely carrying explicit routes for over 110,000 different network addresses—routing can become a nightmare.

The routing issue affects performance, and it affects the Internet's growth far more immediately than the address space squeeze. The IPv4 address space may be depleted in five years, but without help Internet performance could be unacceptable sooner and might even be unacceptable now were it not for some techniques that use hierarchical addressing to aggregate routes and simplify routing.

Subnetting

Judicious use of subnets can increase efficiency of address allocation, but only to a certain extent. To understand why, consider how
network addresses used to be allocated: An organization could
apply to an address authority for a Class A, B, or C address. If they
could justify a need for a considerable number of host addresses,
they might qualify for a Class B address; if not, they would be
assigned a Class C address. It doesn't matter whether the applicant
has to handle 200 host addresses, or 20, or even just 2. They would
get a Class C address, thus tying up 254 host addresses. If they
could convince the authority they needed a Class B address, even if
they only needed to address 1000 hosts, they would get the full
Class B address, thus tying up 65,534 host addresses.

With these addresses, all traffic addressed anywhere within the network from outside is handled at a single router interface, which then
reroutes the traffic to its destination within the organization. This
kind of architecture means that you can design your organizational
network any way you wish. Figure 3.1 shows two alternatives. Both
networks are connected to the Internet, but the Class C network provides a single network of connectivity within the organization. The
Class B network breaks the organization down into three different
subnetted networks, connected to each other through an internal
router and to the Internet through a second router.

The subnet approach is required when the local network medium
approaches its limits in terms of size or number of connected hosts,
but it also can be used to reflect organizational architecture. What
isn't clear from the diagram is that the subnets do not necessarily
have to be in the same building or even the same city. The router can
redirect traffic across long distance data communication links as
well as through more local connections. This means that an organization can share a single network address with different branches,
operating units, or even subsidiaries.

The problem with subnetting is that it only works well for certain
sizes of organization, matched with either Class B or Class C networks. For example, a very large organization can use a Class B net-

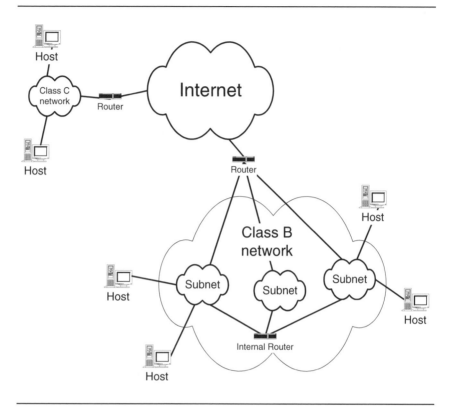

Figure 3.1. Subnets help organize network traffic as well as improve efficiency of network address utilization.

work to great advantage: Using an eight-bit subnet mask (in other words, stealing eight bits of host address from the total of sixteen bits available for a Class B network host) means that you can have up to 256 subnets, each of which can have as many as 254 hosts. Using nine bits for the subnet address doubles the maximum number of subnets to 512, while the maximum number of hosts possible on each of those subnets drops to 126; by increasing or decreasing the number of bits you can fine-tune the subnet architecture to suit the organizational architecture.

Unfortunately for those wanting them, unless you already have a Class B network you are unlikely to be able to get one these days. And addressing authorities are passing out Class C networks in blocks to Internet service providers to be redistributed to their customers. A Class C network can handle no more than 254 hosts (absolute maximum), with even fewer if the network is subnetted. Thus, a subnetted Class C network might work for a small company that needs no more than 8 (or 16) subnets, each with fewer than 30 (or 14) hosts, to give two examples. Even so, these two configurations limit the maximum number of hosts served to no more than 210, cutting the efficiency of the allocation.

Subnets are handy for organizing data traffic within an organization, as well as for making routing of datagrams from external sources simpler. The external source doesn't need to know anything about the destination's subnet, because all subnets are within a single network address, and all datagrams addressed anywhere within that network address are first passed through a single router. The router then determines what subnet to send the datagram to.

An interesting property of subnetting is that you can further subnet an already subnetted network. Consider Figure 3.2, where a Class B network is subnetted into three layers. At the first layer, where the organization's router attaches to the Internet, there is no subnet in operation. Just inside the organization, however, the Internet router recognizes that there are four bits of subnet. This makes possible as many as sixteen subnets; each of those subnets can be further subnetted as shown in the figure. In this example, they each take an additional four bits for the lowest level subnet, but different groups within the organization could choose to allocate their addresses differently. For example, one group with many subgroups, but fewer total hosts, could use an extra six bits for the sub-subnet (making the total subnet mask a total of ten bits) while another group might have fewer subdivisions, but larger subgroups, and thus use only an extra three bits for a total subnet mask of seven bits.

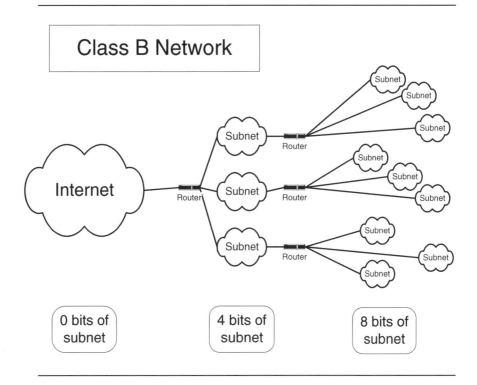

Figure 3.2. A subnet can be further subnetted, yielding a more complex network architecture.

Classless Inter-Domain Routing

Sometimes referred to as *supernetting*, the Classless Inter-Domain Routing (CIDR) protocol extends the idea of subnetting in the opposite direction: taking contiguous blocks of Class C networks and stealing bits from the first three bytes of the address to aggregate routes. In other words, just as all datagrams addressed to a single Class B address are routed to a single router, all datagrams addressed to any of a block of Class C addresses could also be routed to a single router.

This is known as classless routing because it tells the router to ignore the network class (Class C) address and walk up higher in the network address than usual to determine where to send the datagram. And unlike subnetting, where the subnet mask is irrelevant outside the network, the supernet path is used externally for routers to slim down their routing tables. For example, an ISP might be granted a block of 256 Class C addresses. This can be considered the equivalent of a Class B address, only the first three bits will be set to 110, instead of 10x. With supernetting, routers can be set to include the first 16 bits of the address block and treat it as a single route with 8 bits of supernet, instead of having to deal with as many as 256 different routes for each of the included Class C network addresses. ISPs are given these blocks because they often provide the routing for their customers' networks, so all datagrams for those customers will be routed through the ISP's router anyway.

Due to the relative scarcity of Class B networks, the relative abundance of Class C networks, and the fact that Class C addresses can be bundled in blocks that work well for moderate-sized organization, this approach makes a lot of sense. In addition, CIDR offers the added benefit of reducing the size of routing tables—thus improving routing performance. However, while CIDR improves the efficiency of network address allocation, it does not do anything to increase the total number of host addresses possible under IPv4 and should be considered purely a short-term tool rather than a long-term solution to the problems of IPv4.

Network Address Translation

The less information about your network that is available to outsiders, the more likely it is to be secure. For TCP/IP networks, this may mean keeping a firewall between the inside and the outside (Internet), which mediates all requests for internal resources. If you don't ever have direct connectivity between internal hosts and external hosts, it may not really matter if your IP addresses are globally unique—in other words, if your internal hosts do not need to be addressed by anyone on the Internet, you could arbitrarily choose any IP network addresses for them. In fact, many organizations with no intention of ever having *any* contact with the Internet took this approach (much to their chagrin later when they did connect their networks and had to renumber all their hosts).

At one time, such organizations were urged to get globally unique network addresses whether they planned to connect to the Internet or not, so they would not ever have to renumber hosts. However, private IP networks continue to be implemented, and, rather than continue to deplete the global IP address space, a group of IP network addresses has been set aside for private networks. One Class A network (10.0.0.0), 16 Class B networks (172.16.0.0 through 172.31.0.0) and 256 Class C networks (192.168.0.0 through 192.168.255.0) can be used by anyone for private networks. As defined in RFC 1918, routers connecting such private networks with public networks cannot forward packets from these private networks.

Network address translation (NAT) takes place at the interface between public and private networks, where a system (often a firewall or router) keeps track of the addresses of hosts on the private network and translates them into publicly accessible host addresses so that the internal hosts can communicate outside the organization.

While it helps improve the efficiency of IP address allocation, network designers must very carefully determine whether or not a network is a candidate for NAT before deploying it. NAT is most useful for networks that will never, ever, need to be combined with any other network or provide direct access to public networks. An IP network on a submarine would be a good candidate for a private network address: It is unlikely that it will ever be merged with another network, say on another submarine, and it is unlikely to need to have direct access to other, public, networks. Coming up with other pure candidates might be difficult. If two or more networks using these private network addresses were to be combined (for example, if two banks using private network addresses for their ATM machines were to merge) the resulting network would very likely have to be renumbered to avoid IP address collisions.

NAT offers smaller organizations a way to easily manage their own address space without relying on addressing authorities to allocate them sufficient address space for current or future needs. It also allows organizations to define address spaces for temporary or truly private networks quickly and flexibly. Unlike CIDR, NAT offers a mechanism for actually reducing the demand for IP addresses, although if used too haphazardly it can cost organizations dearly in terms of time and expense of renumbering private IP networks down the road.

Network Administration and Configuration

IPv4 and most of the rest of the TCP/IP application protocol suite were never designed, by themselves, to be easy to use. For example, raw FTP (File Transfer Protocol) depends on what appear to be very arcane request and reply codes and uses a set of cryptic-seeming commands. Why do I mention this? Simply because these apparently complicated command and control mechanisms are actually designed to be standard across all platforms, and to *simplify* access to software that understands the protocols. A system running IPv4 must be configured, correctly, with an apparently complicated set of parameters. These usually include a host name, IP address, subnet mask, default router, and some others (depending on the implementation). This is complicated—it means that the person who does the configuration must understand all these parameters or at least be given them by someone who does understand. What it means is that getting a system connected to an IPv4 network can be very complicated, time-consuming, and costly.

The Boot Protocol (BOOTP) took a first step toward simplifying the process of connecting a host to a network. This relatively simply protocol provided a mechanism for a host with minimal preconfiguration (often simply a terminal) to query a BOOTP server to get its IP configuration parameters. This approach failed to solve the entire problem because it only provided a mechanism for the BOOTP server to map IP address and other configuration information to a link layer address (for example, an Ethernet card interface address). To manage 100 hosts with BOOTP, you must assign each host its own IP address.

Address management and host configuration pose at least two big problems: First, if it is difficult to configure hosts, it costs money; second, if each host must tie up an IP address whether or not it is connected, it costs address space. It would be nice if we could make host configuration a plug-and-play operation—in other words, so simple that you simply plug the system into the network and it is automatically configured. It would also be nice if we could figure out a way to share IP addresses among many hosts, so that if no more than half of our 100 hosts were connected at any given time, we could get away with sharing 50 IP addresses among them.

As it turns out, another protocol, called the Dynamic Host Configuration Protocol (DHCP), was built on top of the BOOTP framework in an attempt to address these issues. Still using a client/server model, clients can use DHCP to query a server for configuration information, just as with BOOTP. However, DHCP adds more flexibility in terms of what kind of configuration information can be provided as well as how IP addresses are allocated. There are three mechanisms for allocating addresses:

- ♦ Using automatic allocation, hosts request an IP address and are given a permanent one that they use each time they connect to the network.
- ♦ Using manual allocation, the server assigns specific IP addresses to individual hosts based on a list provided by a network administrator. These IP addresses are reserved, whether or not the hosts request them.
- ♦ Using dynamic allocation, the server doles out IP addresses on a first-come, first-served basis; hosts are allowed to use the addresses for a specific time period after which the address "lease" expires.

Both automatic and manual allocation will tend to inefficiently distribute IP addresses; using automatic allocation may tend to tie up IP addresses. If an organization has more hosts than users, it could burn up as many IP addresses as it has hosts with this scheme. Manual allocation means network administrators must configure an IP address for each host, whether it connects once an hour or once a year to the network. Dynamic allocation, however, enables a relatively large population to share a relatively small number of IP addresses.

Unfortunately, DHCP falls short of enabling true plug-and-play configuration because it is stateful. That is, DHCP maintains the status of different IP addresses and the hosts using them. You have to explicitly set up a DHCP server that knows about your hosts, and the host to be configured with DHCP must know about the nearest DHCP server. True plug-and-play, which is a big part of the portability issue, doesn't happen with IPv4; as we'll see below, the inability of IPv4 to adequately support portability and network administration issues helps prompt the calls for upgrade to IPv6.

Type of Service

IP uses a packet-switched network architecture. This means that a packet might take any of a number of different routes to reach its destination. Those routes differ: Some might cost more, some might allow greater throughput, some might have lower latency, and some might be more reliable than others. IPv4 provides a mechanism, the Type of Service field (TOS) discussed in Chapter 2, that allows applications to tell IP how to handle their data streams. An application that needs lots of throughput, for example FTP, might force the TOS to favor routes that have lots of bandwidth; an application that needs fast responses, for example Telnet, might force the TOS to favor routes that have low delays.

This was a really good idea that never really caught on that well with implementers. For one thing, it requires routing protocols to incorporate notions of preferential routes based on costs as well as the need to track values for latency, throughput, and reliability for available routes. For another thing, it requires that developers implement a function in their application that might request service that, ultimately, could affect performance. TOS is a choice of one, so if you decide that low latency is most important to your application, it might affect your ability to get higher bandwidth or more reliable routes for your application's packets.

IP Options

As mentioned in Chapter 2, the IPv4 header includes a variable-length options field. IP options were meant to be the way to handle certain special functions. The original specifications left these options undefined, but eventually options for things like security as well as certain routing functions were added. Routing options include one (record route) to have each router handling the packet to record its address, another (timestamp) to have each router record its own address as well as the time it handles the packet. Source routing options are also available: Loose source routing specifies a list of routers that the packet must pass through on its way to the packet's destination, while strict source routing requires that the packet be routed *only* by the routers listed.

The problem with options is that they are special cases. IP datagrams without options are the vast majority and are the type of datagrams vendors optimize their routers to handle. The IP header without options is always five bytes long and is easy to process—especially when the router design optimizes for the processing of such headers. Performance is key to router sales, and because most traffic does not use IP options the routers tend to handle those packets as exceptions, shunting them off to the side to be handled when it is convenient—and when it won't affect the router's overall performance.

Despite the benefits of using IPv4 options, the cost in terms of performance has been enough to keep them from being used very often.

IPv4 Security

For a long time, the conventional wisdom about security was that it didn't belong at the internet layer. Security, in this case, means encryption of payload data. Other security functions include digital signatures on payloads, exchange of encryption keys, authentication of entities, and access control to resources. By and large, these functions have been handled at some higher layer, usually the application layer but sometimes the transport layer. For example, the widely used Secure Socket Layer (SSL) protocol operates along with the transport layer just above IP, while less commonly used Secure HTTP (SHTTP) operates at the application layer.

More recently, security tunneling protocols and mechanisms have proliferated as virtual private network (VPN) software and hardware products have been introduced. These products usually work by taking one stream of IP datagrams and encrypting it—turning the packets themselves into the payloads of another set of IP datagrams. Think of an IP datagram as a wrapped box that contains a smaller box, which in turn contains another box. The smallest box inside contains application data; the next box holds transport layer data, and the outside (IP) box contains IP data. Tunneling works by, in effect, putting that IP box inside another IP box with different addressing information on it.

Tunneling protocols like Microsoft's Point to Point Tunneling Protocol (PPTP) encrypt the IP datagrams first before wrapping them up and sending them out the tunnel.

There are problems with all these approaches to IP security. First, encryption at the application layer leaves a lot of information out in the open. Although the application data itself is encrypted, the IP datagrams carrying it will still yield to sniffers information about the processes and systems involved. Transport layer encryption is better and has worked moderately well for web security with SSL, but it still usually requires that the application (both client and server) be rewritten to support SSL. Tunneling protocols also work moderately well but have been hampered by a lack of standards.

The IP Security (IPsec) workgroup of the IETF has been working on devising mechanisms and protocols for securing network traffic for both IPv4 and the IPv6. Although there are mechanisms in place for native IPv4 security, through IP options, they have not been successful in practice. IPsec aims to make these tools available as well as to integrate security more completely in IPv6.

To Transition or Not to Transition

There is no question that IPv4 needs something to make it a viable network protocol going forward. The simple matter of a growing network eating through a limited resource—the IP address space—means that at the very least the address space must be expanded. The previous section listed some of the more prominent mechanisms put into play to help extend IPv4's life span, but it's clear that these are all largely stopgap measures. What is clear is that the address issue is far from the only problem with IPv4: More networks mean longer routing tables, which in turn mean poorer router performance. Likewise, difficulty in implementing IPv4 options means that the functions implemented with those options are not available to users.

Consider what would happen if it were possible to simply double the length of IP addresses, leaving all the rest of the protocol intact. All TCP/IP stacks would have to be updated at the same time. Anyone lagging behind would lose connectivity with the rest of the Internet. Despite the relative simplicity of the change, there would be huge reverberations as systems failed due to misconfiguration. The cost in any case would be massive, because it would mean that all organizations using IPv4 would have to locate every one of their systems (not always an easy task for large organizations with many computers and many users). Further complicating matters will be the fact that many of those systems will be older, outdated, or obsolete, and they will be running outdated and unsupported network software.

Any change requiring an upgrade of existing systems is going to be disruptive. Fixing IPv4, therefore, will be disruptive, whether we fix it temporarily with a patch or more permanently with a redesigned protocol. Therefore, why bother with a patch when a more robust fix is possible, without any significant increase in pain of upgrading?

IPv6 protocol specifications were submitted to and accepted by the IETF as early as the end of 1995. Software vendors started making beta versions of IPv6 network stacks available as early as 1996. Testbed implementations as well as an experimental IPv6 backbone (the 6BONE) were well in place by 1997, but momentum for the upgrade gathered very slowly in 1998. In any case, a "cutover" date is unlikely to be set any time soon. Instead, as will be discussed in later chapters, the migration to IPv6 will be relatively gradual and will see coexistence and interaction between IPv4 and IPv6.

The transition to IPv6 is likely to begin much higher in the food chain than the individual user, as organizations and Internet service providers start implementing it on their backbones. Even so, some of these organizations may now find themselves preoccupied with the year 2000 problem, further slowing the transition. However, once applications developers begin rolling out their new products based on IPv6, the move to IPv6 will accelerate. No matter what and despite far greater flexibility than the deadline for year 2000 problems, the schedule for IPv6 cannot be postponed for long.

4

The Roads to IPng

IPng, or IP Next Generation, did not spring into being fully formed but rather evolved over time, with several previous proposals. This chapter examines the different approaches proposed to upgrade IPv4 and discusses how those proposals contributed to the ultimate form of IPv6.

Birth of a Notion

By the early 1990s, it was clear that the Internet was outgrowing its protocols. RFC 1287, "Towards the Future Internet Architecture" was published in December 1991. It outlined directions that grew out of a January 1991 meeting of the Internet Activities Board (IAB—later renamed the Internet Architecture Board) and the Internet Engineering Steering Group (IESG), including what basic assumptions could be made about the future of the Internet and what were the most important areas for development of the Internet protocols.

Assumptions for the Internet Environment

The group came up with four assumptions, meant to characterize the best guess about what networking would be like during the next five to ten years. Agreement on what the networking environment would be like would lead to appropriate planning for the future. The assumptions were:

- ◆ That the TCP/IP protocol suite would coexist with its main rival, OSI, for some time. The International Organization for Standards (ISO) developed the Open System Interconnection (OSI) architecture (see Chapter 2 where the seven-layer OSI network stack is discussed). Despite the market success and acceptance of TCP/IP, OSI continued to have significant influence for some time.
- ◆ That the Internet itself would become more complex, incorporating more diverse and a greater number of different types of networking technologies. In other words, instead of settling on one or a handful of network connectivity media, an increasing population of network connectivity media would become available and used over time.
- ◆ That access to the Internet would be provided by a variety of different carriers, including both public and private providers, for a wide variety of different networks. In other words, networks for many different types of organizations, including corporations, government agencies, educational institutions, and public services, will be connected through common carrier service providers as well as by privately maintained network connections.
- ◆ That the Internet needs to be able to interconnect as many as one billion (10^9) networks, though the consensus seemed to encompass a relatively broad range of anywhere from ten million to ten billion networks.

Looking back from 1998, these assumptions have largely held up quite well. The biggest exception is the assumption that OSI would maintain its significance; while it has not disappeared, OSI has clearly been losing ground in relation to IP for several years. The complexity of the Internet has indeed increased considerably, with newer network technologies like Asynchronous Transfer Mode

(ATM) and xDSL (a generic acronym for various Digital Subscriber Line services) becoming increasingly common. The diversity of network connectivity has also increased as predicted.

The number of networks to be interconnected is still not entirely clear, though it has become clear that the IPv4 address space is insufficient. On the one hand, we could allot one network to every company and organization in the world with under a billion networks; on the other hand, the rapid decrease in cost and increase in distribution in computers could create a demand for at least one network *per person* in the world, thus requiring on the order of at least 10 billion networks just for people. Factoring in unforseeable circumstances such as these leads some to call for an address space that can handle at least one trillion networks.

Designated Areas for Internet Evolution

The January 1991 IAB/IESG meeting generated another list, this one of the areas that were deemed most important to further architectural growth. The intention was to identify the areas on which development efforts should be focused. These included:

- Routing and addressing concerns.
- Multiprotocol architecture.
- Security architecture.
- Traffic control and state.
- Advanced applications.

These areas, approaches to development, and other issues are discussed next.

Addressing and Routing

The address space was already clearly a problem, but the issue of ballooning routing tables was already of great concern. Another RFC coming out about this time cited routing tables with 5000 and 7000 entries as a looming impediment to performance on networks that were still growing rapidly. The authors of RFC 1287 suggest not only that the IPv4 address will be depleted but also that at some point before then IPv4 routing algorithms will fail due to the large number of networks. They also suggest that multiple routes between sources and destinations will make possible type of service (TOS) variations and therefore require some mechanisms to control route selection.

Aggregation of network routes, through some mechanism, is suggested as one possible solution to the explosion of routes. Using some method of defining boundaries between large domains would help improve routing efficiency. Another suggestion solicits some efficient mechanism for the computation of network routes, as well as some mechanism for routers to maintain state associated with specific streams that are routed in some special way.

Potential addressing fixes include the use of the existing 32-bit address as a non–globally unique identifier. In other words, addresses might be reused in different parts of the network that don't interoperate directly. For example, dividing the world into different domains would allow a host address to be used once in each domain, with interoperation between the domains mediated by protocol gateways that rewrite the addresses as they pass over domain boundaries.

Another suggestion for addressing simply increased the size of the host address field and incorporates an administrative domain as part of the network address. A third suggestion expands the host address field and uses the entire field as a nonhierarchical address space, with a connection setup that gives routers the opportunity to map a host address to an administrative domain.

Multiprotocol Architecture

Support for interoperable transmission of OSI as well as TCP/IP traffic was thought to be an important criteria for further development. The sense was that up to 1991, Internet connectivity meant that a host had an Internet address. If you didn't have an IP address and weren't running IP, you weren't connected. This viewpoint was already eroding by 1991, with the authors of RFC 1287 suggesting that connectivity could be based on access to the Internet through e-mail gateways, or, more simply, through some application. For example, users on NetWare networks can run Internet applications like web browsers and e-mail clients on their systems but use the Internetwork Packet eXchange (IPX) protocol to transport the data on their local Novell NetWare networks.

In practice, acceptance of TCP/IP as an internetworking protocol suite by most software and hardware vendors during the 1990s has largely driven out competing internetworking protocol suites. Even Novell finally deployed its NetWare network operating system as a native TCP/IP product by 1998.

More important, at least in hindsight, was the comment that TCP/IP could integrate or cross-pollinate with other application protocols. Interoperability, particularly between applications rather than at lower layers, was deemed to be a good thing.

Security Architecture

Department of Defense funding of significant research and development work that produced IP meant that the protocols were built with military security in mind. However, the security needs of a commercial Internet are different from those of a military network, and the authors note that adding security to a protocol suite is much harder than building a secure protocol suite from the ground up.

One specific suggestion for a desired security service is distinguished names (an OSI construct used in X.500 directory specifications) that can be authenticated in order to implement access controls. Integrity enforcement was also suggested, with mechanisms to prevent modification of transmissions, spoofing of transmission origins, and defense against replay attacks (where an interceptor replays data stolen from an authorized stream). Other services include confidentiality (encrypted transmission), nonrepudiation (use of digital signature to prevent a sender from denying having sent a message), and protection from denial of service attacks.

Other security issues raised in the RFC include router/gateway protocol filtering (firewalls) and encryption key management and storage.

Traffic Control and State

IPv4 is a connectionless protocol, but some applications—audio and video, for example—depend on some degree of traffic control to work properly. A video stream must arrive at its destination at a relatively dependable rate, not too fast and not too slow; otherwise it doesn't work well at all. RFC 1287 specifies that some sort of packet queuing mechanisms to provide traffic control are necessary, as well as some method of maintaining status of different streams, to facilitate the extension of IP to these real-time applications.

Noting that IPv4 implements a Type of Service (TOS) field, the authors also note that not only is TOS not generally implemented, it is not clear how to implement it.

Advanced Applications

Rather than putting forward suggestions for new applications, the RFC authors suggest that improving and simplifying the processes involved in developing new and advanced applications would be more productive. As a starting point, they suggest that the creation of common data formats for different types of data, particularly text, images and graphics, audio and video, workstation displays, and data objects. Also important to developing advanced applications are mechanisms for exchange of this data. Suggested mechanisms include store and forward services, global file systems, interprocess communications, data broadcast, and a standard method for accessing databases.

The First Round

Up to 1994, quite a few different proposals were made for the successor to IPv4. By 1992, the three dominant proposal families that would eventually be considered by the IETF in 1994 had already taken shape. RFC 1347, *TCP and UDP with Bigger Addresses (TUBA), A Simple Proposal for Internet Addressing and Routing*, outlines one. TUBA can be characterized as simply replacing IP with the OSI internetwork protocol, Connection-Less Network Protocol (CLNP). CLNP uses Network Service Access Point (NSAP) addresses that can be any length but that are often implemented in 20 bytes, providing more than enough address space. Furthermore, using CLNP would help IP and OSI to converge, while at the same eliminating the need to build an entirely new protocol.

Another was first known as IPv7 in 1992 and in 1993 was described in detail in RFC 1475 under the title *TP/IX: The Next Internet*. It's not clear what TP/IX stands for; according to Christian Huitema in *IPv6: The New Internet Protocol* (Prentice Hall PTR, 1998) the name expresses the desire of its proposer, Robert Ullman, to change not only IP but also TCP with the upgrade. TP/IX uses 64-bit addresses and adds an addressing layer to the hierarchy, above organizations, for administrations. The IPv7 eight-byte addresses allocate three bytes to administrative domain, three to the organization's network, and two bytes for the host identifier. The IPv7 datagram header simplifies the IPv4 header, while adding a forward route identifier to be used by intermediate routers to determine how to handle datagrams. For example, the forward route identifier may be associated with a particular route based on certain values relating to the route itself (throughput or value) or to be associated with a particular datagram stream or even to be associated with data from a mobile host—that is, a host that moves from one network to another while maintaining open TCP connections. TP/IX not only modified TCP and UDP, but it also included a new routing protocol called RAP.

TP/IX later evolved into another proposal, described in RFC 1707, *CATNIP: Common Architecture for the Internet*. CATNIP seems to have little in common with TP/IX, however, except that it retains the IPv7 designation. In its goal of providing a common architecture, the CATNIP specification makes allowances for the three most commonly used internetwork architectures: TCP/IP, OSI, and IPX, as well as discussion of how to integrate a competing proposed standard for the next generation of IP. The stated objective is to make it possible for all existing systems to continue to interoperate with *no* modifications, no changes in address, and no software upgrades for individual hosts. By making allowance for different network architectures, the CATNIP proposal meant to minimize impact on the actual infrastructure; however, it meant adding a layer of complexity in order to implement true interoperable internetworking.

The third proposal stream started out as something called IP in IP, or IP Encaps (for IP encapsulation). Under this proposal, there would be two layers of IP: One would be used for a global backbone, while the other would be used in more limited areas. The IP to be used in limited areas could continue to be IPv4, while the backbone would use a new layer with different addressing. Ultimately, this evolved and merged with other proposals to become the Simple Internet Protocol Plus (SIPP) proposal. As explained in RFC 1710, *Simple Internet Protocol Plus White Paper*, this was SIPP's history:

> The SIPP working group represents the evolution of three different IETF working groups focused on developing an IPng. The first was called IP Address Encapsulation (IPAE) and was chaired by Dave Crocker and Robert Hinden. It proposed extensions to IPv4 which would carry larger addresses. Much of its work was focused on developing transition mechanisms.
>
> Somewhat later Steve Deering proposed a new protocol evolved from IPv4 called the Simple Internet Protocol (SIP). A working group was formed to work on this proposal which was chaired by Steve Deering and Christian Huitema. SIP had 64-bit addresses, a simplified header, and options in separate extension headers. After lengthly interaction between the two working groups and the realization that IPAE and SIP had a number of common elements and the transition mechanisms developed for IPAE would apply to SIP, the groups decided to merge and concentrate their efforts. The chairs of the new SIP working group were Steve Deering and Robert Hinden.
>
> In parallel to SIP, Paul Francis (formerly Paul Tsuchiya) had founded a working group to develop the "P" Internet Protocol (Pip). Pip was a new internet protocol based on a new architecture. The

motivation behind Pip was that the opportunity for
introducing a new internet protocol does not come
very often and given that opportunity important new
features should be introduced. Pip supported variable length addressing in 16-bit units, separation
of addresses from identifiers, support for provider
selection, mobility, and efficient forwarding. It
included a transition scheme similar to IPAE.

After considerable discussion among the leaders of
the Pip and SIP working groups, they came to re-
alize that the advanced features in Pip could be
accomplished in SIP without changing the base SIP
protocol as well as keeping the IPAE transition
mechanisms. In essence it was possible to keep the
best features of each protocol. Based on this the
groups decided to merge their efforts. The new
protocol was called Simple Internet Protocol Plus
(SIPP). The chairs of the merged working group are
Steve Deering, Paul Francis, and Robert Hinden.

Briefly, SIPP offers several changes from IPv4. These include:

- *Routing and addressing expansion.* SIPP specifies 64-bit
  addresses, double the size of IPv4. The intention is to
  provide greater degrees of hierarchy within which routing can be accomplished. Another feature is the addition
  of "cluster addresses," which identify regions of the network topology. SIPP address extensions, available in
  units of 64 bits, work with the cluster addresses to create
  the possibility of a much larger address space.
- *IP header simplification.* SIPP does away with some IPv4
  header fields, while streamlining the structure to help
  improve routing efficiency.
- *Improvement in option implementation.* SIPP uses a more
  flexible approach to encoding and implementing IP
  options.
- *Quality of service.* SIPP makes it possible to label datagrams as belonging to specific data flows. Hosts can
  request special handling for the routing of these flows,

especially useful for applications that depend on real-time delivery like that required by video or audio transmission.

- ♦ *Authentication and privacy.* SIPP adds extensions for authentication, data integrity, and confidentiality.

SIPP was the result of many people from several different groups working together. The finished specification includes many interesting new mechanisms, while still not straying too far from the goal of being an upgrade to IPv4 rather than an entirely new protocol built from the ground up. Notable is the use of routing similar to that in IPv4, still using CIDR to add flexibility and improve routing performance. Also important are new routing extensions that allow choice of routes from different providers based on various criteria (including performance, cost, provider policies for traffic, and so on). Other routing extensions include support for mobile hosts as well as automatic readdressing and extended addressing.

One other notable mechanism is the the SIPP approach to IP options: Rather than including them as part of the basic IP header, SIPP segregates any IP options from the main header. The options headers, if any, are simply inserted into the datagram after the header and before the transport layer protocol header. This way, routers can process datagrams without having to process the options headers unless it is necessary—thus improving performance overall for all datagrams.

RFC 1710 provides both a technical overview to the SIPP specification and a readable justification and narrative of the protocol. It is worth a look, if only to see how IPv6 as we know it came to be—because SIPP, with some modifications, was the specification recommended to and accepted by the IESG as the basis for IPng.

Pick of the Litter

RFC 1752, *The Recommendation for the IP Next Generation Protocol,* was published in January 1995. It is a fascinating document that lays out very clearly what was needed and what was available, in terms of the candidate proposals for successors to IPv4. In its summary, the authors of RFC 1752 outline what IPng would look like:

```
This protocol recommendation includes a simpli-
fied header with a hierarchical address structure
that permits rigorous route aggregation and is
also large enough to meet the needs of the Inter-
net for the foreseeable future. The protocol also
includes packet-level authentication and encryp-
tion along with plug and play autoconfiguration.
The design changes the way IP header options are
encoded to increase the flexibility of introduc-
ing new options in the future while improving per-
formance. It also includes the ability to label
traffic flows.
```

The fifth item in a long list of specific recommendations is that IPng be based on SIPP with 128-bit addresses. The rest of the RFC provides an excellent resource for further historical background on how the Internet research community identified and approached the problems associated with IPv4, as well as detailed analysis of the three contenders, TUBA, CATNIP, and SIPP. The RFC examines each proposal and discusses how it meets (or fails to meet) the requirements, as well as what the results of the proposal review process were.

All three proposals are praised in some way and all ultimately contributed something to the final recommendation. For example, SIPP did not include a strong transition plan or a totally acceptable mechanism for autoconfiguration, so the recommendation draws on the TUBA proposal for those areas. And SIPP was not accepted in all its glory: The concept of address extensions was ultimately considered too experimental and potentially risky to incorporate into the IPng work, while the 64-bit address space was replaced with a 128-bit address space to cope with any future uncertainties.

The recommendations described in RFC 1752 include a variety of further tasks related to the actual design of the IPng and related protocols. SIPP and the others could be considered only as starting points, particularly if IPng were to be sufficiently robust to serve the Internet for years to come.

IPv6, Round 1

The first proposed standard RFCs (RFCs 1883–1887) to describe IPv6 and supporting protocols were published by early 1996 and some are included in Appendix B of this book. However, they were not entirely complete and were soon followed by various additions and some slight modifications. Appendix A includes a list of RFCs related to IPng and IPv6. The next chapter describes the basics of IPv6, and the chapters following it provide more of the details based on these and later protocol specifications.

IPv6, Round 2

By the end of the summer of 1998, new IPv6 RFCs were being approved for publication. In particular, RFC 2373, *IP Version 6 Addressing Architecture*, replaces RFC 1883 and RFC 2374, *An IPv6 Aggregatable Global Unicast Address Format*, replaces RFC 2073. Other new RFCs approved for publication describe ICMPv6, neighbor discovery and stateless autoconfiguration for IPv6.

5

The Shape of IPv6

This chapter introduces the update to IPv4, examining the fields of the new protocol header and the IPv6 address space and highlighting the changes and new features of IPv6. IPv4 had two "helper" protocols: the Internet Control Message Protocol (ICMP) and the Internet Group Management Protocol (IGMP). These protocols defined mechanisms for hosts and routers to report IP layer errors as well as to perform other, diagnostic, functions. IPv6 uses the ICMPv6 protocol, which updates ICMP; ICMPv6 originally incorporated IGMP functions, but these functions are likely to disappear as they are now handled by IGMPv2.

The first part of this chapter presents the basic outline of the IPv6 protocol and introduces the IPv6 header fields and IPv6 options and extensions as defined in RFC 1883, *Internet Protocol, Version 6 (IPv6) Specification* and by the successor specification (not assigned an RFC number as of September 1998). The second part of this chapter presents an overview to ICMPv6, as defined in RFC 1885, *Internet Control Message Protocol (ICMPv6) for the Internet Protocol Version 6 (IPv6) Specification*. IGMPv2 is described in RFC 2236, *Internet Group Management Protocol, Version 2*, and relates to both IPv4 and IPv6.

IPv6 addressing is introduced in Chapter 6, while more details on the use of IPv6 options and header extensions are provided in Chapter 7. Chapter 8 examines routing with IPv6, Chapter 9 goes into greater detail on security and authentication with IPv6, and Chapter 10 discusses how the upgrade to IPv6 will affect protocols above and below IP.

IPv6

The upgrade to IPv4 was initially described in two RFCs. RFC 1883 decribes the protocol itself, while RFC 1884 describes the IPv6 address architecture; RFC 1884 has been superseded by RFC 2373, and during the summer of 1998 the IETF approved a draft to replace RFC 1883. The change from 32-bit addresses to 128-bit addresses represents a very major shift, and exactly how IPv6 addresses are to be assigned and distributed was not clear even as of the autumn of 1998; more details about IPv6 addressing are provided in Chapter 6. This section provides an introduction to the most important changes to the actual IPv6 protocol, without worrying about addressing details.

Overview of Changes

IPv6 embodies change in five important areas:

- ◆ Expanded addressing.
- ◆ Simplified header format.
- ◆ Improved extension and option support.
- ◆ Flow labeling.
- ◆ Authentication and privacy.

These changes to IP improve IPv6 in most of the directions originally charted by the IAB back in 1991. IPv6's expanded addressing means that IP can continue to grow without concern about depletion of resources; the addressing architecture helps improve the situation for routing efficiency. The simplified header format improves routing efficiency by requiring less processing of routers, while the improvements in extension and option support mean that special needs can be accommodated without significantly affecting performance either of routing of normal packets or of the special-needs packets. Flow labeling provides another mechanism for treating streams of packets efficiently, particularly useful for real-time applications. Authentication and privacy improvements make IPv6 a more desirable protocol for commercial uses that require special treatment of sensitive information or resources.

Expanded Addressing

In addition to moving from a 32-bit address space to a 128-bit address space, the IPv6 addressing architecture makes some adjustments to the different types of address available to an IP host. As will be explained in more detail in Chapter 6, IPv6 eliminates broadcast addresses while adding the concept of *anycast* addresses. Unicast addresses, specifying a single network interface, and multicast addresses, specifying an address to which one or more hosts may be listening, continue basically unchanged from their IPv4 incarnations.

Simplified Header

IPv6 headers consist of eight fields (two of which are source and destination addresses) spread over 40 bytes. Contrast this with IPv4 headers, which contain at least 12 different fields and which may be as short as 20 bytes if no options are in use or as long as 60 bytes if options are being used. Efficient routing is more easy with a uniformly sized header and with fewer fields to examine and process.

The header could be simplified as a result of some changes in the way IP works. For one thing, making all headers the same length eliminates the need for the header length field. For another, by changing the rules about packet fragmentation, several fields can be removed from the header. Fragmentation in IPv6 may only be done by source nodes: Intermediate routers along the packet's path can no longer fragment them. Finally, eliminating the IP header checksum shouldn't affect reliability in any way, particularly because header checksums are performed by higher level protocols (UDP and TCP).

Improved Extension and Option Support

Unlike IPv4, in which options may be added at the end of the actual IP header, IPv6 adds options in separate extension headers. In this way, the option header need only be examined and processed as necessary. These will be discussed at greater length below and in Chapter 7.

To illustrate, consider two different types of extensions supported: the fragmentation header and the routing header. Fragmentation in IPv6 occurs only at a source node, so the only nodes that need to concern themselves with fragmentation extension headers are the source node and the destination node. The source node does the fragmentation and creates the headers, which are placed after the main IPv6 header and before the next higher layer protocol header. The destination node accepts the packets and uses the fragmentation extension header to reassemble the packet. All intermediate nodes can safely ignore the fragmentation extension headers, thus improving efficiency as the packets are routed.

Alternatively, a hop-by-hop option extension header requires that every node along the packet's route process that header. In that case, each router must process the option as well as the main IPv6 header. The first such hop-by-hop option is defined for handling extra-large IP packets (*jumbo payloads*). Packets with jumbo payloads (over 65,535 bytes) require special treatment because not all links will be capable of handling such large size transmission units, and routers want to avoid attempting to send them out on networks that cannot handle them. Thus, it is necessary for the option to checked at every node the packet traverses.

Flows

In IPv4, all packets are treated roughly equally, which means each is handled on its own by intermediate routers. Routers do not keep track of packets sent between any two hosts so they can "remember" how to handle future packets. IPv6 implements the concept of the *flow*, which is, according to RFC 1883:

> A flow is a sequence of packets sent from a particular source to a particular (unicast or multicast) destination for which the source desires special handling by the intervening routers.

Routers are supposed to keep track of flows and maintain a certain amount of information that remains constant for each packet in a flow. This helps make it possible for the router to efficiently handle the packets in the flow. Packets in a flow may be handled differently from other packets, but in any case, they can be handled more quickly because the router does not have reprocess each packet's header. Flows and flow labels are discussed in more detail in the following sections.

Authentication and Privacy

RFC 1825, *Security Architecture for the Internet Protocol*, describes a security architecture for IP, both versions 4 and 6. Since it was published in August 1995, it has been undergoing modification and update. An updated version of an Internet draft was published in March 1998. While the basic structure of IP security remains fairly solid, significant changes and additions have been made. This architecture, and how it is implemented in IPv6, is covered in Chapter 9.

IPv6 uses two security extensions: the IP authentication header (AH) first described in RFC 1826, *IP Authentication Header*, and the IP encapsulating security payload (ESP) first described in RFC 1827, *IP Encapsulating Security Payload (ESP)*.

Message digest functions provide authentication by providing what is, in effect, a secure and reliable checksum calculation on packets. The sender calculates the message digest and inserts it into the authentication header (AH); the recipient recalculates the message digest of the packet received and compares it to the value contained in the AH. If the two values are identical, the recipient can be assured that the packet was unchanged during its transmission. If the two values are different, the recipient can assume that the packet was either damaged during transmission or purposely modified by some interloper.

The encapsulating security payload provides a mechanism to encrypt the payload of an IP packet or to encrypt an entire IP packet and tunnel it over the Internet. The difference is that when encrypting only the payload of a packet, the rest of the packet—the headers—is transmitted in the clear. This means that intercepters may be able to identify the source and destination hosts, as well as other information about the packet. Tunneling IP with ESP means that the entire IP packet is encrypted and then encapsulated within another IP packet by a system operating as a security gateway. In this way, all details of the encrypted IP packet are obscured. This mechanism is fundamental to the creation of virtual private networks (VPNs), which allow organizations to use the Internet as their own private backbone for sharing what may be sensitive information.

IPv6 Header Structure

In IPv4, all headers terminated on a 32-bit boundary; in other words, the basic unit of measurement was four bytes. In IPv6, header boundaries are placed at 64-bit boundaries, with IPv6 headers being a total of 40 bytes long. The IPv6 protocol specifies the following fields for its header:

- ♦ *Version.* This is a four-bit value, and for IPv6 must be equal to six.
- ♦ *Class.* An eight-bit value specifies that some form of "differentiated service" be provided for the packet. RFC 1883 originally defined this field as only four bits long and called it the Priority field; later, the name was changed to Class, with the latest IPv6 Internet draft referring to it as

Traffic Class. Use of this field is defined separately from IPv6 and has not yet been specified in any RFCs. The default value for this field is all zeros.

♦ *Flow label.* This is a 20-bit value used to identify packets that belong to the same flow. A node can be the source for more than one simultaneous flow. The flow label and the address of the source node uniquely identify flows. This field was originally (in RFC 1883) set to 24 bits, but when the class field was increased in size to eight bits, the flow label field was decreased to compensate.

♦ *Payload length.* This is a 16-bit field that contains an integer value equal to the length of the packet payload in bytes; that is, the number of bytes contained in the packet after the end of the IPv6 header. This means that IPv6 extensions are included as part of the payload for the purposes of calculating this field.

♦ *Next header.* This field indicates what protocol is in use in the header immediately following the IPv6 packet. Similar to the IPv6 protocol field, the next header field may refer to a higher-layer protocol like TCP or UDP, but it may also indicate the existence of an IPv6 extension header.

♦ *Hop limit.* Every time a node forwards a packet, it decrements this eight-bit field by one. If the hop limit reaches zero, the packet is discarded. Unlike in IPv4, where the time-to-live field fulfills a similar purpose, sentiment is currently against putting a protocol-defined upper limit on packet lifetime for IPv6. This means that the function of timing-out old data should be accomplished in upper-layer protocols.

♦ *Source address.* This is the 128-bit address of the node originating the IPv6 packet.

♦ *Destination address.* This is the 128-bit address of the intended recipient of the IPv6 packet. This address may be a unicast, multicast, or anycast address. If a routing extension is being used (which specifies a particular route that the packet must traverse), the destination address may be one of those intermediate nodes instead of the ultimate destination node.

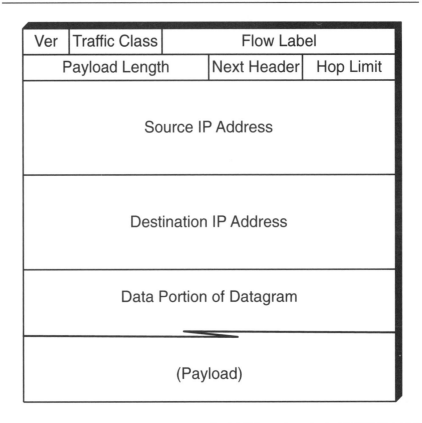

Figure 5.1. IPv6 headers are significantly simpler than IPv4 (see Figure 2.3).

Figure 5.1 shows the IPv6 header format. The next section provides a more detailed comparison with the IPv4 header fields.

IPv4 versus IPv6

Look again at Figure 2.3, showing the IPv4 header. Although some of the fields are similar to those found in IPv6, the only field that remains entirely unchanged is the first one, the version field, which must remain the same for IPv4 and IPv6 to be compatible on the same wires. The next field, header length, is irrelevant to IPv6 because all

IPv6 headers are the same length; IPv4 requires this field because its headers can be as short as 20 bytes and as long as 60 bytes.

The Type of Service field is similar to the IPv6 traffic class field, but ToS is positioned later in the header than that field (and it also has not found wide acceptance from implementers). The next field, datagram length, evolves into the payload length field in IPv6. The IPv6 payload length includes extension headers, while the IPv4 datagram length field specifies the length of the entire datagram including headers. Thus, routers can calculate the length of the IPv4 datagram payload by subtracting the header length from the datagram length; this calculation is unnecessary in IPv6.

The next three fields, datagram identification, flags, and fragment offset, all pertain to IPv4 datagram fragmentation. Because IPv6 calls for an end to fragmentation by intermediate nodes (see the following for more on fragmentation), these fields become unnecessary and are missing from the main IPv6 packet header.

The time-to-live field, as mentioned above, has become the hop limit field. The time-to-live field was originally meant to be an upper bound, in seconds, of the lifetime of a packet in the Internet cloud. If the time-to-live counter reached zero, the packet was to be discarded. The rationale was that packets might be caught in circular routes, and if they did not expire in some way they would continue to be routed forever (or until the network crashed). The original specification called for routers to decrement this value by the number of seconds it took from receipt of a packet until the packet was forwarded. In practice, most routers have been implemented to simply decrement this value by one rather than attempting to measure the actual time spent in the router.

The protocol field, as mentioned above, refers to the next-higher layer protocol encapsulated within the IPv4 packet. The values for different protocols are available in the most recent version of the *Assigned Numbers* RFC (currently RFC 1700). This field evolved into the next header field in IPv6, where it specifies the next header, whether an IPv6 extension header or another layer's protocol header.

With upper-layer protocols like TCP and UDP calculating their own checksums on headers, the IPv4 header checksum was deemed superfluous, so that field disappears in IPv6. For those applications that actually require content authentication, the authentication header is available in IPv6.

The 32-bit IPv4 source and destination addresses reappear in IPv6, but they have been enlarged to 128 bits. The IP options field disappears entirely, however, to be replaced with IPv6 extension headers.

Flow Labels

IPv4 is often described as a connectionless protocol. Like any packet-switched network, IPv4 is designed to let each packet find its own path to its destination. Each packet is handled separately, and as a result any two packets sent from the same source to the same destination could easily be routed over entirely different paths. This is a good thing for network robustness, as it means that any given route could be down at any given time, but as long as there is *some* route between two hosts the data they transmit to each other will get through.

However, this approach may seem a bit inefficient, particularly when packets do not stand alone but in fact represent portions of a stream of data flowing between applications on the communicating systems. To go a step further, consider what happens when a stream of packets passes from along its route from one host to another: Processing of each packet by each intermediate router contributes slightly to added latency in the link. For most of the traditional Internet applications, such as file transfer or terminal emulation, latency is mostly an inconvenience, but for newer applications that provide interactive audio or video, even relatively small increases in latency can significantly degrade service.

Another problem that the independent handling of IPv4 datagrams presents is the difficulty of assigning certain traffic to lower-cost links. For example, e-mail transmissions are usually done in the background and are not real-time applications, but there is no simple way for IPv4 network administrators to identify these packets and route them along a lower-cost Internet link while reserving higher-cost links for real-time applications.

IPv6 implements the concept of flows to help with these and other problems. A flow label in this field in the IPv6 header identifes the packet as part of a stream of packets that share the same source address and destination address. All packets in the same flow have the same flow label.

IPv6 Traffic Classes

The original IPv6 RFC (1883) specified a four-bit priority field, in which one of 16 different priority classes could be specified for the packet. However, after much discussion the name of this field was changed to "class" and expanded to a full byte. The most recent Internet draft revision for RFC 1883 changes the name again, to "traffic class."

Values and precise use of the IPv6 class field is yet to be determined. Experimentation using the IPv4 type of service field, as well as using class with IPv6, should eventually produce usable results. The object of using traffic classes is to allow nodes that originate traffic as well as routers that forward traffic to mark packets for different treatment than the default. Generally, it is assumed that eventually packets may receive special treatment in terms of the cost, bandwidth, latency, or some other characteristic of the links over which they are routed.

While IPv6 implementations are very likely to require or recommend that upper-layer protocols be permitted to specify a desired traffic class for their data, those implementations may also allow intermediate routers to change the value of this field depending on circumstances.

Fragmentation

Fragmentation in IPv6 is permitted only between the originating node and the destination; this simplifies the header and reduces overhead for routing. Hop-by-hop fragmentation is considered harmful. For one thing, it can generate more fragments than end-to-end fragmentation. For another, the loss of a single fragment means all the fragments must be retransmitted. IPv6 does support fragmentation through an extension header, though, as described below. Understanding how IPv4 fragmentation works will clarify why it has been changed in IPv6.

IPv4 packet fragmentation happens when the unfragmented packet is too long to traverse a network link along its route from source to destination. To illustrate, a source node may create a packet of 1500 bytes and send it to a remote destination somewhere on the Internet. The packet is transmitted on the source's local Ethernet network to the default router for that node. This router forwards the packet on its link to the Internet, which may be a point-to-point connection with an Internet service provider. Somewhere inside the Internet cloud, or somewhere closer to the destination node, there may be a network link that cannot handle data in chunks that large. In that case, the router using that network link would have to break up the 1500-byte datagram into fragments no larger than the next network's *link maximum transmission unit* (MTU) size. So, if the next link could handle packets no larger than, say, 1280 bytes, the router would break the original packet up into two pieces. The first would be 1260 bytes long, leaving 20 bytes for the IPv4 header. The second fragment would be the length of the remainder of the original packet, 240 bytes, plus another 20 bytes for another IPv4 header.

Fragmentation in IPv4 is done as needed by intermediate routers along a packet's path. The fragmenting router modifies the packet's header as necessary to include the original packet's datagram identification, as well as setting the fragmentation flags and the fragment offset field appropriately. When the resulting fragmented packets are received by the destination node, that system must reassemble the packets using the fragmentation data in the IPv4 headers of each packet fragment.

Using fragmentation, it is possible to interoperate between nodes that exist on very different types of networks, with any kind of network in between—the source node doesn't need to know anything about the destination node's network, nor does it need to know

anything about the networks in between. This has always been considered a relatively good thing, as not requiring nodes or routers to
store information or maps of the entire Internet helps make the
Internet very scalable. On the other hand, it also poses a performance problem for routers: Fragmenting IP packets costs processing power and time along the route as well as at the destination.
There is the overhead of keeping track of IP datagram identifiers,
calculating fragment offsets, and actually dividing up a packet into
fragments and then reassembling it at its destination.

The problem is that for any given route, while the source can know
what the link MTU is, there is no way to know ahead of time what
the *path MTU* will be. The path MTU is the size of the largest packet
that can be carried over any network along the route between the
source and the destination, without having to fragment it.

There are, however, two ways to reduce or eliminate the need for
fragmentation. The first, which is available in IPv4, is to use a
method called *path MTU discovery*. With this approach, a router can
send out a packet to the destination the size of the link MTU for the
router. If the packet reaches a link at which it must be fragmented,
using the Internet Control Message Protocol (ICMP) the fragmenting router will send back a message indicating how much smaller
the fragmenting router's link MTU is. This process can be repeated
until the router can determine the path MTU. (ICMP is discussed at
greater length below.)

The other way to cut down on the need for fragmentation is to
require that all links supporting IP be able to handle packets of some
reasonable minimum size. In other words, if a link MTU could be
anything from 20 bytes on up, then all nodes would have to be prepared to do a considerable amount of fragmenting of packets. On the
other hand, if you could come up with some reasonable size which
all network links could accommodate and set that as the absolute
minimum permitted packet size, you could eliminate fragmentation.

IPv6, in fact, uses both these approaches. In the original RFC, the
IPv6 specification calls for every link to support an MTU of at least
576 bytes. The resulting payloads for these packets would then be

536 bytes, allowing 40 bytes for the IPv6 headers. Since RFC 1883 was published in 1995, compelling arguments have been made for a larger MTU. Huitema reports (in *IPv6: The New Internet Protocol*, 2nd ed., Prentice-Hall) that as of 1997, Steve Deering was campaigning for an MTU of 1500 bytes. The most recent Internet draft, published November 1997, set the MTU at 1280 bytes. Clearly, this is a major point of contention: Advocates of shorter MTUs want to ensure that networks unable to support longer MTUs are not made entirely obsolete, while advocates of longer MTUs want to avoid hobbling the entire Internet with performance constraints just to accommodate a small population of nearly obsolete networks.

In part to compensate for what may turn out to be a shorter MTU, the IPv6 specification also strongly recommends that all IPv6 nodes implement path MTU discovery. Described first in RFC 1191, *Path MTU Discovery*, this mechanism uses the "Don't Fragment" bit in the fragment flags field to cause intermediate routers to return ICMP error messages indicating that the packet is too large.

The IPv6 version of path MTU discovery is described in RFC 1981, *Path MTU Discovery for IP version 6*. This upgrade is largely based on the original RFC 1191 specification, but some changes have been made to make it work with IPv6. Most important, because IPv6 doesn't support fragmentation in its header, there is no "Don't Fragment" bit to set. The node doing the path MTU discovery simply transmits the largest packet permissable on its own network link to the destination. If an intermediate link cannot handle packets of that size, the router attempting to forward the path MTU discovery packet will return an ICMPv6 error message back to the source node. The source node will then send another, smaller, packet. The process is repeated until no ICMPv6 error messages are received, and the source node then can use the most recent MTU as the path MTU.

It should be noted that there will be instances where path MTU discovery is not implemented. For example, terminals using minimal IPv6 implementations for remote network booting may simply use a path MTU of 576 bytes. IPv6 fragmentation, from source to destination nodes, is implemented as an extension header and is discussed in the following section.

IPv6 Extension Headers

The problem with IPv4 options is that they change the shape of the IP headers and thus make it more of a "special case," meaning it must get special handling. Routers must optimize for performance, which means they optimize for the best performance for the most common packets. The result is that IPv4 options tend to cause a router to shunt the optioned packet onto a side track and deal with it later, when it has time.

Extension headers implemented in IPv6 should eliminate, or at least drastically reduce, the performance hit that options cause. By moving the options out of the IP header and into the payload, routers can forward packets with options just as they forward nonoptioned packets. With the exception of hop-by-hop options, which by definition must be processed by each forwarding router, the options on IPv6 packets are hidden from intermediate routers.

What Options Are Available

In addition to reducing the impact that options have on IPv6 packet forwarding, the IPv6 specification makes it easier to define new extensions and options. Other options and extensions may be specified in the future, as needed. This section lists the defined extensions, but the use of extension headers and options is discussed in greater detail in Chapter 7; the security headers are discussed in Chapter 9. RFC 1883 defines the following options extensions for IPv6:

- ♦ *Hop-by-hop options header*. This header must always appear just after the IPv6 header; it contains optional data that every node on the packet's path must examine. Because it requires processing by every intermediate router, the hop-by-hop option is to be avoided except where absolutely necessary. So far, two options have been specified: the Jumbo payload option and the router alert option. The Jumbo payload option identifies the payload of the packet as being longer than normally allowed in IPv6 by the length of the 16-bit payload length field. Whenever a packet payload is larger than 65,535 bytes (including the hop-by-hop option header), this option must be included. If the node cannot forward the packet, it must return an ICMPv6 error message. The router alert option is used to notify routers when there is information inside an IPv6 datagram that is intended to be viewed and processed by an intermediate router even though the datagram is addressed to some other node (for example, control datagrams that contain information pertaining to bandwidth reservation protocols).

♦ *Routing header.* The routing header indicates that the packet will be visiting specific nodes on its route to its destination. The routing header includes, among other information, a list of addresses to be visited along the packet's path. The initial destination address of the IPv6 header is not the same as the ultimate destination of the packet but rather is the first address in the list contained in the routing header. When that node receives the packet, it processes the IPv6 header and the routing header and resends the packet to the second address listed in the routing header. This process continues until the packet reaches its ultimate destination.

♦ *Fragment header.* The fragment header contains a fragment offset, a "More Fragments" flag, and an identification field; it is used to allow a source node to fragment a packet too large for the path MTU between the source and the destination.

♦ *Destination options header.* This header stands in for the IPv4 options field. At present, the only destination options specified are padding options to fill out the header on a 64-bit boundary if the (future) options require it. The destination options header is meant to carry information intended to be examined by the destination node.

♦ *Authentication header (AH).* This header provides a mechanism for calculating a cryptographic checksum on some parts of the IPv6 header, extension headers, and payload.

♦ *Encapsulating Security Payload (ESP) header.* This header will always be the last, unencrypted, header of any packet. It indicates that the rest of the payload is encrypted, and provides enough information for the authorized destination node to decrypt it.

ICMPv6

IP nodes need a special protocol to exchange messages that pertain to IP-related conditions. The Internet Control Message Protocol (ICMP) fulfills this need; with the upgrade from IPv4 to IPv6, ICMP also underwent modification. ICMPv6 is defined in RFC 1885, *Internet Control Message Protocol (ICMPv6) for the Internet Protocol Version 6 (IPv6) Specification*. ICMP messages are used to report error and informational conditions, as well as for diagnostic functions like the Packet Internet Groper (Ping) and traceroute.

Originally folded into the ICMPv6 specification, the Internet Group Management Protocol (IGMP) was updated in November 1997 in RFC 2236, *Internet Group Management Protocol, Version 2* (and as of early fall 1998, IGMP version 3 is in the works). IGMP is required to support multicast transmissions, and it provides a mechanism for hosts to report their membership in multicast groups to local routers.

ICMPv6 Messages

ICMP messages are generated as a result of some error condition. For example, if a router is unable to process an IP packet for some reason, it would probably generate some type of ICMP message directed back at the packet's source. The source would then be able to take some action to remedy the error condition being reported. For example, if a router is unable to process an IP packet because it is too large to be sent out on a network link, the router is expected to generate an ICMP error message indicating that the packet is too large. The source host, on receiving this message, can use it to determine a more appropriate packet size and resend the data in a series of new IP packets.

RFC 1885 defines the following message types (excluded are group-related messages defined in that document):

- ◆ Destination Unreachable.
- ◆ Packet Too Big.
- ◆ Time Exceeded.

- ◆ Parameter Problem.
- ◆ Echo Request.
- ◆ Echo Reply.

These messages are discussed in greater detail below.

Destination Unreachable

This message is generated by a router or by the source host when there is some reason other than traffic congestion for inability to deliver a packet. There are five different codes defined for this error message. They include:

- ◆ 0: No route to destination. This message occurs when a router does not have a route defined for the destination address of the IP packet. This message can only be generated by a router without a default route—the default route is used to route packets being sent to networks that have not been explicitly defined in the router's routing table.
- ◆ 1: Communication with destination administratively prohibited. This message may be generated by a packet-filtering firewall when a prohibited type of traffic is sent to a host inside a firewall.
- ◆ 2: Not a neighbor. This code is used when the IPv6 routing header extension is being used and strict routing is in force (see Chapter 8). It occurs when the next destination in the list does not share a network link with the current forwarding node.
- ◆ 3: Address unreachable. This code signifies that there is some problem resolving the destination address into a link layer (network) address or that there is some problem reaching the destination at the link layer on the destination network.
- ◆ 4: Port unreachable. This code is generated by the destination node when an upper layer protocol (e.g., DP) is not listening for traffic on the packet's destination port but only if the transport protocol doesn't have some other mechanism for notifying the source of this problem.

Packet Too Big

A router generates the Packet Too Big message when it receives a packet that cannot be forwarded because it is larger than the MTU of the link it should be forwarded onto. This ICMPv6 error message includes a field containing the value of the MTU of the link that causes the problem. This is the relevant error message used in the process of path MTU discovery.

Time Exceeded

When the hop limit of an IP packet is one and it is received by a router, the router must decrement the value before forwarding it. If the value of the hop limit field becomes zero as a result of the router decrementing it (or if the router receives a packet whose hop limit field contains the value zero), the router must discard it and send an ICMPv6 Time Exceeded message to the source node. This message, when received by the originating node, can be considered either to indicate that the hop limit was initially set too low (the actual route for the packet is longer than the source node was expecting) or that there is a routing loop causing the packet to fail to be delivered.

This message is useful for building the *traceroute* function. This function allows a node to identify all routers along the path that a packet takes between the source and the destination. It works like this: First, a packet is sent to the destination with a hop limit of one. The first router it reaches will decrement the hop limit and respond with a Time Exceeded message, and the source node will have identified the first router in the path. The source resends the packet with a hop limit of two, and if the packet must pass through a second router, that router will decrement the hop limit to zero and generate another Time Exceeded message. This continues until the packet eventually reaches its destination; in the meantime, the source node has received a Time Exceeded message from each intermediate router.

Parameter Problem

When there is some problem with some part of the IPv6 header or extension headers that keeps a router from completing the processing of the packet, the router must discard the packet. It is recommended that the router implementation should generate an ICMP parameter problem message that indicates the type of problem (bad header field, unrecognized next header type, or unrecognized IPv6 option), with a pointer value that indicates at which byte of the original packet the error condition was encountered.

ICMPv6 Echo Function

ICMPv6 includes a function that is not related to error conditions. Two types of messages, the echo request and echo reply, are required for all IPv6 nodes. The Echo Request message can be sent to any valid IPv6 address and can include an echo request identifier, a sequence number, and some data. The Echo Request identifier and sequence may be used to differentiate replies to different requests, though both are optional. The data is also optional and can be used for diagnostic purposes.

When an IPv6 node receives an Echo Request message, it is required to respond by sending an Echo Reply message. The reply must contain the same request identifier, sequence number, and data as were contained in the original request message.

The ICMP Echo Request/Reply message pair is the basis of the *ping* function. Ping is an important diagnostic function, as it provides a method of determining whether or not a particular host is connected to the same network as some other host.

6

IPv6 Addressing

Before this chapter introduces IPv6 addressing, it presents some of the issues related to IP addressing in general as they are used to identify and locate nodes on IP networks. For many years, IP addresses were treated as ultimately unique and persistent identifiers of nodes on IP networks. Over the past few years, particularly with the development of the next generation of IP, that view of IP addresses has been changing; it may not be necessary or efficient to allocate network and node addresses as we have been doing for the past 20 years.

After introducing the IPv6 addressing architecture as described in RFC 2373, *IP Version 6 Addressing Architecture*, I present some of general issues related to IP addressing. A discussion of some of the possibilities for address assignment follows. This chapter breaks IPv6 addressing into several different pieces: the structure and nomenclature of the 128-bit address itself and the different types of IPv6 addresses (unicast, multicast, and anycast).

The designers of IPv6 could have simply grafted a larger address space onto the existing IPv4 addressing architecture. Of course, doing so would cause us to miss out on a huge opportunity for improving IP. Changing the entire addressing architecture provides an incredible opportunity not only for improving efficiency of address allocation but also for improving IP routing performance. These improvements are discussed here in this chapter, with special attention to IPv6 routing issues to follow in Chapter 8. Address allocation, mobile networking, and autoconfiguration are discussed in detail in Chapter 11.

RFC 2373, *IP Version 6 Addressing Architecture*, was published in July 1998 and made obsolete the original IPv6 addressing architecture document, RFC 1883, published in December 1995. Most of the changes are clarifications, corrections, and modifications that had been deemed necessary during the two and a half years since publication of the original RFC.

The IPv6 Address

The most obvious difference between IPv4 and IPv6 addresses is their length: IPv4 addresses are 32 bits long, IPv6 addresses are 128 bits long. RFC 2373 explains not only how those addresses are expressed in print but also the different types of addresses that are allowed and how they are structured. Where the IPv4 address can be divided into only two or three variable parts (the network identifier, the node identifier, and sometimes a subnet identifier), IPv6 addresses are large enough to support fields within the address.

There are three types of IPv6 addresses, the unicast, multicast, and anycast addresses. These will all be discussed in more detail in the next section. The unicast and multicast addresses are quite similar to the IPv4 versions; the IPv4 broadcast address is no longer supported, while a new type of address, the *anycast* address, is added. This section introduces the IPv6 addressing model, the IPv6 address types, IPv6 address representation, and special cases of IPv6 addresses.

IPv6 Address Representation

IPv4 addresses are almost always represented as a four-part, dot-delimited value: in other words, four numbers, separated by periods. For example, these are all valid IPv4 addresses, all represented in decimal integers:

```
10.5.3.1
127.0.0.1
201.199.244.101
```

IPv4 addresses are also often represented as a set of four two-digit hexadecimal integers and far less frequently as a set of four eight-digit binary integers.

IPv6 addresses, four times as long as IPv4 addresses, are four times more cumbersome. The basic representation of an IPv6 address is of the form X:X:X:X:X:X:X:X, where X refers to a four-digit hexadecimal integer (16 bits). Each digit consists of four bits, each integer consists of four digits, and each address consists of eight integers and totals 128 bits (4 x 4 x 8 = 128). For example, the following are valid IPv6 addresses:

```
CDCD:910A:2222:5498:8475:1111:3900:2020
1030:0:0:0:C9B4:FF12:48AA:1A2B
2000:0:0:0:0:0:0:1
```

Note that the integers are hexadecimal integers, so the letters A through F represent the digits 10 through 15. Each integer must be included, but leading zeros are not required.

This is the preferred format for IPv6 address representation, but there are two additional methods that may be used for clarity and ease of use.

It is expected that some IPv6 addresses will consist of long series of zeros (as in the second and third examples above). When this is the case, the specification allows the address to be represented with a "gap" that stands in for the series of zeros. In other words, the address

```
2000:0:0:0:0:0:0:1
```

could be represented as

```
2000::1
```

The double colon means that the address should be expanded out to a full 128-bit address. This method replaces zeros only when they fill a complete 16-bit group, and the double colon can be used only once in any given address.

A third option is expected to be useful in mixed IPv4/IPv6 environments. The lowest-order 32 bits of the IPv6 address can be used to refer to an IPv4 address, and such addresses would be expressed as a combination with the form of X:X:X:X:X:X:d.d.d.d, where X represents a 16-bit integer and d represents an 8-bit decimal integer. For example, the address

```
0:0:0:0:0:0:10.0.0.1
```

is a valid IPv4 address. Combining both alternate representation methods, this address could also be expressed as:

```
::10.0.0.1
```

Because IPv6 addresses are broken out into two portions—the subnet prefix and the interface ID—an IPv6 node address is expected to be represented as an address with a separate value indicating how much of the address is to be masked, similar to the way CIDR addresses are represented. In other words, an IPv6 node address indicates a prefix length, separated from the IPv6 address with a backslash, like this:

```
1030:0:0:0:C9B4:FF12:48AA:1A2B/60
```

This indicates that the first 60 bits refers to a prefix, for routing purposes.

IPv6 Addressing Model

The IPv6 addressing model is much the same as the IPv4 addressing model. Each unicast address identifies a single network interface. IP addresses are assigned to network interfaces rather than nodes, so a node with more than one network interface can have more than one IPv6 address. Any of those IPv6 addresses identify that node. A unicast address is associated with only one network interface, though a network interface can be associated with more than one unicast address. Each network interface must have at least one unicast address associated with it.

There is one important clarification and one important exception. The clarification relates to the use of point-to-point links. In IPv4, all network interfaces, including point-to-point links that connect a node with a router (as in most dial-up Internet connections), require a dedicated IP address. With many organizations using point-to-point links to connect branch offices, each link is often given its own subnet—thus burning a lot of address space. In IPv6, specific addresses are unnecessary for the endpoints of point-to-point links if the nodes at either end of the link are not originating or receiving IPv6 packets from non-neighbors. In other words, if the two nodes are merely passing traffic, they do not need to have IPv6 addresses.

The requirement that each network interface have a globally unique unicast address presents an impediment to scalability for IPv4. A server providing a popular service can easily be overwhelmed by high demand. As a result, the IPv6 addressing model incorporates an important exception: Multiple network interfaces can share a single IPv6 address if the hardware is able to appropriately share the network load across those multiple interfaces. This makes it possible to scale servers with load-sharing server farms rather than requiring a hardware upgrade when server demand rises.

Multicast and anycast addresses, discussed below, are also associated with network interfaces. A network interface can be associated with multiple addresses of any type.

IPv6 Address Space

RFC 2373 includes an IPv6 address space "map" that shows how the address space is allocated, showing type of address allocation, the prefix (the values of the first bits of the address allocation), and the size of the allocation as a fraction of the total address space. Figure 6.1 shows the IPv6 address space allocation map.

Several points should be noted in reference to the IPv6 allocation. Originally, in RFC 1884, a full quarter of the address space was allocated for two different types of addresses: one-eighth for provider-based unicast and one-eighth for geographic-based unicast addresses. It was intended that addresses would be assigned based on who the network service provider is or on the physical location of the subscribing net-

```
Allocation                             Prefix        Fraction of
                                       (binary)      Address Space
------------------------------------   --------      -------------
Reserved                               0000 0000     1/256
Unassigned                             0000 0001     1/256

Reserved for NSAP Allocation           0000 001      1/128
Reserved for IPX Allocation            0000 010      1/128

Unassigned                             0000 011      1/128
Unassigned                             0000 1        1/32
Unassigned                             0001          1/16

Aggregatable Global Unicast Addresses  001           1/8
Unassigned                             010           1/8
Unassigned                             011           1/8
Unassigned                             100           1/8
Unassigned                             101           1/8
Unassigned                             110           1/8

Unassigned                             1110          1/16
Unassigned                             1111 0        1/32
Unassigned                             1111 10       1/64
Unassigned                             1111 110      1/128
Unassigned                             1111 1110 0   1/512

Link-local Unicast Addresses           1111 1110 10  1/1024
Site-local Unicast Addresses           1111 1110 11  1/1024

Multicast Addresses                    1111 1111     1/256
```

Figure 6.1. Allocation for IPv6 addresses, from RFC 2373.

work. Provider-based aggregation, as it was originally called, would require networks to take on aggregatable IP addresses based on whom they buy their Internet access from. However, this approach was seen to be less than a perfect solution for very large organizations with far-flung branches, some of which would require service from different providers. Provider-based aggregation would add even more IP address management headaches for these large organizations.

Steve Deering proposed the geographic-based allocation alternative as part of the Simple Internet Protocol (SIP, a precursor to SIPP, as discussed in Chapter 4). These addresses, unlike provider-based addresses, would be allocated on a permanent basis much as IPv4 addresses have been allocated. These addresses would be based on geographic location, and providers would have to maintain additional routes to support these networks outside the aggregatable portion of the IPv6 address space.

The ISP community really didn't care for this solution, as it meant a significant increase in complexity (and costs) to manage the geographic addressing. On the other hand, most of the objections to the provider-based allocation grew out of difficulties of configuring and reconfiguring nodes with provider-based addresses. Without wider use of IPv4-based solutions for autoconfiguration (like DHCP), this would truly pose a mammoth administrative issue for any organizational network. However, with far better support for autoconfiguration in IPv6, the geographic allocation option did not to make it into the final mix.

Note that most of the address space is unassigned; the first allocation in the table is listed as reserved. The types of addresses listed, as well as some addresses that fit into the reserved allocation, will be discussed in the following section.

IPv6 Address Types

As mentioned before, IPv6 addresses are of three types: unicast, multicast, and anycast. Broadcast addresses are no longer available. The three IPv6 address types are defined in RFC 2373 as follows:

```
Unicast:      An identifier for a single interface. A packet sent
              to a unicast address is delivered to the interface
              identified by that address.

Anycast:      An identifier for a set of interfaces (typically
              belonging to different nodes). A packet sent to an
              anycast address is delivered to one of the interfaces
              identified by that address (the "nearest" one, according
              to the routing protocols' measure of distance).

Multicast:    An identifier for a set of interfaces (typically
              belonging to different nodes). A packet sent to a
              multicast address is delivered to all interfaces
              identified by that address.
```

These three address types are discussed in greater detail in the following section.

Whither Broadcast?

Broadcast addresses created problems for IPv4 networks almost from the start. Broadcasts were intended to be used to carry information intended for more than one node or for making requests when the requesting node doesn't know exactly where that information may come from. However, broadcasts can be a drag on network performance; lots of broadcasts on the same network link mean that every node on that link must process all broadcasts, and almost all are likely to ignore them because they are not relevant. Forwarding of broadcasts across subnets can cause even more problems with routers being flooded with traffic.

The IPv6 solution to the broadcast problem is to use an "all nodes" multicast addresses to replace those broadcasts that are absolutely necessary, while resorting to more limited multicast addresses for other situations in which broadcasts were previously used. This way, nodes interested in the traffic formerly carried in broadcasts can subscribe to a multicast address; all other uninterested nodes can ignore packets sent to that address. Broadcasts never adequately solved the problem of propagating information across the

Internet, for example, routing information, but multicasting provides a more viable alternative.

Unicast

Unicast addresses identify a single IPv6 interface. A node can have more than one IPv6 network interface. Each separate interface must have its own unicast address associated with it. Unicast addresses can be viewed as containing a single piece of information, contained in a 128-bit field: an address that completely identifies one particular interface. Alternatively, the data in the address can be parsed out into smaller pieces of information. However, all that information, when put together, will result in a 128-bit field that identifies a node's interface.

The IPv6 address itself may offer a node more or less information about its structure, depending on who or what is looking at the address. For example, a node might simply be aware that the entire 128-bit address is a globally unique ID, without being aware of the node's existence in a network. On the other hand, a router would presumably be able to determine, from the address, that part of the address identifies a unique node on a specific network or subnetwork.

For example, an IPv6 unicast address may be viewed as a two-field entity, with one field for the network and the other for an identifier of the node's interface on that network. As will be seen later when specific types of unicast addresses are discussed, the network identifier can be split into different pieces, identifying different network units. IPv6 unicast addresses function like IPv4 addresses that are subject to CIDR—in other words, they can be divided into two parts (on a specific boundary within the address). The most significant bits of the address contain the prefix used for routing, while the least significant bits of the address contain the network interface identifier.

If the simplest view of the IPv6 address is as an undifferentiated 128-bit chunk of data, a slightly more formatted view divides it into two pieces: the interface ID and the subnet prefix, shown in Figure 6.2 as it is expressed in RFC 2373. The length of the interface

Figure 6.2. A simple view of the IPv6 unicast address, from RFC 2373.

ID depends on the length of the subnet prefix, and both may vary depending on who is doing the interpreting. A router that is situated very close to the addressed node's interface (or far from a backbone) will probably need relatively fewer bits to identify the interface. A router closer to a backbone will need less of the address to specify the subnet prefix, and as a result the interface ID will take a greater part of the address. The aggregatable global unicast address, to be discussed below, has a more complex structure.

Different types of IPv6 unicast addresses to be discussed here include:

- ◆ Aggregatable global addresses.
- ◆ The unspecified address, or the all-zeros address.
- ◆ The loopback address.
- ◆ IPv6 addresses with embedded IPv4 addresses.
- ◆ Provider- and geographic-based provider addresses.
- ◆ OSI network service access point (NSAP) addresses.
- ◆ Internetwork Packet Exchange (IPX) addresses.

IPv6 Unicast Address Formats

Based on RFC 1884, one might expect to see several different types of IPv6 addresses in general use. With allocations for NSAP and IPX addresses, networks based on the OSI and on NetWare could be accommodated and incorporated seamlessly into the IPv6 architecture. With one-eighth of the address space each, provider-based and geographic-based allocations were expected to constitute the bulk of assigned addresses. Link-local and site-local addresses offer an institutionalized version of Network 10-style network address translation.

However, as RFC 2373 shows, the IPv6 address allocation has changed and simplified. For one thing, the geographic-based address allocation is gone, while the term *provider-based unicast address* has been changed to *aggregatable global unicast address*. The change in name makes clear that it allows aggregation as defined previously for provider-based addresses as well as for a new type of exchange-based aggregation. It also reflects a more neutral vision of that address category. Space for NSAP and IPX addresses is still reserved, and one-eighth of the address is assigned to aggregatable addresses. Otherwise, except for multicast addresses and certain categories of reserved addresses, the rest of the IPv6 address space is unassigned—leaving plenty of room for future growth.

Interface Identifiers

The IPv6 addressing architecture requires an *interface identifier* in any IPv6 unicast address. An interface identifier is very much like the 48-bit media access control (MAC) addresses that are hard-coded into network interface cards. These addresses are burned into the network boards by the vendor and are globally unique—no two network cards should ever have the same MAC address. These addresses can be used to uniquely identify the interface at the network link layer.

IPv6 host addresses are based on the IEEE EUI-64 format for interface identifiers. This format builds on existing MAC addresses to create 64-bit interface identifiers that can be unique across a local or global scope. RFC 2373 includes an appendix explaining how to create the interface identifiers; more about the IEEE EUI-64 standard is available on the IEEE standards web site at:

```
http://standards.ieee.org/db/oui/tutorials/EUI64.html
```

These 64-bit interface identifiers can globally address each and every network interface uniquely. This means that in theory as many as 2^{64} different physical interfaces—roughly 18 billion billion (18,000,000,000,000,000,000) different addresses—can be uniquely addressed, taking only half of the IPv6 addressing space. This should be enough, at least for the foreseeable future.

Aggregatable Global Unicast

Provider-based aggregation has already been mentioned in this chapter, and the concept will be encountered again in Chapter 8. However, aggregatable global unicast addresses allow another type of aggregation that is independent of Internet service providers. While provider-based aggregatable addresses must be changed when the provider is changed, exchange-based addresses are allocated directly by an IPv6 exchange entity. The exchange provides the address block, while the subscriber contracts with a separate provider for actual network access. The network access is provided either directly, through the provider, or indirectly, through the exchange, but routing is through the exchange. This makes possible arrangements by which the subscriber can change providers without address renumbering. It also allows the subscriber to use more than one Internet service provider to handle a single block of network addresses.

Aggregatable global unicast addresses will include all = addresses starting with 001 (though this format may in the future be used for other unicast prefixes that have not yet been assigned). The address is formatted into fields, as shown in Figure 6.3.

```
| 3|  13  | 8 |    24     |   16   |            64 bits               |
+--+------+---+-----------+--------+----------------------------------+
|FP| TLA  |RES|   NLA     |  SLA   |          Interface ID            |
|  |  ID  |   |   ID      |  ID    |                                  |
+--+------+---+-----------+--------+----------------------------------+
```

Figure 6.3. The format for IPv6 global aggregatable unicast addresses, from RFC 2373.

The fields shown in Figure 6.3 include:

♦ FP. The format prefix is the three-bit prefix to the IPv6 address that identifies where it belongs in the IPv6 address space. Currently, 001 in this field identifies it as an aggregatable global unicast address.

♦ TLA ID. The top-level aggregation identifier contains the highest-level routing information of the address. This refers to the grossest level of routing information in the internetwork, and as currently defined (at 13 bits) there can be no more than 8192 different top-level routes.

♦ RES. The next eight bits are reserved for future use. They may ultimately be used to expand the top-level or next-level aggregation ID fields.

♦ NLA ID. The next-level aggregation identifier is 24 bits long, and it is meant to be used by organizations that control top-level aggregation IDs to organize that address space. In other words, those organizations (probably to include large Internet service providers and others providing public network access) can carve that 24-bit field into their own addressing hierarchy. Such an entity might break itself down into four top-level routes (internal to the entity) by taking two bits for those routes and leave itself 20 bits of address space to allocate to other entities (likely to be smaller-scale, more local, service providers). Those entities, in their turn, could also subdivide the space they are allocated in the same way—if there is enough room.

♦ SLA ID. The site-level aggregation identifier is the address space given to organizations for their internal network structure. With 16 bits available, each organization can create its own internal hierarchical network structure using subnets in the same way they are used in IPv4. As many as 65,535 different subnets are available using all 16 bits as a flat address space. Using the first eight bits for higher-level routing within the organization would allow 255 high-level subnets, each of which has as many as 255 sub-subnets.

♦ Interface ID. This 64-bit field contains a 64-bit value based on the IEEE EUI-64 interface ID discussed above.

As should be clear by now, the IPv6 unicast address can contain significant complexity even beyond the explicit fields that are likely to be specified in future RFCs. Both the site-level aggregation and the next-level aggregation IDs offer plenty of room for network access providers and organizations to add additional topological structure through hierarchical subdivision of these two fields.

Special and Reserved Addresses

The first 1/256th of the IPv6 address space—all those addresses whose first eight bits are 0000 0000—is reserved. Most of the space is empty, but there are some "special" addresses to be found here as well. The special addresses include:

♦ The *unspecified address*. This is the "all-zeros" address that actually is used when there is no valid address—for example, when a host that boots from the network first starts up and has not yet been assigned an IPv6 address, it might use this address in the source field of the IPv6 header when sending out a request for configuration information. This address is represented as 0:0:0:0:0:0:0:0; it can also be abbreviated as :: using the conventions discussed earlier.

♦ The *loopback address*. In IPv4, the loopback address is defined as 127.0.0.1; any packets addressed to the loopback address must be passed down through the protocol stack to the network interface—but not transmitted on the network link. The network interface itself must accept these packets as if they were received from outside the node and pass them back up the protocol stack. Loopback is useful for testing software as well as configurations. The IPv6 loopback address is all zeros, except for the lowest-order bit. In other words, the loopback address is represented as 0:0:0:0:0:0:0:1, or ::1.

♦ *IPv6 addresses with embedded IPv4 addresses*. There are two types of these addresses, which allow IPv6 nodes to address IPv4 nodes that don't support IPv6 and allow IPv6 routers to tunnel IPv6 packets over IPv4 networks. Both these types of addresses are discussed next.

IPv6 Addresses with Embedded IPv4 Addresses

No matter what anyone might like, the transition to IPv6 will be a gradual one. This means that IPv4 and IPv6 nodes must find some way to coexist. One of the most obvious points of difference, of course, is that between the addresses of the different versions of IP. From the beginning, as specified in RFC 1884 and carried over to RFC 2373, IPv6 provides two types of special addresses that embed IPv4 addresses. Both of these addresses begin with the 80 high-order bits set to zero; the 32 low-order bits contain the IPv4 address. The 16 bits in the middle, when set to zero (or 0000), indicate that the address is what is called an *IPv4-compatible address*. When those 16 bits are set to one (or FFFF), the address is an *IPv4-mapped IPv6 address*. Figure 6.4 shows the structure of these two addresses, from RFC 2373.

IPv4-compatible addresses are intended to be used by nodes that need to tunnel IPv6 packets through IPv4 routers. These nodes understand IPv4 as well as IPv6. IPv4-mapped addresses are used by IPv6 nodes to address nodes that support only IPv4. Both these types of addresses will be discussed in Chapter 12.

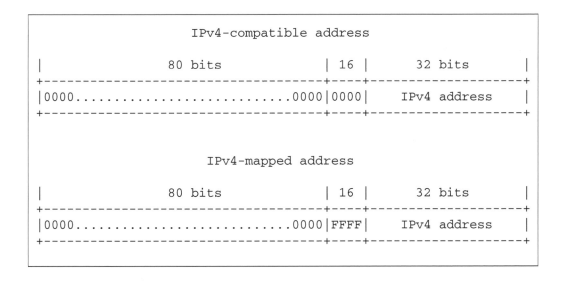

Figure 6.4. IPv6 addresses with embedded IPv4 addresses, from RFC 2373.

Link- and Site-local Use Addresses

We've seen that in IPv4 network address translation through the use of Network 10 addresses provides an option for organizations that do not wish to apply for a globally unique IPv4 network address. These addresses are not supposed to be forwarded by routers outside the organization that uses them, but there is nothing about these addresses that would prevent them from being forwarded nor is there anything about them that distinguishes them from other valid IPv4 addresses. A router could relatively easily be configured to allow these addresses to be forwarded.

In response to this type of use, IPv6 allocates two different segments of the address space entirely separate from the globally unique Internet space. Figure 6.5, from RFC 2373, shows how the link-local and site-local addresses are structured.

```
                    Link-local Addresses:

|   10     |
|  bits    |            54 bits        |          64 bits          |
+----------+-------------+-------------+---------------------------+
|1111111010|             0             |       interface ID        |
+----------+-------------+-------------+---------------------------+


                    Site-local Addresses:

|   10     |
|  bits    |    38 bits   |  16 bits   |          64 bits          |
+----------+-------------+-------------+---------------------------+
|1111111011|      0      |  subnet ID  |       interface ID        |
+----------+-------------+-------------+---------------------------+
```

Figure 6.5. Link-local and site-local network addresses, from RFC 2373.

Link-local addresses are intended to be used to number hosts on a single network link. The first ten bits of the prefix identify the address as a link-local address; routers can safely ignore packets with link-local addresses in their source or destinations, because these packets must never be forwarded. The middle portion of 54 bits is set to zero, while the interface ID uses the same IEEE structure described earlier. This portion of the address space allows individual networks with as many as $(2^{64}-1)$ hosts attached.

While link-local addresses can be used only for a single network link, site-local addresses can be used for a site. This means that they can be used to route traffic on an intranet without allowing any direct routing from the site to the global Internet. Routers internal to the site can forward packets within the site but not outside the site. Site-local addresses have a slightly different ten-bit prefix, followed by a series of bits that are set to zero. The subnet ID for site-local addresses is 16 bits, while the interface ID will be the same 64-bit IEEE-based address discussed earlier.

NSAP and IPX Allocations

One of the goals of IPng was to unify the networking world and make it possible for IP, IPX, and OSI networks to interoperate. To support that interoperabity, IPv6 reserves 1/128th of the address space to each of OSI and IPX. At this writing, the precise format of the IPX addresses has yet to be determined; the NSAP (for Network Service Access Point) allocation is described in RFC 1888, *OSI NSAPs and IPv6*. Discussion of OSI and NSAP is outside the scope of this book, but the interested reader should find a more complete discussion in that RFC.

Multicast

Like broadcast addresses, multicast addresses are particularly useful in local networks like old-fashioned Ethernets, where all nodes can sense all transmissions on the wire. Each node checks for the destination address at the beginning of each transmission, and if the destination is the same as the node's interface address, the node will pick up on the rest of the transmission. This makes it relatively simple for a node also to pick up on broadcast and multicast transmissions. Broadcasts are easy, as there is no decision to make: If it is a broadcast, the node listens. Multicasts, however, are a bit more complicated: The node subscribes to a multicast address, and if it senses that the destination address is a multicast address, it must determine if it's a multicast address to which the node is subscribed.

IP multicast is more complicated. For one thing, an important reason for IP's success is that traffic does not indiscriminately get forwarded to all nodes on an internetwork (let alone the Internet). It would bring most or all connected networks to their knees if it did. This is why broadcasts are not supposed to be forwarded by routers. However, with multicast, you can selectively forward packets as long as the routers can subscribe to multicast addresses on behalf of other nodes.

When a node subscribes to a multicast address, it announces that it wants to be a member, and any local routers will subscribe on behalf of that node. When a transmission is sent to that multicast address from another node that is on the same network, the IP multicast packet is encapsulated into a link layer multicast data transmission unit. On an Ethernet, the encapsulated unit is addressed to an Ethernet multicast address; on other types of networks that use point-to-point circuits for all transmissions (like ATM), the packet will be transmitted to subscribers through some other mechanism, usually through some sort of server that transmits the packet to each individual subscriber. Multicasts from outside the local network are handled the same way, only they are delivered to the router, which forwards the packet to subscribing nodes.

IPv6 Multicast Address Format

Unlike IPv6 unicast addresses, which have different formats, IPv6 multicast addresses adhere to a more rigid format, shown in Figure 6.6. Multicast addresses must be used only as destination addresses; no datagram should ever be originated with a multicast address as its source.

The first octet, which is all ones, identifies the address as a multicast address. Multicast addresses include a full 1/256th of the IPv6

```
|   8    | 4  | 4  |                   112 bits                       |
+------ -+----+----+-------------------------------------------------+
|11111111|flgs|scop|                   group ID                      |
+--------+----+----+-------------------------------------------------+
```

Figure 6.6. The IPv6 multicast address format, from RFC 2373.

address space, as shown in Figure 6.1. The rest of the multicast address consists of three fields:

- `flgs`. This is actually a set of four single-bit flags. Only the fourth flag is currently assigned, and it represents whether or not the address is a well-known multicast address—one that has been assigned by the Internet numbering authority—or is a temporary ("transient") multicast address being used in an *ad hoc* fashion. If this flag is set to zero, it means the address is well-known; being set to one signifies a transient address. The other three flags are currently being reserved for future use.
- `scop`. This four-bit field contains a value that indicates what the scope of the multicast group is, in other words, whether the multicast group can include only nodes on the same local network, same site, same organization, or anywhere within the IPv6 global address space. Possible values range from 0 to 15 (hexadecimal F) and are shown in Figure 6.7.
- `group ID`. This 112-bit field identifies the multicast group. The same group ID can represent different groups, depending on whether the address is transient or well-known, and also depending on the scope of the address. Permanent multicast addresses use assigned group IDs with special meanings, and the membership in such groups will depend both on the group ID and on the scope.

```
Hex   Decimal      Value

0     0            reserved
1     1            node-local scope
2     2            link-local scope
3     3            (unassigned)
4     4            (unassigned)
5     5            site-local scope
6     6            (unassigned)
7     7            (unassigned)
8     8            organization-local scope
9     9            (unassigned)
A     10           (unassigned)
B     11           (unassigned)
C     12           (unassigned)
D     13           (unassigned)
E     14           global scope
F     15           reserved
```

Figure 6.7. Values for IPv6 multicast scope, from RFC 2373.

All IPv6 multicast addresses start out with FF to represent that the first eight bits of the address are all ones. At present, the third hexadecimal digit of the address can be either zero (representing a well-known address) or one (representing a transient address). This is because no other flags are defined. The fourth hexadecimal digit represents the scope and can have any assigned, unreserved value as shown in Figure 6.7.

IPv6 Multicast Groups

IPv4 already uses multicasting for applications that require a high bandwidth to send the same data to multiple nodes, for example, video conferencing or distribution of financial news and stock quotes. Other applications are possible, with some of the possibilities apparent from the implications of assigned multicast addresses combined with multicast scopes. Some of the early registered multicast addresses include those grouping routers, DHCP services, audio and video services, and networked game services, among others, as detailed in RFC 2375, *IPv6 Multicast Address Assignments*.

To illustrate, consider what happens when working with the multicast group ID for "all DHCP servers." This group is represented by the group ID of 1:3. When used with a scope of two, representing the link-local scope (the local network link), the resulting IPv6 multicast address would be:

```
FF02:0:0:0:0:0:1:3
```

This address can be interpreted to mean: "all DHCP servers on the link-local scope"; in other words, all DHCP servers on the same network. Change the scope to site-local, and this address changes its meaning to "all DHCP servers at the same site."

This means that the reserved multicast group IDs can become more inclusive as the scope increases. A group ID that specifies all servers of a particular type will include only those servers that exist on the local node if the scope is set to one, while it will include the same servers, plus all other servers connected to the same network, if the scope is set to two. For example, using the group ID for all Network Time Protocol (NTP) servers with a scope of one will have an active member only if there is an NTP server running on the local node. Increase the scope to two, and it will include any nodes running an NTP server that are connected to the same network. Increase the scope to eight, and it includes all NTP servers running in the entire organization. Increase the scope to E (14 in decimal notation), and it includes all NTP servers anywhere on the internetwork.

On the other hand, group IDs for transient multicast addresses have no meaning outside their own scope. A transient multicast group that exists on a global scope does not bear any relation to a group on a link-local scale, even though they may have the same group ID.

Anycast

Multicast addresses can be, in a sense, shared by more than one node. All nodes that are members of a multicast address expect to receive all packets sent to that address. A router that connects five different local Ethernet networks will forward a copy of a multicast packet to each of those networks (assuming that there is at least one subscriber to that multicast address on each of those networks). Anycast is the same, but different. Multiple nodes may be sharing the anycast address, like a multicast address. However, only one of those nodes can expect to receive a datagram sent to the anycast address.

Anycast is particularly useful for providing certain types of services, in particular, services that do not require a particular relationship between the client and server. For example, consider domain name servers and time servers. A name server is a name server, and the nearest name server should work as well as one further away. Likewise, a closer time server is preferable for maximum accuracy. When a host issues a request to an anycast address for some information, the closest server associated with that anycast address will respond.

Anycast Address Allocation and Format

Anycast addresses are allocated out of the normal IPv6 unicast address space. Because anycast addresses cannot be differentiated in their form from unicast addresses, members of an anycast address must each be explicitly configured to recognize that address as an anycast address.

Anycast Routing

To figure out how to route anycast packets, the lowest common routing denominator must be extracted from the set of hosts assigned to a single anycast address. In other words, there will be some number of network addresses in common, and this prefix defines the region in which all of the anycast nodes exist. To illustrate: An ISP may require that each of its subscriber organizations provide a time server with a single shared anycast address. In this case, the anycast region is defined by the prefix that has been assigned to the ISP for redistribution.

Routing occurs within this region, defined by the distribution of hosts sharing an anycast address. Within its region, an anycast address must be carried as a routing entry: The entry includes pointers to the network interfaces of all nodes that share the anycast address. The region may be limited, as above, or the anycast hosts may be spread throughout the global Internet—in a case like that, the anycast address must be added to all routing tables throughout the world.

7

IPv6 Extension Headers

This chapter discusses the implications of the IPv6 extension headers, how they work and how extension headers differ from IPv4. Particular attention will be paid to the proper order and use of header extensions, as well as discussion of the use of jumbograms, hop-by-hop options, destination options, routing, and fragmentation headers. Security headers (authentication headers and encapsulating security payload headers) are discussed at greater length in Chapter 9.

IPv6 Extension Headers

Chapter 5 introduced the new IPv6 extension headers as a means of streamlining the IPv6 headers for the vast majority of network traffic that works without options while improving the ability of the network to handle those packets that do require options. To recap from Chapter 5, the new IPv6 extension headers include:

- *Hop-by-hop options header.* This header must always appear just after the IPv6 header; it contains optional data that every node on the packet's path must examine. So far, only one option has been specified: the jumbo payload option. This option identifies the payload of the packet as being longer than normally allowed in IPv6 by the length of the 16-bit payload length field. Whenever a packet payload is larger than 65,535 bytes (including the hop-by-hop option header), this option must be included. If the node cannot forward the packet, it must return an ICMPv6 error message.

- *Routing header.* The routing header indicates that the packet will be visiting specific nodes on its route to its destination. The routing header includes, among other information, a list of addresses to be visited along the packet's path. The initial destination address of the IPv6 header is not the same as the ultimate destination of the packet but rather is the first address in the list contained in the routing header. When that node receives the packet, it processes the IPv6 header and the routing header and resends the packet to the second address listed in the routing header. This process continues until the packet reaches its ultimate destination.

- *Fragment header.* The fragment header contains a fragment offset, a More Fragments flag, and an identification field; it is used to allow a source node to fragment a packet too large for the path MTU between the source and the destination.

- *Destination options header.* This header contains options that must be processed by the final destination node only. At present, the only destination options specified are padding options to fill out the header on a 64-bit boundary if the (future) options require it.

- *Authentication Header (AH).* This header provides a mechanism for calculating a cryptographic checksum on some parts of the IPv6 header, extension headers, and payload.

♦ *Encapsulating Security Payload (ESP) header.* This header will always be the last, unencrypted, header of any packet. It indicates that the rest of the payload is encrypted, and provides enough information for the authorized destination node to decrypt it.

In addition to understanding what the extension headers do, it's helpful to understand how they are used, how they work, and how they can be used to extend IPv6 in the future. The next section covers the proper use of extension headers, while the sections that follow explain specifically how each extension header works (security-related headers are discussed in Chapter 9).

Using IPv6 Extension Headers

IPv4 options created a fairly complicated scheme for incorporating options within the standard IPv4 packet header. That header could be as short as 20 bytes or as long as 60 bytes, and the extra data includes IPv4 options, which must be interpreted by routers in order to process the packet. This tended to produce two effects. First, router implementations tend to shunt optioned packets, thus causing reduction in efficiency in processing. Second, because packets with options would thus be subject to worse performance, applications developers tended not to use options in their applications.

IPv6 extension headers make it possible to implement options without affecting performance substantially. With IPv6 extension headers, developers can use options where necessary without worry that routers will treat their packets any differently than other packets—unless the routing extension header or hop-by-hop options are in place, in which case the router can still do the necessary processing more easily than when using IPv4 options.

Identifying Extension Headers

All IPv6 headers are the same size and look pretty much the same. The difference is in the Next Header field. In an IPv6 packet with no extension headers, the value of this field will refer to the next layer's protocol. In other words, if the IP packet contains a TCP segment, then the Next Header field will contain the eight-bit value (six) from RFC 1700, *ASSIGNED NUMBERS*. If the packet contains a UDP datagram, this value will be 17. Table 7.1 shows some of the possible values for the Next Header field.

The Next Header field value will indicate whether, and what, the next extension header is. Thus, IPv6 headers can be chained together, starting from the IPv6 header itself and linking extension headers. Figure 7.1 shows how these header chains can develop. The first packet shown has no extension headers, but the second packet shows a routing header extension, followed by the TCP header and the rest of the packet. The last packet shown demonstrates a more complex possible header chain, with a fragment header extension appended to the IPv6 header, followed by an authentication extension header, followed by an encapsulating security payload (ESP) header extension, finally followed by the TCP header and the remainder of the packet.

Ordering Extension Headers

A single IPv6 packet can have more than one extension header. However, there is only one instance in which the same type of extension header can appear more than once in a packet—and there

Next Header Value	Description
0	Hop-by-Hop Header
43	Routing Header (RH)
44	Fragmentation Header (FH)
51	Authentication Header (AH)
52	Encapsulated Security Payload (ESP)
59	No next header
60	Destination Options Header

Table 7.1. Some possible values that indicate an extension header in an IPv6 Next Header field.

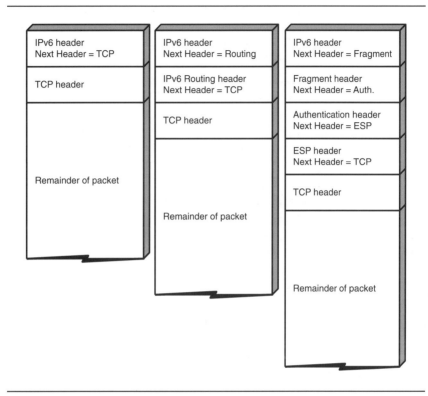

Figure 7.1. Three different IPv6 packets. The first has no extension headers, the second has a routing header extension, and the third has three header extensions.

is a preferred order in which header extensions should be chained together. From RFC 1883, extension headers should be ordered as follows:

- ◆ IPv6 header.
- ◆ Hop-by-Hop Options header.
- ◆ Destination Options header (to be appled at the first destination in the IPv6 destination address field, plus any additional destinations that may be listed in a routing header).
- ◆ Routing header.
- ◆ Fragment header.

♦ Authentication header.
♦ Encapsulating Security Payload (ESP) header.
♦ Destination Options header (to be applied only at the packet's final destination when a routing header is in use).
♦ Upper-layer header.

As this listing makes apparent, only the destination options header can appear more than once in the same packet, and that can occur only when a routing header is present.

It may not be immediately obvious that this ordering of extension headers is more than arbitrary. For example, as has been noted already, the ESP header *must* be the last header inasmuch as the rest of the packet will be encrypted. Likewise, the hop-by-hop options header has priority over all other extensions because it must be processed by every node that receives the packet.

Creating New Options

Header extensions must be identifiable through the Next Header field in the IPv6 headers. This means that there can be no more than 256 different values, as this is an eight-bit field. Even further reducing the number of possible values here is the fact that this value must also support all possible values of next-level headers. In other words, not only does this value identify header extensions, but also all other protocols that can be encapsulated within IP. Thus, many of these values have already been assigned, and unassigned values for this field can be considered a very limited resource.

Some of the protocol identifiers that IPv6 uses for extension headers carry over from IPv4; the authentication and ESP headers for example. So far, a handful of specific extension headers have been assigned, but provision has been made through the hop-by-hop options and the destination options header extensions to create new options.

In addition to conserving protocol values for the Next Header field, using these options header extensions makes it easier to robustly implement new options. Consider what would happen if an entirely new extension header type was being used to send a packet. If the destination node supports the new header type, then everything is fine. But if the destination node doesn't know about the new extension header protocol type, then it has no option but to discard the entire packet. On the other hand, all IPv6 nodes must support support the hop-by-hop and destination options extension headers, along with very basic options (see next section). In this way, if a destination node receives a packet with a destination options extension header, it can respond to it even if it does not support the options in the header. In other words, the options are designed to solicit an appropriate response from a recipient node that doesn't understand the option. For example, the option may be of the form, "Do X; if you don't understand X then discard this packet," or it may be of the form "Do X; if you don't understand X then just skip over this option, and finish processing the header." The option may also solicit an ICMP error message from the destination node to indicate that the option is not understood.

Options Extension Headers

The hop-by-hop and destination extension headers can contain special options. RFC 1883 defines two padding options that are used to make sure fields in the extension headers fall on the correct boundaries. In other words, if the option uses three eight-bit fields followed by one 32-bit field, an extra eight bits must be inserted (padded) so that the 32-bit field doesn't get broken across a 32-bit word boundary. Figure 7.2 shows how this works. Otherwise, only one functional option is defined, the jumbo payload option used in the hop-by-hop options extension header.

All options extensions headers, both the hop-by-hop and destination options headers, have a similar format, shown in Figure 7.3. Very simply, these extension headers have only two predefined fields, the Next Header field (in common with all IPv6 headers), and the header extension length field, an eight-bit field that indicates the length of the option header. The length indicated here is in eight-byte units and does not include the first eight bytes of the header. Thus, this value would be zero for an option header that is only eight bytes long; this field limits the header to a maximum of

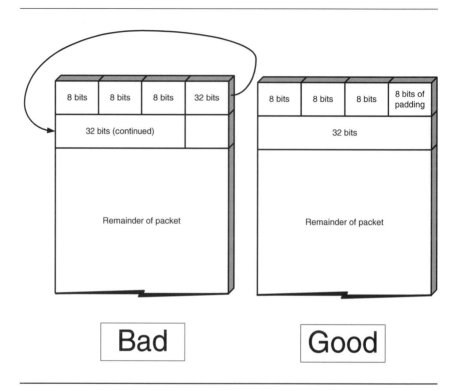

Figure 7.2. Options headers may need padding so that fields are not split across 32-bit word boundaries.

2048 bytes. The rest of the header consists of any options contained within the header.

Options

An IPv6 option consists of three fields:

♦ *Option type.* This is an eight-bit identifier that specifies the option type. The first three bits of this value encode information about the option type that a destination node can interpret even if it does not recognize the option itself. These are discussed below.

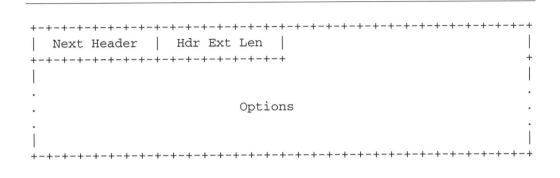

Figure 7.3. The standard options header format, from RFC 1883.

♦ *Option data length.* This is an eight-bit integer that indicates the length of the option data field; its maximum value is 255.

♦ *Option data.* This field contains data specific to the option, and can be no more than 255 bytes long.

The option type field uses the first two bits to indicate how the destination node should respond if it does not recognize the option specified. These different option types are:

♦ 00. Ignore this option and finish processing the rest of the header.

♦ 01. Throw away this entire packet.

♦ 10. Throw away the packet, and send an ICMP message to the packet's source address. Do this whether or not the destination address was a multicast address.

♦ 11. Throw away the packet, and send an ICMP message to the packet's source address. Do this only if the destination address was a unicast or anycast address (not a multicast address).

The third bit of the option type field indicates whether or not the value of the option data can change during transit from source to destination. If this bit is zero, the option data cannot change; if this bit is one, then the option data may change.

The only two generalized options defined for both hop-by-hop and destination options extension headers are padding options. These are the Pad1 option and the PadN option. The Pad1 option is a special option in that it consists of only eight bits, all set to zero. This option pads out the header by a single byte and does not have an option data length field or any option data.

The PadN option is identified by the option type value of one, and is used for padding a header by two or more bytes. If N bytes are required to pad out a header, then the option data length field contains the value $N–2$, and the option data field contains $N–2$ bytes, all set to zero. With one byte used by the option type field and another byte used by the option data length field, N bytes of padding require only $N–2$ bytes of option data.

Hop-by-Hop Options

The hop-by-hop option carries information that is intended to be examined by every node en route from the source to the destination—in other words, all the routers that forward the packet. So far, only one option has been defined: the jumbo payload option. Figure 7.4, from RFC 1883, shows how the hop-by-hop extension header looks when the jumbo payload option is being used.

As with any options extension header, the first two fields indicate the Next Header protocol and the header extension length (in this case,

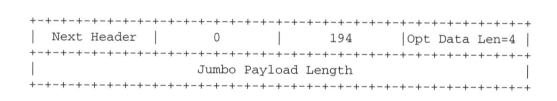

Figure 7.4. The hop-by-hop extension header containing the jumbo payload option (from RFC 1883) allows IPv6 payloads to exceed 65,535 bytes in length.

zero, because the entire option is only eight bytes long). At the third byte of this header, the options begin; in this case, the jumbo payload option type is 194, and the jumbo payload option data length is four bytes. The last field, jumbo payload length, indicates the actual length of the packet (not just the payload) in bytes, excluding the IPv6 header but including the hop-by-hop options extension header.

Nodes can use the jumbo payload option to send large packets, but only if every router along the way is able to handle packets that large. Thus, this option is used with the hop-by-hop header, which requires that every router along the way must check the information in the header.

The jumbo payload option allows payload lengths of over 65,535 bytes to as many as $2^{32}-1$ (well over four billion) bytes. When this option is being used, the 16-bit payload length field in the top IPv6 header must be set to zero, and the payload length in the option field must be at least 65,536 or greater; if either of these conditions is not met, the node receiving such a packet is supposed to send an ICMP error message indicating a problem to the source node. One other limitation: If a packet has a fragment extension header, it cannot also use the jumbo payload option. Using the jumbo payload means that the packet cannot be fragmented.

Routing Header

The routing header replaces source routing as it was implemented in IPv4. Source routing allows you to specify routers that the packet must traverse on its way to its destination. In IPv4 source routing, using IPv4 options, was limited by the number of intermediate routers that you could specify (no more than ten 32-bit addresses fit into the extra 40 bytes allowed for IPv4 headers with extensions). Furthermore, processing of source-routed packets tended to be slow, because every router in the path had to process the entire address list, whether the router was on the list or not.

IPv6 defines a generic routing extension header, with two one-byte fields: a routing type field, indicating what kind of routing header is in use, and a segments-left field, which indicates how many addi-tional routers listed in the rest of the header must still be visited before the packet reaches its ultimate destination. The rest of the header is type-specific data, which may vary depending on the type of routing header specified. RFC 1883 defines one type, the type 0 routing header.

The type 0 routing extension header fixes problems both major problems with IPv4 source routing. The routing header itself is pro-cessed only as it arrives at each router in the list, and there can be as many as 256 nodes specified in the list. The routing header works something like this:

- The source node builds a list of routers that the packet must traverse and then builds a type 0 routing header. This includes the list of routers and the final destination node address and the number of segments left (an eight-bit integer) indicating the number of specified routers that must still be visited before the packet can be deliv-ered to its final destination.
- When the source node transmits the packet, it sets the IPv6 header destination address equal to the address of the first router in the routing header list.
- The packet is forwarded until it arrives at the first stop in the path. Intermediate routers ignore the routing header; only when the packet arrives at the IPv6 destination (a router) does that router examine the routing header.
- At the first stop (and all other stops), the router checks to make sure that the number of segments left jibes with the address list. If the value of segments left is equal to zero, it means that the node is actually the final destination of the packet, and the node can then continue processing the rest of the packet.
- Assuming that the node is not the final destination and everything else checks out, it takes its own address out of the IPv6 header destination field and replaces it with the node that is next in the routing header list. The node also decrements the segments-left field, and sends the packet on its way to the next stop where the process is repeated.

The RFC 1883 definition of the type 0 routing header reserved one byte after the segments-left field and added a 24-bit strict/loose bit map field. This field essentially mapped a series of 24 flags onto up to 24 intermediate destinations, allowing the source node to specify whether to use strict routing (no intermediate routers not on the list) or loose routing (intermediate routers allowed between routers on the list). This scheme has been dropped, and the entire 32-bit field after segments left is reserved. Dropping the strict/loose bit-map field means that the number of routers that can be listed in the header is limited only by the eight-bit segments-left field, although it does mean that strict routing cannot be specified with the type 0 routing header.

Fragment Header

By allowing fragmentation only by the source node, IPv6 stream-lines the processing of packets by intermediate routers. In IPv4, intermediate routers can fragment packets that are too large for transmission over a local link. This means routers must do extra work and can result in packets that have been fragmented by more than one intermediate router. Fragmentation occurs when a node sends a packet that is too large to fit in a single data transmission unit along a local link. For example, Ethernet allows a maximum transmission unit (MTU) of 1500 bytes. You couldn't send an IP packet of 4000 bytes without fragmenting it on an Ethernet link; your system would probably break the packet into three fragments, none of them larger than 1500 bytes. Some link further downstream might have an even smaller MTU, perhaps 576 bytes, which would mean that the router on that link would have to fragment the fragments of that original 4000 byte packet, breaking up those 1500 byte fragments into even smaller pieces.

Fragmentation in IPv4 can be an annoyance. It adds to the overhead processing necessary by intermediate routers as well as by the destination node. What's more, a node can avoid fragmentation by using path MTU discovery to determine the maximum packet size that can be transmitted without fragmentation by intermediate routers. RFC 1883 specifies a minimum MTU of 576 bytes, but this value is being raised to 1280 bytes in the draft that is expected to replace RFC 1883, with a recommendation that any link that can be configured should be set to handle packets at least 1500 bytes long.

This means that nodes can confidently send packets that are as large as 1280 bytes without any concern that they will be fragmented. Packets as large as 1500 bytes have a pretty good chance of passing unfragmented, too. However, the IPv6 specification recommends that all nodes implement path MTU discovery and allows fragmentation only at the source node. In other words, before you can send a packet of any size, you have to check the path to your destination node to figure out the size of the largest packet you can send without fragmenting. Then, if you need to send a packet larger than that MTU, you can fragment it at the source so it will fit.

Fragmentation in IPv6 occurs only at the source node and uses the fragment header. Figure 7.5, from RFC 1883, shows what the fragment header looks like. Fragment header fields include:

- *Next header field.* This eight-bit field is common to all IPv6 headers.
- *Reserved.* The next eight bits is unused at this time and set to zero.
- *Fragment offset field.* This is very similar to the fragment offset field in IPv4 headers. This 13-bit field indicates, in units of eight bytes, where the data included in this packet (a fragment) begins in relation to the beginning of

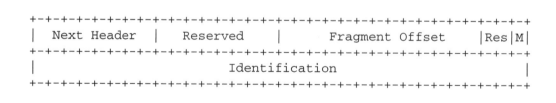

Figure 7.5. The IPv6 fragment header fields, from RFC 1883.

the fragmentable portion of the data of the original packet. In other words, if this value is 175, it means that the data in the fragment fits into the original packet 1400 bytes from its start.

♦ *Reserved field.* This two-bit field is set to zero and is not currently used.

♦ *M flag.* This single bit indicates whether or not more fragments are to come; a one in this field indicates that more fragments are on their way, while a zero indicates that this is the last fragment.

♦ *Identification field.* This is like the IPv4 identification field except that it is 32 bits long rather than 16 bits. Each IPv6 packet that is fragmented is assigned a 32-bit identifier that is intended to uniquely identify any packet sent recently (within the likely lifetime of a packet) from the source address to the destination address.

Only part of the entire IPv6 packet can be fragmented: the fragmentable portion includes the payload as well as any extension headers that are to be processed only when the packet has arrived at its final destination. The IPv6 header, as well as any extension headers that must be processed by routers while the packet is on its way to its final destination—for example, routing or hop-by-hop options headers—must not be fragmented.

Destination Options

The destination options header provides a mechanism, like the hop-by-hop options header, to deliver optional information along with IPv6 packets. Rather than attempt to define additional specific extension headers every time someone comes up with a good reason to do so—for example, as was done for the fragment, authentication, and ESP headers—the destination options header makes it possible to define new options intended for the destination node. Destination options will use the format described earlier for building options.

So far, no destination options (other than the padding options discussed earlier) have been defined in published RFCs, but they have been defined in Internet drafts, particularly relating to mobile IP (see Chapter 11 for more about mobile IP).

8

IPv6 Routing

This chapter begins with a discussion of how addressing—and how addresses are allocated—affects IP networks. The rest of the chapter discusses how IPv6 routing differs from IPv4 routing, and routing protocols for IPv6 are examined briefly. The different transmission types, unicast, anycast, and multicast, are also discussed here as they relate to routing.

Impact of Addresses on IP Networks

Back in the late 1970s and early 1980s when IP was being born, few people imagined that IP and the Internet would grow to accommodate tens of millions of hosts on tens of thousands of different networks. Consider RFC 814, *NAME, ADDRESSES, PORTS, AND ROUTES*, which describes early IP implementations that use only eight bits of 32-bit addresses to identify networks. In other words, these internetworks could support no more than 256 networks. Even more sophisticated implementations still used a fairly simple set of addressing mechanisms: Individual networks were each specified by a single routing table entry, and, within each network, individual hosts each were specified by a single hosts table entry.

Host names and network domain names are linked with host addresses and network addresses through simple tables. When a host changes its network address (for example, as a result of a network reorganization), the tables must be updated. When a network domain changes its address, routing tables must be updated. The host changes need only be updated within the host's domain; the network changes need to be updated in external routers' tables. The yet to be fully specified and implemented Domain Name System (DNS) would simplify matters, by mandating DNS servers. These servers can be queried by nodes looking for a network address that is associated with a host name. This means that applications need not be concerned with IP addresses but only with host names whose IP addresses may change over time.

However, there is a long history of sentiment that identifies IP addresses as globally unique and temporally stable. In other words, not only is every IP host and network identifiable by a unique address, but that address tends to remain the same over time. This scenario held fairly well up until about the mid-1990s. Once Internet access became available on a large scale to organizations and individuals who used it as a medium for communication, much the same way they use telecommunications services, the way IP addresses were used and distributed also changed. Prior to that, most companies using IP and the Internet applied directly to addressing authorities for their network addresses and network domains and took on responsibility for their Internet (or predecessor network, like NSFNet or ARPAnet) connections either directly or in partnership with networking specialist firms like Bolt, Beranek and Newman (BBN).

As the Internet became available commercially, however, things started to change. Individual organizations no longer controlled their network address directly, particularly as addressing authorities tightened up the supply. These authorities delegated addressing concerns to Internet service providers, which, in conjunction with the use of CIDR, made it possible to aggregate routes—a very important feature as routing tables ballooned.

This trend changed things drastically for IP addressing. First, if an organization changes its ISP, it may also find itself under pressure to change its network address. Second, with tighter control of IP addresses, an organization may find itself needing to fit a 500-node network into a 255-node address space. The rest of this section explores some of the ramifications of IP addressing as they relate to existing addressing mechanisms as well as how they relate to goals for IPv6 routing.

Identifiers and Locators

RFC 2101, *IPv4 Address Behaviour Today,* was published in February 1997 and describes how the use of IPv4 addresses has changed over time. Most important, it differentiates between the use of *identifiers* and *locators* in IPv4. An identifier is defined in this RFC as "a bit string which is used throughout the lifetime of a communication session between two hosts, to identify one of the hosts as far as the other is concerned." In other words, it sounds very much like the source host's IP address as it is used for Internet communication. A locator is defined as "a bit string which is used to identify where a particular packet must be delivered, i.e. it serves to locate the place in the Internet topology where the destination host is attached." In other words, it sounds very much like a destination host's IP address.

So, the identifier identifies the source, and the locator identifies the destination. This is reasonably straightforward: Host IP addresses tend to be used both as identifiers and as locators. However, the function of location—finding the destination—has been given priority over the function of identification—knowing where something is coming from. In other words, it's more important to be able to deliver a packet and then figure out where it came from than to be able to know the precise source of a packet but not be able to deliver it.

The authors of RFC 2101 identified two important differences in the requirements for identifiers and locators. The first relates to uniqueness, the second to persistence.

First, let's discuss uniqueness. The identifier must be unique with respect to both communicating nodes. This means that identifiers for nodes that communicate among themselves must all be unique. A host with a valid and unique IP address can identify any other host with a valid and unique IP address, and all such hosts connected to the same internetwork must all be unique. On the other hand, locators need to be unique only in respect to the routers that communicate with each other. In other words, locators must be unique within routing realms, but there may be overlap across different routing realms. A router can connect a Network 10 network to other networks but cannot link two or more Network 10 networks to each other (even if there were no specification prohibiting the forwarding of Network 10 packets, the router would never know which link to send out packets addressed to Network 10 addresses).

Second, we consider persistence. The lifetime of an identifier is longer than that of the locator. The identifier must last for at least as long as the complete communication between two nodes. If a node's identifier does change, then the other node won't be able to correctly address any more packets to it. On the other hand, the locator is important only for as long as the pertinent routing mechanisms require it to be. In other words, a router may be able to deal with locators that change during the course of a communication between nodes.

Even though locators and identifiers, at least currently, are derived mostly from nodes' IPv4 addresses, the two have different attributes—and each has different and conflicting ideal properties. For example, an ideal identifier would be assigned once (when the node is first installed on the network) and never change. The ideal identifier is bound to one and only one node and never reused or reassigned. This makes it possible to always link that identifier with that node and no other. After all, the function of the identifier is to identify a node as a source of data.

On the other hand, a locator is used for figuring out where a packet must go—it does not need to last for very long, but it should describe where in the network topology that node actually is. That way, if the host's location in the network topology changes for some reason, the locator would change as well. For example, if a host moved from one network to another, the locator would (in this ideal situation) also change; if the network to which the host is attached was renumbered, again, the locator would also change.

The RFC authors note that IP addresses don't work perfectly either as locators or as identifiers. The IP address is not a perfect identifier because IP addresses can no longer be said to be globally unique: Network 10 addresses represent a sizable portion of IP nodes that share the same network and host addresses. IP addresses also increasingly lack temporal persistence, making them even less suitable as identifiers. In networks that rely on DHCP to assign IP addresses temporarily to nodes, the IP address used by one node today may be used by another node tomorrow.

Likewise, IP addresses are flawed as locators. For one thing, Network 10 addresses say nothing about where in an internetwork the node is located. For another, historically, the network address says nothing about where the network is located in relation to other networks. This is certainly changing as more and more network routes are aggregated with CIDR. A network address within a certain CIDR block is usually handled by the organization responsible for that block. But the address of a class B network, for example, or any network assigned before CIDR came into general use, says nothing about where that network fits into the Internet. Finally, changing ISPs changes the network topology, but the IP address does not reflect the change unless the organization chooses to renumber (which, of course, affects the stability of the IP address as an identifier).

Address Allocation, Seamless Interoperability, and Network Topology

RFC 2008, *Implications of Various Address Allocation Policies for Internet Routing*, was published in October 1996 and raises some of the issues related to IP routing—and describes a "Best Current Practice" for address allocation. This RFC's basic premise is that the pursuit of an "address lending" approach provides significant performance and scalability benefits over the more traditional "address ownership" approach.

In other words, organizations that can do so are urged to use IP addresses as allocated by their ISPs—and change those addresses any time they change ISPs. This means that the organization borrows its IP addresses from a provider, who aggregates traffic to its customers. Aggregation means fewer routes must be maintained and improves the overall scalability of the Internet. However, aggregation also means that when an organization decides to change providers, it must also change its IP addresses so that its routes can be aggregated by its new provider.

The alternative, address ownership, has been responsible for the billowing of routing tables. However, owning an IP address is valuable if traffic is being directed at that particular IP address from other nodes. In other words, address ownership is valuable if you are using IP addresses as identifiers.

Unfortunately, using IP addresses as identifiers can cause a lot of problems. For one thing, it means you lose considerable flexibility in terms of how you can handle network traffic and how you can upgrade or change functions of nodes. Using DNS, you can bind a logical name (for example, www.loshin.com) to an address that may change over time. This means that I can easily change the binding of my web site from a web server running on my outdated 80486 Intel-based microcomputer to a high-end SMP server running at a third-party web presence provider. All I have to do is change the DNS mapping of the logical name from one IP address to another IP address.

This flexibility is very useful. In this example, my Internet presence provider would have to map my domain name to the IP address of its server; my own system would have to be assigned a new host name. More importantly, requiring IP applications to use only logical node names rather than IP addresses allows those applications to more seamlessly interoperate over IPv4 and IPv6 links. If the application cares only about a logical node name, this makes it possible for some other mechanism to perform the mapping between node name and node address. This and other issues related to IPv6-dependent protocols will be discussed in Chapter 10.

The biggest advantage of using address lending is that it allows the IP address to reflect network topology. Consider the example illustrated in Figure 8.1. An IP network address is assigned to Acme Co. using ISP B, which in turn receives connectivity through ISP Q, which in turn connects to the Internet through ISP Z. If all IP network addresses are loaned to customers, significant performance

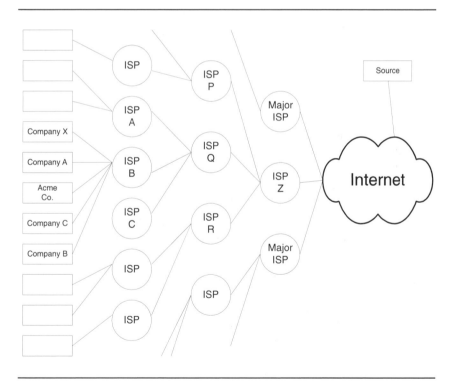

Figure 8.1. IP route aggregation and address lending allow IP addresses to reflect Internet topology.

and scalability improvement can be made. For packets being routed to Acme Co., it means that the source node shown in the figure will know that the route must be to ISP Z—the same route as is being used for all networks on the left that link up with ISP Z. At ISP Z, there are only three routes (in this example) to its customers, ISPs P, Q, and R. ISP Q needs only to have three routes, to ISPs A, B, and C.

Acme Co., borrowing its network IP address from ISP B, will have to renumber if it changes ISPs. For example, it may decide that ISP A offers better price or service. In that case, ISP Q will have to change its routing table to reflect the new address for Acme, but ISPs at higher levels—and routers on the other side of the Internet—will still route packets that have been sent to Acme through ISP Z. Acme might decide it needs a higher level of service available only from a higher-tier ISP, which would change more routes. However, it should be noted that address lending improves scalability and performance at the cost of requiring organizations to renumber their networks any time they change providers—or their providers change providers. The authors of RFC 2008 note that such renumbering of internal hosts is not always necessary if the organization uses some form of NAT or application gateways. They also note that the objective of aggregation and address lending should *not* be to create the smallest possible routing tables but rather to reduce the size and rate of increase of existing routing tables to allow for additional growth without adversely affecting routing performance.

The issues raised in this section relate largely to IPv4 addressing, but the RFCs were written in the shadows of the upgrade to IPv6. Pointing out where IPv4 offers room for improvement helps identify where and how IPv6 addressing can be improved.

Routing Issues for IPv6

Everyone (at least everyone *I* know) seems to know that IPv4 network addresses are running out. What doesn't seem quite as obvious is that default-free routers, or routers that list every route on the

Internet—in other words, routers that route on or near Internet backbones and must therefore know *all* the routes—are dealing with routing tables that are getting way too long. A route to every separate network has to be listed in this table, and that is why CIDR was so welcome. With CIDR, one of these mainline routers could replace 256 routes for 256 Class C networks with a single CIDR route that supernets eight bits of address space. All those 256 routes get passed through the same Internet access provider, so with CIDR you can drastically reduce the number of routes necessary to map the Internet.

IPv6 does not have a notion of classes, as IPv4 had. Whatever utility the existence of Class A, B, and C addresses had for IPv4 seems to have long since dissipated: the ability to sub- or supernet network addresses seems to be a much more useful attribute of a network address architecture. And IPv6 addresses certainly can be rolled up for routing purposes, thus giving the theoretical potential for drastically reducing the size of default-free routing tables.

Of course, the problem with such a highly aggregatable architecture is that it requires that networks be renumbered whenever an organization changes providers. Likewise, multihomed networks may pose additional problems. In fact, opponents of the CIDR-style provider-based aggregation approach refer to it as a "tyranny" and have proposed alternate solutions. It's become clear that these alternatives won't become a part of IPv6, but they have helped make automatic configuration and provider mobility a vital part of the IPv6 migration strategy. Chapter 11 introduces the mechanisms behind automatic configuration and provider mobility.

Perhaps surprisingly, it seems as though IPv6 routing protocols won't be drastically different from IPv4 routing protocols. After all, the IPv6 addressing architecture itself should vastly improve routing efficiency and reduce the size of default-free routing tables, so the routing algorithms and protocols need little modification to perform better. Most of the changes to these protocols to make them support IPv6 are related to adapting them to handle the longer IPv6 addresses.

IP Routing Protocols

IP routing protocols can essentially be categorized as either *link state* protocols or as *vector distance* (or *path vector*) protocols. They can also be classified as either *interior* routing protocols or as *exterior* routing protocols. These categories may be a bit oversimplified, but for the purposes of this book they should suffice.

Interior and Exterior Routing

The concepts of interior and exterior routing are vitally important to the structure of the Internet. They are bound up with the way the Internet and connected internetworks interact. A corporate intranet, for example, may be connected to the Internet, but it is connected through a single link; if that link goes down, there is no external connectivity to that intranet, and all traffic between that intranet and the global Internet passes through that link. This type of network is called an *autonomous system* (AS) because everything that goes on inside it is the responsibility of a single administering organization. It is also autonomous because on the global Internet routers need only know a single route to get any node within that system—and because any node inside the AS can use a *default route*, which identifies a router that links the AS with the global Internet, when sending packets to any node outside the AS.

Interior routing is concerned with the routing of packets within an AS. In other words, routing within relatively small internetworks—small, at least, when compared with the global Internet. Routers inside the AS keep routing tables that are relatively small. These tables include routes to subnets and networks within the AS, and one or more default routes that are used when a packet is addressed to a network that is not otherwise explicitly listed.

Exterior routing, on the other hand, happens outside the normal AS environment. A backbone router cannot have a default route. It must know the explicit route to every destination network if it is to function properly as a backbone router. This means far longer routing tables, which is why the use of aggregation mechanisms like CIDR are so important to improving backbone routing performance.

All routing protocols use some element of either the link state or vector distance routing algorithms, as discussed below. IPv4 exterior routers currently rely on the Border Gateway Protocol 4 (BGP-4, defined in RFC 1771), which is a vector distance routing protocol that supports CIDR. Despite some initial sentiment that BGP was optimized for IPv4's 32-bit addresses and thus entirely unsuitable for IPv6 (see Huitema's *IPv6 The New Internet Protocol*), it appears that BGP-4 will be used for exterior routing under IPv6. With some extensions (described in an Internet draft) to appropriately handle scoped IPv6 unicast addresses (link-local, site-local, and global) and other relatively minor modifications to support multiprotocol routing, specified in RFC 2283, BGP-4 will be capable of handling IPv6 exterior routing.

Another important exterior routing protocol is the Inter-Domain Routing Protocol (IDRP) that grew out of the ISO/OSI effort. IDRP allows more flexibility for describing networks of virtually unlimited size and with greater flexibility for supported network address architecture. Some saw in IDRP a better exterior routing protocol for IPv6, though whether it is likely to continue to be an important protocol as the global Internet continues to grow is open to question.

Link State and Vector Distance Protocols

Vector distance protocols are often relatively simple. An important vector distance protocol is the Routing Information Protocol, or RIP. RIP is both simple and limited because it requires each router in an internetwork to periodically broadcast routing information to all other routers in the network. As the vector distance protocol appellation implies, the information broadcast by each router consists of a list of routes and an integer that indicates how far away the route is. Consider router 1 in the network shown in Figure 8.2. This router would advertise that it has a single-hop path to network A; a two-hop path to each of networks B, D, and F; and a three-hop path to each of networks C and E. Router 2 shows a single-hop path to network B but a two-hop path to network A (among other routes).

Using this information, router 2 knows that any packets intended for network A should be routed through router 1—no other router will be able to advertise a shorter path to that network. Likewise, router 2 will also know that it should avoid sending packets intended for network A to router 5, which is three hops away from network A. It should also be clear that router 3, which is three hops from router 2, is a further three hops from network A—thus, sending a packet via router 3 would take a full six hops.

Now, some of the drawbacks of RIP become apparent. First, it is a noisy protocol. Every router frequently sends out status information (by default, messages go out every 30 seconds), and the amount of traffic increases very quickly as the internetwork expands and the number of routers increases. Second, RIP is limited by definition to supporting routing in internetworks that are no wider than 16 hops across—in other words, if there are routes longer than 16 hops, RIP cannot be used. Although the RIP header can support hop lengths as high as $(2^{32} - 1)$, routing convergence problems helped developers come to an early determination that RIP should be limited to 16 hops. Routing convergence problems arise when messages relating to connectivity problems cannot be relayed to all routers before incorrect routes are propagated through the network.

Routing protocols are necessary to allow packets to be routed independently of network topology. This means that the source node should not have to keep a map of the Internet in storage to be able to send a packet to a destination anywhere on the network. Intermediate routers are supposed to keep track of connectivity so that they can forward packets appropriately—but they still don't necessarily need to track the entire structure, just the local portions of it. Thus, we have protocols like RIP that allow routers to keep other routers apprised of the status of their various connections. IP was designed to work in a networking infrastructure that was expected to not be entirely dependable as well as not entirely redundant. What this means is that, using the example in Figure 8.2, if router 6 fails, packets can still go to network A from network E through an alternate route (instead of from router 5 to router 6 to router 1, from router 5 to router 2 to router 1).

So, what's the problem? If router 1's link to network A fails, there is *no* connectivity to network A from *anywhere*—the network is cut off.

However, router 1 has been receiving information about other routers' links to network A. All of these routes are at least two hops, so up to now router 1 has ignored them (because it had a one-hop route to network A). This, and similar, problems have to be remedied by assorted different complications to make the protocol work.

This is not to say that RIP is not useful: It is quite important as a routing protocol for small and medium internetworks (also known as intranets), where limitations on network width is unimportant. However, it is not enough for larger intranets—and woefully inadequate for routing backbone traffic where there are many different routes to consider.

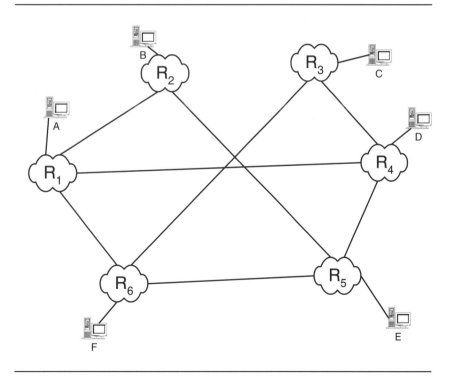

Figure 8.2. A simple internetwork linked by routers using RIP.

Link state routing protocols like the Open Shortest Path First (OSPF) protocol were largely created to answer the shortcomings of vector distance approaches. Instead of periodically notifying all other routers of all their routes, a router limits itself to advertising its own direct links. Using Figure 8.2 again, router 1 would advertise that it has direct connections with network A and with routers 2, 4, and 6. The other routers would advertise their own connections, and all would then be able to derive appropriate and ideal routes. If router 5 knows that router 2 (with which it has a direct connection) is connected to router 1, and that router 1 is connected directly to network A, then it has derived a route from network E to network A. Routers advertise their connections when they change, and when they are asked by another router, so the noise level associated with routing drops with a protocol like OSPF. OSPF can also support much larger internetworks because it is free from RIP's hop limitation and because it does not generate as much traffic between routers. However, OSPF is also much more complex. Other important characteristics of OSPF are that it supports multiple layers of hierarchy and type-of-service based routing.

Routing protocols may also allow more information about routing links. For example, routers may assign different values to certain links depending on things like available bandwidth, latency, even cost. Thus, router 5 in Figure 8.2 might prefer to route traffic to network A through router 4 if that link appears to be better in some way (shorter, faster, or cheaper).

IPv6 Updates for Routing Protocols

As mentioned earlier, BGP-4 and IDRP are likely to continue as the exterior routing protocols of choice for IP, with relatively minor modifications to accommodate IPv6 addresses and address scopes. Likewise, RIPng is described in RFC 2080, *RIPng for IPv6*, and it is quite similar to the existing protocol. OSPF is most recently defined as an Internet standard in RFC 2328, *OSPF Version 2*, though a version of OSPF for IPv6 is in the works. OSPF for IPv6 is expected to retain the general look and feel of OSPF, with all the same basic features and functions, while adapting it to handle IPv6 routing.

9

IPv6 Authentication and Security

The desirability and utility of authentication and security features at the IP layer have been debated for years. This chapter discusses how authentication and security, including secure password transmission, encryption, and digital signatures on datagrams, are implemented under IPv6 through the authentication headers (AH) and encapsulating security payload (ESP) headers. Before examining the IPv6 security headers, however, we will take a look at the IP security architecture first described in RFC 1825, *Security Architecture for the Internet Protocol*, and the different pieces of that architecture that are likely to be implemented under IPv6.

Adding Security to IP

IPv4 incorporated no real security features; it was intended simply as an internetworking protocol. This is not necessarily a drawback for a research tool or even for a production networking protocol used in relatively restricted venues that include research, military, educational, and government networks. However, the increase in importance of IP networking to the general business and consumer networking environments makes the potential harm resulting from attacks more devastating than ever. This section examines:

- The security goals that have been defined for IP.
- How those goals are going to be met.
- How those goals and related topics are defined in relation to IP.

The next section takes a look at the specifics of the IP security architecture itself, also known as IPsec, as well as some of the tools being assembled to achieve these goals.

It should be noted that IPsec, as defined in RFC 1825 and successor documents, provides a security architecture for the Internet Protocol—not a security architecture for the Internet. The distinction is important: IPsec defines security services to be used at the IP layer, both for IPv4 and IPv6. IPv4 can use authentication headers and ESP headers, as long as they are implemented in proper IPv4 options formats. It just happens that these security functions can be more easily implemented under IPv6.

Security Goals

When speaking of security, three broadly stated goals can be defined:

- *Authentication.* The ability to reliably determine that data has been received as it was sent and to verify that the entity that sent the data is what it claims to be.
- *Integrity.* The ability to reliably determine that the data has not been modified during transit from its source to its destination.
- *Confidentiality.* The ability to transmit data that can be used or read only by its intended recipient and not by any other entity.

Integrity and authentication are often closely connected, and confidentiality is sometimes achieved through the use of public key encryption, which can also help authenticate the source.

The authentication header and the encapsulating security payload (ESP) header offer help in achieving these goals over IP. Very simply, the authentication header provides a mechanism for a source node to digitally sign packets. All data that follows an authentication header remains in plaintext and may be intercepted by attackers. Upon receipt by the destination node, however, the data can be authenticated with the data included in the authentication header.

The ESP header, on the other hand, makes it possible to encrypt the contents of a packet. The ESP header holds enough data to allow the recipient to decrypt the rest of the packet (all data following an ESP header is encrypted).

The problem with Internet security (indeed, with any kind of security) is that creating security is difficult, particularly in an open network where packets may traverse any number of unknown networks and where packet sniffers may be at work, undetected, on any of those networks. There are significant threats to security, even where encryption and digital signatures are in use, in such open environments. Also, while attacks on IP traffic include things like interception, where data being transmitted from one entity to another is stolen by an unauthorized third entity, there are other security threats that IP security should attempt to address:

- ◆ Denial of service attacks occur when an entity uses network transmissions to somehow keep an authorized user from having access to network resources. For example, an attacker may flood a host with requests and thereby crash a system, or the attack may consist of repeated transmission of very long e-mail messages with the intention of filling up a user's or site's bandwidth with nuisance traffic.
- ◆ Spoofing attacks occur when an entity transmits packets that misrepresent the packets' origins. For example, one type of spoofing attack occurs when the attacker sends an

e-mail message with the "From:" header indicating the source of the message as, say, the president of the United States. More insidious are those attacks that occur when packets are sent out with an incorrect source address in the headers.

Further complicating matters is the issue of handling keys. The IP security architecture demands the use of keys for both authentication purposes and for encryption. One of the thorniest issues facing the Internet community is how to securely administer and distribute keys and at the same time correctly associate keys with entities in such a way as to avoid man-in-the-middle attacks. In this type of attack, an attacker (call it C) positions itself between two communicating entities (call them A and B), intercepting all transmissions, posing as A when resending data to B, and posing as B when resending data to A. If C convinces A that it is really B by authenticating itself with a public key that might appear to be B's (and vice versa), then A and B will believe their transmissions to be secure when in fact they are not.

IPsec by itself will not make the Internet secure, and this chapter addresses only a few of the most pressing issues relating to Internet security. For more details about Internet security, the interested reader should see the author's *Personal Encryption Clearly Explained* (AP Professional, 1998) for general discussions of encryption, digital signatures, and Internet security issues.

RFC 1825 and Proposed Updates

Published in August 1995, RFC 1825, *Security Architecture for the Internet Protocol*, weighed in at 22 pages; the fifth draft update to this RFC (dated May 1998) runs 66 pages long. The reason for the expansion is mostly that doing security properly requires exquisite attention to the details, and the updated document, when it is finally published, will provide far more detail about how to implement all of IP, including ICMP and multicast, as well as more details relating to key management and keeping track of security associations (see the following discussion).

IPsec

The goal of IPsec is to provide security mechanisms to be used by IPv4 as well as IPv6. IPsec provides security services at the IP layer. A system can use IPsec to require that other systems interact with it in a secure way, using particular security algorithms and protocols. IPsec offers the tools necessary for a system to negotiate an acceptably secure interaction with other systems. This means that a system may have more than one acceptable encryption algorithm, which lets it negotiate with other systems for its preferred algorithm but allows it to accept some alternate algorithm if the other system doesn't support the first system's first choice.

The security services that are likely to be considered a part of IPsec include:

- *Access control.* If you don't have the right password, you can't get access to a service or system. Security protocols can be invoked that govern the secure exchange of keys, allowing authentication of users for access control purposes.
- *Connectionless integrity.* It is possible to use IPsec for verifying the integrity of any individual IP packet without need to reference any other packet; each packet can stand alone and be validated on its own. This function can be carried out through use of secure hashing techniques, similar to the use of check digits but with greater reliability and less likelihood of tampering from unauthorized entities.
- *Data origin authentication.* Identifying the source of the data contained in an IP packet is another security service provided by IPsec. This function is accomplished through the use of digital signature algorithms.
- *Defense against packet replay attacks.* As a connectionless protocol, IP is subject to the threat of replay attacks, where an attacker sends a packet that has already been received by the destination host. Replay attacks can harm system availability by tying up receiving system

resources. IPsec provides a packet counter mechanism that protects against this ploy.

♦ *Encryption.* Data confidentiality—keeping access to data from anyone but those with proper authorization—is provided through the use of encryption.

♦ *Limited traffic flow confidentiality.* Encrypting data is not always sufficient to protect systems; merely knowing the end points of an encrypted exchange, the frequency of such interaction, or other information about the transmissions can provide a determined attacker with enough information to disrupt or subvert systems. IPsec provides some limited traffic flow confidentiality through the use of IP tunneling, especially when coupled with security gateways.

All of these functions are possible through proper use of the encapsulating security payload (ESP) header and the authentication header (AH). A handful of cryptographic functions are used, described very briefly in the next section, as is a key management infrastructure, described very briefly in the section following that.

Encryption and Authentication Algorithms

Security algorithms and protocols are hard to design because there are so many different ways to attack them—and the designers can't always imagine them all. The prevailing wisdom in security holds that a good encryption or authentication algorithm should be secure even if an attacker knows what algorithm is being used. This is particularly important for Internet security, as an attacker with a sniffer will often be able to determine exactly what kind of algorithm is being used by listening as systems negotiate their connections.

In general, there are five types of important cryptographic functions related to Internet security. These include symmetric encryption, public key encryption, key exchange, secure hashes, and digital signature.

Symmetric Encryption

The type of encryption most people are familiar with is symmetric encryption. Each party uses the same key to encrypt and decrypt data. If you have the key, you can decrypt all data that has been encrypted with that key. This is also sometimes known as *secret key encryption*. Symmetric encryption is usually quite efficient and is the most frequent type of encryption for network transmission of volumes of data.

Symmetric encryption algorithms commonly in use include:

♦ *Data Encryption Standard (DES)*. First developed during the 1970s by IBM, DES is an international standard with 56-bit keys. A variation called triple-DES encrypts data three times with the DES algorithm, providing improved security.
♦ *RC2, RC4, and RC5*. These ciphers are available for licensing from RSA Data Security (a Security Dynamics company) and provide variable key-length encryption. They are used for example, in Netscape's Navigator browser, as well as many other Internet client and server products.
♦ Other algorithms include CAST (developed in Canada and used by Nortel's Entrust products), IDEA (the International Data Encryption Algorithm), GOST (an algorithm reportedly developed by a Soviet security agency), Blowfish (an algorithm developed by Bruce Schneier and released to the public domain), and Skipjack (an algorithm developed by the National Security Agency for use with the Clipper chip's escrowed key system).

Using a secure encryption requires using sufficiently long keys. Shorter keys are vulnerable to *brute force attacks* in which an attacker simply uses a computer to try all the different possible keys. Key lengths on the order of 40 bits, for example, are considered to be insecure because they can be broken by brute force attacks in very short order by relatively inexpensive computers. Single DES has been brute-forced, as well; in general, 128-bit keys are likely to be secure against such attacks for the foreseeable future.

Symmetric encryption algorithms can be vulnerable to other types of attacks. Most applications that use symmetric encryption for Internet communications use *session keys*, meaning that a key is used for only a single session data transmission (or sometimes several keys are used for a session). In that way, loss of a session key compromises only the data that was sent during that session rather than potentially compromising a much larger volume of data exchanged over a longer period.

Public Key Encryption

Public key encryption uses a pair of keys. The *public key* is associated with a secret key; the public key is intended to be made public. Any data encrypted with the public key can only be decrypted with the secret key—and any data encrypted with the secret key can be decrypted with the public key. As long as an entity can keep its secret key a secret, other entities can be sure that any data encrypted with the public key will be accessible only to the holder of the associated secret key. Public key encryption tends to be inefficient and is most often used to encrypt session keys for network transmissions as well as for digital signatures (see the following discussion).

The most common type of public key encryption is the RSA algorithm (developed by Ron Rivest, Adi Shamir, and Len Adleman and available for license from RSA Data Security). RSA defines a mechanism for choosing and generating the secret/public key pairs, as well as for the actual mathematical function to be used for encryption.

Key Exchange

An open channel (an communication medium over which transmissions can be overheard) like the Internet complicates the process of sharing a secret. This process is necessary when two entities need to share a key to be used for encryption. Some of the most important cryptographic algorithms relate to the process of sharing a key over an open channel securely, in a way that keeps the secret from anyone but the intended recipients.

Diffie-Hellman key exchange is an algorithm that allows entities to exchange enough information to derive a session encryption key. Alice (the customary entity name for the first participant in a cryptographic protocol) calculates a value using Bob's public value and her own secret value (Bob is the second participant in cryptographic protocols). Bob calculates his own value and sends it to Alice; they each then use their secret values to calculate their shared key. The mathematics are relatively simple (but outside the scope of this book); the bottom line is that Bob and Alice can send each other enough information to calculate their shared key but not enough for an attacker to be able to figure it out.

Diffie-Hellman is often called a public key algorithm, but it is not a public key *encryption* algorithm. It can be used to calculate a key, but that key must be used with some other encryption algorithm. Diffie-Hellman can be used for authentication, though, and is used by the Pretty Good Privacy (PGP) public key software (from Network Associates).

Key exchange is integral to any Internet security architecture, and candidates for the IPsec security architecture include the *Internet Key Exchange* (IKE) and the *Internet Security Association and Key Management Protocol* (ISAKMP). These and other related standards and proposed standards will be discussed later.

Secure Hashes

A hash is a sort of digital summary of some amount of data. Simple types of hashes include check digits; secure hashes produce somewhat longer results (often 128 bits). Good secure hashes are hard for attackers to reverse-engineer or to subvert in other ways. Secure hashes can be used with keys or without, but their purpose is to provide a digital summary of a message that can be used to verify whether some data that has been received is the same as the data sent. The sender calculates the hash and includes that value with the data; the recipient calculates the hash on the data received. If the results match the attached hash value, the recipient can be confident in the data's integrity.

Commonly used hashes include the MD2, MD4, and MD5 *message digest* functions available from RSA Data Security. The Secure Hash Algorithm (SHA) is a digest function developed as a standard by the National Institute of Standards and Technology (NIST). Hashes may be used on their own or as part of digital signatures.

Digital Signature

Public key encryption, as noted previously, relies on key pairs. Digital signatures rely on the property of public key encryption that allows data encrypted with an entity's secret key to be decrypted with the public key of the pair. The sender calculates a secure hash on the data to be signed then encrypts the result using a secret key. The recipient calculates the same hash and then decrypts the encrypted value attached by the sender. If the two values match, the recipient knows that the owner of the public key was the entity that signed the message and that the message was not modified during transmission.

The RSA public key encryption algorithm can be used for digital signatures: The signing entity creates a hash of the data to be signed and then encrypts that hash with its own secret key. The certifying entity then calculates the same hash on the data being received, decrypts the signature using the signing entity's public key, and compares the two values. If the hash is the same as the decrypted signature, then the data is certified.

Digital signatures carry with them several implications:

- ♦ A signature that can be certified indicates that the message was received without any alteration from the time it was signed to the time it was received.
- ♦ If a signature cannot be certified, then the message was corrupted or tampered with in transit, the signature was calculated incorrectly, or the signature was corrupted or tampered with in transit. In any case, an uncertifiable signature does not necessarily imply any wrongdoing but does require that the message be resigned and resent in order to be accepted.
- ♦ If a signature is certified, it means that the entity associated with the public key was the *only* entity that could have signed it. In other words, the entity associated with the public key cannot deny having signed the message. This is called *nonrepudiation* and is an important feature of digital signatures.

There are other mechanisms for doing digital signatures, but RSA is probably the most widely used one and is implemented in the most popular Internet products.

Security Associations

Fundamental to IPsec is the concept of *security association*. The security association, or SA, contains a combination of data that can uniquely identify a connection for security purposes. The connection is one way only, and each security association is defined by a destination address and a *Security Parameter Index* (SPI); an identifier indicating the type of IP header the security association is being used for (AH or ESP) is called for in Internet drafts for the revision of RFC 1825. The SPI is a 32-bit value that simply identifies a security association and differentiates security associations linked with the same destination address. For secure communication between two systems, there would be two different security associations, one for each destination address.

Each security association includes more information related to the type of security negotiated for that connection. This means that systems must keep track of their SAs and what type of encryption or authentication algorithms, key lengths, and key lifetimes have been negotiated with the SA destination hosts.

Key Management

One of the most complex issues facing Internet security professionals is how to manage keys. This includes not only the actual distribution of keys through a key exchange protocol but also the negotiation of key length, lifetime, and cryptographic algorithms between communicating systems. This is an area in which a great deal of work has been done by Internet working groups and the research community at large; however, there has not been enough consensus yet to enable publication of any RFCs.

The Internet Security Association Key Management Protocol (ISAKMP) defines an entire infrastructure for the secure exchange of keys. ISAKMP is an actual application protocol, using UDP as its transport, which defines different types of messages that systems send to each other to negotiate the exchange of keys.

The mechanisms and algorithms for doing the actual exchanges, however, are not defined in ISAKMP—it is a framework to be used by the specific mechanisms. The mechanisms, often based on Diffie-Hellman key exchange, have been defined in a number of different proposals over the years. These include:

- *Photuris.* This proposal is based on Diffie-Hellman but adds the requirement that the requesting node send a cookie (a random number) first, which the server then acknowledges. This reduces the risk from denial-of-service attacks made by attackers forging their source addresses. Photuris also requires all parties to sign their negotiated key to reduce the risk of a man-in-the-middle attack (in which an attacker pretends to be Bob to one system's Alice, while pretending to be Alice to the other system's Bob).
- *Sun's Simple Key-management for Internet Protocols (SKIP).* This is also based on Diffie-Hellman key exchange, but, rather than requiring parties to use random values to calculate their keys, SKIP calls for the use of a secret table that remains static. The parties look up secret values in this table and then transmit calculated values based on some secret value from the table.
- *OAKLEY.* Although this mechanism shares some features with Photuris, it provides different modes of key exchange for situations where denial-of-service attacks are not of concern.

As of autumn 1998, it appeared that Internet key exchange would ultimately be defined in the Internet Key Exchange specification, based on OAKLEY and SKEME (Secure Key Exchange Mechanism for Internet).

It should be noted that manual key management is an important option and in many cases the only option. This approach requires individuals to personally deliver keys and configure network devices to use them. Even after open standards have been firmly determined and implemented, particularly as commercial products, manual key management will continue to be an important choice.

Implementing IPsec

IP layer security protects IP datagrams. It does not necessarily have to involve the user or any applications. This means that users may be merrily using all of their applications without ever being aware that all their datagrams are being encrypted or authenticated before being sent out to the Internet (of course, that situation will only occur as long as all the encrypted datagrams are properly decrypted by hosts at the other end).

As a result, one question that comes up is how to implement IPsec. Three possibilities include:

   ♦ Implement IPsec as a part of the IPv4 or IPv6 stack. This approach incorporates IP security header support into the IP network stack and makes it a complete and integral part of any IP implementation. However, it also requires that the entire stack be updated to reflect the changes.
   ♦ Implement IPsec as a "bump in the stack" (BITS). This approach inserts special IPsec code into the network stack just below the existing IP network software and just above the local link software. In other words, this approach implements security through a piece of software that intercepts datagrams being passed from the existing IP stack to the local link layer interface. This software then does the necessary security processing for those datagrams and hands them off to the link layer. This approach can be used to upgrade systems to IPsec support without requiring that their IP stack software be rewritten.
   ♦ Implement IPsec as a "bump in the wire" (BITW). This approach uses external cryptographic hardware to perform the security processing. The device is usually an IP

device that acts as a sort of a router or, more accurately, security gateway for all IP datagrams from any system that sits behind it. When such a device is used for a single host, it works very much like the BITS approach, but implementation can be more complex when a single BITW device is used to screen more than one system.

These options differ more in terms of where they are appropriate than in subjective terms. Applications that require high levels of security may be better served with a hardware implementation. Applications run on systems for which new IPsec-compliant network stacks are not available may be better served by the BITS approach.

Tunnel Mode vs. Transparent Mode

We'll be returning to the concept of *protocol tunnels* later, when we discuss migration strategies. However, tunneling is important for IP security as well. As shown in Figure 9.1, two systems can set up

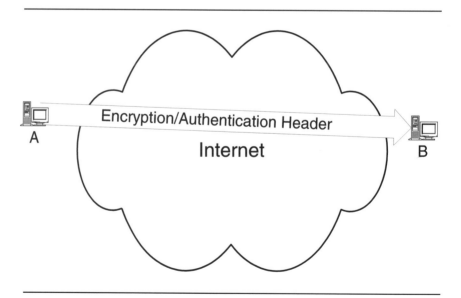

Figure 9.1. A pair of hosts using IPsec to communicate transparently.

security associations so that they can communicate securely over the Internet. Network traffic originates on one system, is encrypted or signed, and is then sent to the destination system. On receipt, the datagram is decrypted or authenticated, and the payload is passed along up the receiving system's network stack where it is finally processed by the application using the data. This is a *transparent mode* use of security associations, because the two hosts could be communicating just as easily without security headers—and because the actual IP headers of the datagrams must be exposed to allow them to be routed across the Internet.

A security association can also be used to tunnel secure IP through an internetwork. Figure 9.2 shows how this works. All IP packets from system A are forwarded to the security gateway X, which creates an IP tunnel through the Internet to security gateway Y, which unwraps the tunneled packets and forwards them. Security gateway Y might forward those packets to any of the hosts (B, C, or D) within its own local intranet, or it could forward them to an external host, like M. It all depends on where the originating host directs

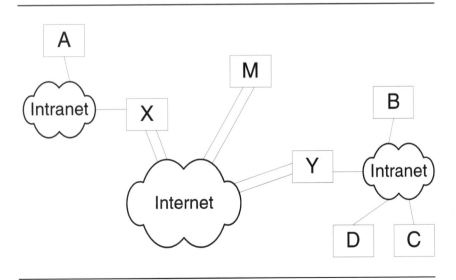

Figure 9.2. IP security tunneling.

those packets. Whenever an SA destination node is a security gateway, it is by definition a tunneled association. In other words, tunneling can be done between two security gateways (as shown in Figure 9.2), or it can be done between a regular node and a security gateway. Thus, host M could create a tunneled connection with either security gateway, X or Y. It is tunneled by virtue of the fact that datagrams sent from M are passed first to the security gateway, which then forwards them appropriately after decrypting or authenticating.

IPv6 Security Headers

As already mentioned, IPsec security services are provided entirely through the mechanism of the authentication header and the encapsulating security payload header in conjunction, of course, with appropriate and relevant key management protocols. The authentication header is described in RFC 1826, *IP Authentication Header*; the encapsulating security payload header is described in RFC 1827, *IP Encapsulating Security Payload (ESP)*. As with the IP security architecture RFC, these RFCs are merely first passes at the problems. The IPsec working group members continue to refine these header specifications, and the current drafts of these documents are both roughly double the size of the original RFCs. The current drafts retain much of the language and intent of the original RFCs but have been expanded to describe the headers and their functions more completely and comprehensively.

The security headers may be used by themselves or together. If they are used together, the authentication header should come before the ESP header—that way, the authentication can be checked prior to decrypting the ESP header payload. These headers can also be nested, when using IPsec tunneling. In other words, an originating node can encrypt and digitally sign a packet, then send it to the local security gateway. That gateway may then re-encrypt and re-sign the packet as it sends it off to another security gateway.

It is important to remember that the authentication and ESP headers are defined for use with both IPv4 and IPv6. This section discusses how these headers are used with IPv6. For use with IPv4, the security headers are added to the normal IPv4 header as options.

Authentication Header (AH)

The authentication header can be used to do the following:

♦ *Provide strong integrity services for IP datagrams.* This means that the AH can be used to carry content verification data for the IP datagram.
♦ *Provide strong authentication for IP datagrams.* This means that the AH can be used to link an entity with the contents of the datagram.
♦ *Provide nonrepudiation for IP datagrams,* assuming that a public key digital signature algorithm is used for integrity services.
♦ *Protect against replay attacks* through the use of a sequence number field.

The authentication header can be used in tunnel mode or in transport mode, which means that it can be used to authenticate and protect simple, direct datagram transfers between two nodes, or it can be used to encapsulate an entire stream of datagrams that is sent to or from a security gateway.

Authentication Header Syntax

The authentication header in IPv6, when used with other extension headers, must be placed after any headers intended to be processed at intermediate hops but before any headers intended to be processed only at the datagram's destination. This means that the authentication header should be placed after hop-by-hop, routing, or fragmentation extension headers. Depending on circumstances, the authentication header may appear before or after any destination option extension headers.

In transport mode, the authentication header protects the payload of the original IP datagram as well as the parts of the IP header that do not change from hop to hop (e.g., the hop limit field or routing

```
Datagram prior to calculating AH
-------------------------------------------
| dest IP hdr | ext headers | TCP | Data |
-------------------------------------------

Datagram after inserting AH
-------------------------------------------------------------
| dest IP hdr | ext headers | AH | dest options | TCP | Data |
-------------------------------------------------------------
|<---- authenticated except for fields that change --------->|
```

Figure 9.3. Adding an authentication header to an IP datagram in transport mode.

headers). Figure 9.3 shows what happens to a transport-mode IP datagram as the authentication header is calculated and added to it (the destination options header may also appear before the authentication header). The destination IP address and extension headers are protected only insofar as they do not change from hop to hop.

When the authentication header is used in tunnel mode, however, it is used differently. Figure 9.4 shows the difference. The original destination IP address, along with the entire original IP datagram, is encapsulated into an entirely new IP datagram that is sent to the security gateway. Thus, the entire original IP datagram is fully protected, as are the portions of the encapsulating IP headers that don't change.

Authentication Header Fields

Figure 9.5 shows the format and fields of the authentication header. As with all IPv6 extension headers, the first field is the eight-bit Next Header field, which indicates the protocol of the header that follows. The other fields of the authentication header include:

◆ *Payload length.* This eight-bit field indicates the entire length of the authentication header in units of 32-bit

```
Original IP datagram
---------------------------------------
| orig IP hdr | ext hdrs | TCP | Data |
---------------------------------------

IP datagram for tunneling to security gateway (GW)
------------------------------------------------------------------
| GW IP hdr | ext hdrs | AH | orig IP hdr | ext hdrs | TCP | Data |
------------------------------------------------------------------
```

Figure 9.4. Adding an authentication header to an IP datagram in tunnel mode.

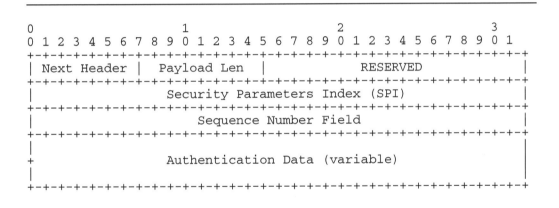

Figure 9.5. Authentication header format and fields.

words, minus two. As originally defined, the authentication header consisted of 64-bits of header with the rest devoted to authentication data (see the following). Thus, the payload length field merely indicated the length (in 32-bit words) of the authentication data. With the addition of the sequence number field (see the following), this value now equals the length of the authentication data plus the length of the sequence number field.

♦ *Reserved.* The next 16 bits are reserved for future use; at present, they must be set to all zeros.

♦ *Security Parameters Index (SPI).* This 32-bit value is an arbitrary number. Together with the destination IP address and security protocol (in this case, AH to indicate the authentication header), the SPI uniquely identifies the security association to be used for the authentication header. An SPI value of zero is for local use only and should never be transmitted; values from one through 255 are reserved by the Internet Assigned Numbers Authority (IANA) for future use.

♦ *Sequence Number.* This 32-bit value is a mandatory counter; it is also included by the sender, though it may not always be used by the recipient. Starting from zero, this counter is incremented with every datagram sent and is used to prevent replay attacks. When the recipient is using it for anti-replay purposes, it will discard any datagrams that duplicate a sequence number that has already been received. This means that when the counter is ready to cycle through (when 2^{32} datagrams have been received), a new security association must be negotiated—otherwise, the receiving system will discard all datagrams once the counter is reset.

♦ *Authentication Data.* This field contains the *Integrity Check Value* (ICV), which is the heart of the authentication header. The contents must be a multiple of 32 bits in length and may contain padding to attain that length. Calculation of this value is discussed in the next section.

Calculating the Integrity Check Value (ICV)

RFC 1826 is relatively vague on how the integrity check value is to be calculated and with what mechanisms. In fact, the term *Integrity Check Value* (ICV) does not appear in that document, but is taken from later drafts of documents intended to replace RFC 1826. The ICV is expected to be the result of an appropriate authentication algorithm. Suggested algorithms include:

♦ Message Authentication Codes (MACs), the result of which are then encrypted with an appropriate symmetric encryption algorithm (for example, DES).

♦ Secure hash functions like MD5 or SHA-1 (an updated version of SHA).

To comply with the standard, it is expected that any implementation of the authentication header will have to support MD5 and SHA-1 keyed hashing. The authentication data is calculated on the entire IP datagram payload, as well as on the parts of the IP header that cannot change or that can be predicted.

Encapsulating Security Payload (ESP) Header

The Encapsulating Security Payload (ESP) header is designed to allow IP nodes to send and receive datagrams whose payload is encrypted. More specifically, the ESP header is designed to provide several different services (some overlapping with the authentication header), including:

♦ Confidentiality of datagrams through encryption.
♦ Authentication of data origin through the use of public key encryption.
♦ Antireplay services through the same sequence number mechanism as provided by the authentication header.
♦ Limited traffic flow confidentiality through the use of security gateways.

The ESP header can be used in conjunction with an authentication header. In fact, unless the ESP header uses some mechanism for authentication, it is recommended that the authentication header be used with the ESP header.

ESP Header Syntax

The ESP header must follow any headers that need to be processed by nodes intermediate to the destination node—all data that follows the ESP header is likely to be encrypted. In fact, the encrypted payload appears as the last ESP header field (see below).

ESP can be used in tunnel or transport mode, similar to the authentication header. In transport mode, the IP header and any hop-by-hop, routing, or fragmentation extension headers precede the authentication header (if present), followed by the ESP header. Any destination options headers can either precede or follow the ESP header, or even both; any headers that follow the ESP header are encrypted.

The result appears, in many respects, to simply be a regular IP datagram transmitted from source to destination, with an encrypted payload. This use of ESP in transport mode is appropriate in some cases, but it allows attackers to study traffic between the two nodes, noting which nodes are communicating, how much data they exchange, when they exchange it, and so forth. All this information may potentially provide the attacker with some information that helps defeat the communicating parties.

An alternative is to use a security gateway, much as described above for the authentication header. A security gateway can operate directly with a node or can link to another security gateway. A single node can use ESP in tunnel mode by encrypting all outbound packets and encapsulating them in a separate stream of IP datagrams that are sent to the security gateway. That gateway then can decrypt the traffic and resend the original datagrams to their destinations, as shown in Figure 9.6, where node A encrypts all traffic for nodes B, C, and D and sends them to GW1. Alternatively, node E can send all datagrams through GW2, which does the encryption and sends that traffic to GW1—which decrypts the traffic and resends it to its destinations.

When tunneling, the ESP header encapsulates the entire tunneled IP datagram and is an extension to the IP header directing that datagram to a security gateway. It is also possible to combine ESP headers with authentication headers in several different ways; for example, the tunneled datagram may have a transport-mode authentication header.

ESP Header Fields

The ESP header differs from other extension headers. For one thing, the Next Header field appears near the end of the ESP header. For another, the header that precedes the ESP header specifies that an

ESP header follows by placing the value 50 in its Next Header field. The rest of the ESP header will probably consist of the following:

- *Security Parameters Index (SPI)*. This is the same 32-bit value referred to in the section on the authentication header. This value is used by the communicating nodes to refer to a security association, which can be used to determine how the data should be encrypted.
- *Sequence Number*. This 32-bit value is set to zero to start and is incremented by one with each datagram sent. As described above for the authentication header, the sequence number can be used to protect against replay attacks, and before it cycles through all 2^{32} values a new security association must be set up.
- *Payload Data*. This is a variable length field and actually contains the encrypted portion of the datagram, along with any supplementary data necessary for the encryption algorithm (e.g., initialization data).
- *Padding*. The encrypted portion of the header (the payload) must end on the appropriate boundary, so padding may be necessary.
- *Padding Length*. This field indicates how much padding has been added to the payload data.
- *Next Header*. This field operates as it normally does with other IPv6 extension headers; it just appears near the end of the header rather than at the beginning.
- *Authentication Data*. This is an ICV, calculated on the entire ESP header (except for the authentication data). This authentication calculation is optional.

Doing the Encapsulation

It is expected that, at a minimum, support for DES encryption as well as SHA-1 authentication will be required to be a compliant ESP implementation. Other algorithms may be supported, but these are expected to be part of the minimum requirements.

10

Related Next-Generation Protocols

Protocols within the TCP/IP suite that interoperate directly and indirectly with the Internet Protocol include various application protocols and link layer protocols as well as the Transmission Control Protocol (TCP) and the User Datagram Protocol (UDP). This chapter examines how these protocols must be modified, or whether they must be modified at all, to accommodate IPv6.

Protocol Layers

As you'll recall from Chapter 2, TCP/IP networking relies on the concept of layering. At each layer, two entities can communicate with each other, using the next lower layer to encapsulate their data. Application protocols define the way that applications communicate with each other, usually from one node to another. Data from the applications is encapsulated by transport layer protocols, which in turn is encapsulated within internet layer protocols, which is encapsulated within link layer protocols.

To understand how IPv6 impacts protocols at other layers, it is important to understand how those protocols use IP. Because so many systems rely on a wide range of TCP/IP networking and application protocols, it was important that an upgrade to IP not necessarily require extensive upgrades to the protocols above or below. As a result, most existing TCP/IP applications, software, and hardware (with the exception, of course, of IPv4) will work with IPv6 with minimal modifications.

Application Layer

The most commonly used applications today are the World Wide Web and e-mail. Web and e-mail clients must be pointed to servers on the Internet in order to function. These clients traditionally have been able to accept either a node's host name or its IP address. When a domain name is used, the Domain Name System (DNS) is invoked to get an IP address for the host name, which is then used at transport and internet layers.

Fixing simple applications to work with IPv6 is very simple: Either rewrite the software to accept both IPv4 and IPv6 addresses and deal with them appropriately, or require that hosts be referred to only by their host name. The former solution retains the ability to address a node directly from an application but tends to be more complicated than the latter solution, which can be implemented simply by taking out a function that most users do not use or even need.

However, applications that expect to use IPv6 services for security, quality of service, or other special features provided by IPv6 will require more extensive updates.

Transport Layer

While IP addresses are (mostly) irrelevant to application layer protocols, they are quite relevant to the transport layer. Consider UDP and TCP, both of which use both the source and destination IP addresses in their pseudoheaders; TCP circuits are defined by the port numbers and IP addresses of the source and destination nodes. At the very least, both UDP and TCP must be modified to accommodate 128-bit IPv6 addresses if they are to interoperate with IPv6. This means that they need to be able to recognize IPv6 addresses and calculate appropriate pseudoheaders; for TCP, this means that implementations must be able to manage circuits based on IPv6 addresses as well.

After the first IPv6 RFCs were published, there was some concern that a "TCPng" would be necessary to supplement IPng. One problem cited was that of dealing with mobile nodes: TCP circuits are partially specified by the IP addresses of the source and destination nodes. If you change one or both of those addresses in the middle of a TCP interaction, the identity of that circuit will be in question. The appropriate use would be a mobile node that actually shifted from one network address to another, for example, a node using wireless network access from a train or car or a node attached to a network that changes Internet service providers in the evening to take advantage of better rates.

The problem arises because TCP, at least as it stands now, does not have a mechanism that allows such changes in IP address in the middle of a connection. If a node receives a TCP segment with a different source IP address than the one originally negotiated during the setup of the TCP circuit, then it is assumed to be part of a different circuit. This means that mobile IP won't currently support the shift of live TCP circuits from one network address to another.

The question of TCPng is more complex than simply allowing a TCP connection to support shifts in network addresses. The problem is that supporting such shifts opens an enormous security hole: I can just as easily be an authorized node shifting from one network to another as I can be an attacker pretending to be that node shifting from one network to another. To fix this would require a significant upgrade to TCP, which incorporated mechanisms for nodes to authenticate themselves to each other even if their IP addresses changed.

As it stands currently, a mobile host switching networks in the middle of a TCP connection would have to renegotiate that connection after the switch. At some point, a TCPng may become necessary to support seamless interoperability for mobile hosts.

Link Layer

Even more so than upper layers, link layer protocols like Ethernet and ATM are affected minimally by the upgrade to IPv6. This is because they simply encapsulate the upper-layer datagrams into link layer frames. This is not to say that IPv6 will have no impact on link layer protocols. For example, ATM, which uses what appear to be point-to-point circuits for transmitting data across networks, requires special attention to provide IPv6 services that call for delivery of IPv6 packets to more than one node. More information about ATM over IP is available in RFC 1680, *IPng Support for ATM Services*, and RFC 1932, *IP over ATM: A Framework Document*. See also the IP over ATM working group's Internet drafts, some of which specifically address IPv6 over ATM.

Other link layer issues that may be affected are path MTU discovery (see Chapter 5) as well as the Address Resolution Protocol (ARP), which requires modification to support 128-bit IPv6 addresses.

Domain Name System Extensions for IPv6

The Domain Name System (DNS) is an important factor in the ease of use of Internet applications: It facilitates the mapping of names onto IP addresses. DNS uses a hierarchical namespace, in which there are servers at each level of the hierarchy to help map names to addresses. Host names may be of the form *host.organization.com*; the host (*host*) exists within the domain (*organization.com*). A node within *organization.com*, looking for *host*, would query its local DNS server. That server, which maintains name and address information for hosts on *organization.com*, would simply look up *host* and reply to the request with the 32-bit IP address associated with *host*.

If a node outside of *organization.com* needed an IP address for *host.organization.com*, it would query its local DNS server, which would have to query a higher-level server that maintains information about *.com* network domains—that server would reply to the local DNS server's request by pointing it to the *organization.com* DNS server, which would finally reply by sending the requested IP address to the local DNS server, which would pass the information along to the node that made the original request.

So far, so good. However, DNS is designed to handle 32-bit, IPv4 addresses. RFC 1886, *DNS Extensions to support IP version 6*, describes the modifications necessary to make DNS support IPv6. This short RFC very briefly states that three changes are to be made to enable DNS for IPv6:

- Creation of a new resource record type, called the AAAA record type, to map names to 128-bit IPv6 addresses (IPv4 resource records use the A record type).
- Creation of a new domain (.IP6.int) to which IPv6 host addresses can be appended in order to support lookups based on the address (in which the requesting node wants to know the domain name for the requested IPv6 address). A similar facility is available for IPv4 addresses (.in-addr.arpa).
- Existing DNS queries must be revised to locate or process not just IPv4 addresses but IPv4 and IPv6 addresses (if they exist).

Address Resolution Protocol and Neighbor Discovery

IPv6 doesn't do Address Resolution Protocol (ARP) or Reverse ARP (RARP) any more. These protocols are used in IPv4 to figure out what IP address is associated with what local link network address, in other words, to link an Ethernet MAC address (as an example) with the IP address of its node. Such a protocol is necessary for a node to figure out where to send IP packets to nodes on the same local subnet, using the link layer.

ARP is a simple, straightforward, protocol. It works for Ethernet and for any network medium that uses 48-bit MAC addresses and can be used for any length MAC addresses. Why not just continue to use it for IPv6? For one thing, it relies on IPv6 and ICMPv6 messages using multicast. This means that there is no need to rebuild ARP for every different type of network that uses ARP—any node that supports IPv6 and multicast should also support neighbor discovery. Multicast support, particularly on the link layer, is also important. Multicast, like broadcast, is easy for networks like Ethernet that support multiple simultaneous access to the same media. However, so-called *non-broadcast multi-access* (NBMA) networks—like ATM and frame relay—are harder to deal with. These networks rely on circuits rather than packets and require a separate circuit for every node that is intended to receive a transmission. This makes multicast more complicated—but as long as there is a mechanism in place to provide a multicast function, nodes on these networks will also be able to support neighbor discovery without having to explicitly create an ARP-like service.

Described in RFC 1970, *Neighbor Discovery for IP Version 6 (IPv6)*, *neighbor discovery* serves several different purposes, including support for:

- *Router discovery.* It helps hosts to identify local routers.
- *Prefix discovery.* It is used by nodes to figure out which address prefixes indicate local link addresses and which must be sent to a router for forwarding.
- *Parameter discovery.* It helps nodes figure out information like the local link MTU.
- *Address autoconfiguration.* It is used for IPv6 node autoconfiguration (see Chapter 11).
- *Address resolution.* It replaces ARP and RARP in helping nodes figure out the link layer address of local nodes (in other words, neighbors) from the destination IP address.
- *Next-hop determination.* It can be used to figure out what the next destination for a packet should be—in other words, to determine whether the destination of the packet is on the local link, and thus the next hop should be the destination; or whether the packet needs to be routed, in which case the next hop is a router and neighbor discovery can be used to figure out which router should be used.
- *Neighbor unreachability detection.* Neighbor discovery can help nodes to figure out whether a neighbor, either a destination node or a router, is still reachable.

◆ *Duplicate address detection.* Neighbor discovery is used to help a node figure out whether or not the address it wants to use is already in use on the local link.

◆ *Redirect.* Sometimes a node sends packets to a router for forwarding, even though the router is not the best one for those packets. In those cases, the router can redirect the node to send those packets to a better router. For example, when a node sends packets destined for the Internet to a default router serving the node's intranet, the intranet router may redirect the node to send those packets to an Internet router connected to the same local link.

Neighbor discovery works by defining special ICMP message types. These include:

◆ *Router advertisement.* Routers are required to periodically advertise their availability, as well as various link and Internet parameters for configuration purposes (see Chapter 11). These advertisements contain indication of thenetworkaddressprefixesinuse,suggestedhoplimitvalue, and local MTU; they also contain flags that indicate what kind of autoconfiguration a node should use.

◆ *Router solicitation.* A host may request that local routers send out their router advertisements immediately. Routers must send out these advertisements periodically, but when they receive a router solicitation message, they send out an advertisement without waiting for the next scheduled transmission.

◆ *Neighbor advertisement.* Nodes send out neighbor advertisement messages when they have been requested (through a neighbor solicitation message) or when their link-layer address has just changed.

◆ *Neighbor solicitation.* A node sends out neighbor solicitations to request the link-layer address of a neighbor, to verify that a neighbor is still reachable at a link-layer address previously acquired (and stored in a cache), or to verify that its own address is unique on the local link (see Chapter 11).

◆ *Redirect.* Routers send redirect messages to notify hosts that they are not the best router to use for a particular destination.

Routers send out their router advertisement messages via multicast so that nodes on the same link can build up their own lists of available default routers.

Neighbor discovery can also be used to accomplish other goals, including:

- *Link-layer address changes.* A node that is aware that its link-layer address has changed (for example, if it has more than one interface to the same network) can notify its neighbors of the change by sending a few multicast packets.
- *Inbound load balancing.* Nodes that accept lots of traffic may have more than one network interface; with neighbor discovery all these interfaces can be represented by a single IP address. Load balancing for a router can be accomplished by having that router omit its source link-layer address when it sends out its router advertisement packets. This way, nodes looking for that router must do neighbor discovery every time they want to send packets to that router—and the router can respond with whichever link-layer interface it chooses to accept packets on for that node.
- *Anycast addresses.* As discussed in Chapter 6, an anycast address specifies a set of unicast addresses. Packets sent to the anycast address are to be delivered to any one of those addresses; anycast addresses typically identify sets of nodes that provide the same service (in other words, a node sending a packet to an anycast address doesn't care which one of those nodes responds). Because multiple members of anycast addresses may respond to requests for their link-layer addresses, neighbor discovery requires that nodes expect to hear more than one response to such requests and handle them appropriately.
- *Proxy advertisements.* Neighbor discovery makes it possible for a node to act on behalf of another node that can't respond appropriately to neighbor discovery requests. For example, a proxy server might act on behalf of mobile IP nodes (see Chapter 11).

11

Autoconfiguration and Mobile IP

Consider for a moment the most ubiquitous global network: the telephone system. Imagine how much more difficult it would be to use if every time you bought a new telephone you had to have it configured to work with your assigned telephone number in your house. Imagine how much more difficult it would be if every time you moved an extension phone from one room to another you had to reconfigure it. In many ways, IPv4 networking used to require that level of manual configuration: Installing a new computer or other connected device called for a human to manually configure address and other network information. The situation has improved over the past decade, but IP configuration can still be a problem.

One of the important stated goals for IPng was to support "plug-and-play"—to make it possible to plug a node into an IPv6 network and have it boot to the network without any human interference. This goal fits in with computing industry trends: In 1983, the buyer of a personal computer had to install the operating system as well as any and all desired application software. In 1998, most new systems come preinstalled with operating system as well as application software. The change in network readiness of new systems is also apparent. In 1983, if you wanted any kind of connectivity, you had to buy and install a network card or modem—and then configure it to work for your particular application. By 1998, most new systems include a built-in modem and/or network card, fully configured and ready to go.

This improvement in user friendliness is a requirement if networked computing is to become as easy to use as the telephone. Engineers and scientists may be comfortable setting hardware switches on Ethernet cards, but mechanics, physicians, travel agents, and most other nontechnical professionals can't afford to waste hours or days getting their systems to work or to connect to the Internet.

IPv6 Plug-and-Play

IPv6 uses two different mechanisms to support plug-and-play network connection. The first is exemplifed in the Boot Protocol (BOOTP), and later the Dynamic Host Configuration Protocol (DHCP) was designed to allow IP nodes to get configuration information from special BOOTP or DHCP servers. However, these protocols support what is known as *stateful autoconfiguration*—meaning that somewhere, a server must maintain status information about each node and administer that stored data. DHCP is an important tool for IPv4 network configuration, both for ISPs serving many individuals and for large organizations whose employees often change offices.

Stateful vs. Stateless Autoconfiguration

The problem with DHCP, as a stateful autoconfiguration protocol, is that it requires that a DHCP server be installed and administered—and it requires that each new node to be served must be configured on the server. Very simply, the DHCP server keeps a list of nodes that it will supply configuration information to, and if you're not on the list, you don't get an IP address. State is also maintained as nodes use the DHCP server, because the server must keep track of how long each IP address is in use and when the IP address may be available again for reassignment.

The problem with stateful autoconfiguration is that you do have to maintain and administer a special autoconfiguration server in order to manage all that "state" (information about allowed and current connections). This is fine for organizations that have the resources to set up and maintain configuration servers but works less well for smaller organizations without those resources. The better (e.g., easier) solution, at least for most individuals and small organizations, is *stateless autoconfiguration*, that is, some mechanism that allows individual nodes to somehow figure out what their IP configuration should be without having to explicitly query some server that has prior information about each node.

In fact, this is a relatively straightforward procedure, at least in theory and assuming certain things are true. For one thing, if you use IEEE EUI-64 link layer addresses (see Chapter 6), you can be reasonably certain that your host ID will be unique. Thus, all a node needs to do is figure out what its own link-layer address is and calculate an EUI-64 address—and then somehow figure out what is the address of its IPv6 network. One way to figure that out would be to ask the nearest router for that information, and this is how stateless autoconfiguration is done in IPv6 (as we'll see next).

Finally, stateful autoconfiguration and stateless autoconfiguration as defined under IPv6 can coexist and operate together. An update to DHCP, called DCHPv6, is in the works, as we'll see later. Cooperation between the two types of autoconfiguration makes plug-and-play internetwork connections easier than either type on its own. For example, using stateless autoconfiguration, a node can quickly determine its own IP address; once it has this information, it can interact with a DHCP server to get any other network configuration values that it may require. In fact, DHCPv6 is very likely to rely on IPv6 stateless autoconfiguration to simplify stateful autoconfiguration in some cases.

If stateless autoconfiguration is so much easier to use, why bother with stateful autoconfiguration? The answer depends on the requirements of the organization building the network. Stateless autoconfiguration provides minimal oversight of who gets an IP address. Any node can connect to a link, get the network and subnet information that routers advertise to enable stateless autoconfiguration, and build a valid link address. With DHCP servers, however, the organization can maintain tighter control over which nodes can be configured for the network. The only nodes that can be configured through the DHCP server are those that have been explicitly authorized by the network administrator.

IPv6 Stateless Autoconfiguration

Stateless autoconfiguration for IPv6 is described in RFC 1971, *IPv6 Stateless Address Autoconfiguration*. This RFC is being updated, though most changes are either for clarification or to refine the specification, for example, methods of dealing with potential denial of service attacks against routers. The stateless autoconfiguration process calls for nodes to take the following steps. First, the node doing autoconfiguration must figure out its own link-local address (e.g., IEEE EUI-64 address). Then, that link-local address must be verified as being unique on the link. Finally, the node must determine what information is necessary for it to be configured. This may be the node's IP address, other configuration information, or both. If an address is necessary, the node will have to determine whether it must use the stateless or stateful autoconfiguration process to get that address.

Stateless autoconfiguration requires that the local link support multicast and that the network interface be able to send and receive multicasts. The node doing autoconfiguration starts out by appending its link-local address (e.g., IEEE EUI-64 address) to the link-local network prefix (as discussed in Chapter 6; see Figure 6.1). This gives the node a place to start: It can communicate with other nodes on the same network link using IPv6, and it has an IPv6 address that will probably work as long as there are no other nodes on the same link using the same EUI-64 address.

However, before it can take on that address, the node must verify that the starting address is in fact unique to the local link. In other words, the node must determine that no other node on the same network link is using the same EUI-64 address. In most cases this will not be a problem; for nodes using network interface cards (e.g., Ethernet or token-ring adapters), most will have unique 48-bit MAC addresses, and for nodes connecting over point-to-point links, there will only be one end-point node on that link. However, other network media may not have unique MAC addresses, and some network interface cards may improperly use MAC addresses they are not entitled to. The node must send a *neighbor solicitation* message to the link-local address that it wants to use. If it gets any responses, the node trying to autoconfigure knows that address is already in use and must then be configured in some other way.

If the node is on a network that is not served by a router—in other words, if the local network is isolated from any other network—then the node has to look for a configuration server to complete its configuration. Otherwise, the node must listen for a *router advertisement*. These are messages periodically sent to the all-hosts multicast address (see Chapter 6) that indicate configuration information like the network and subnet address. The node can either wait for the router to advertise, or it may solicit the router to send its advertisement by sending a multicast request to the all-routers multicast address. Once a router has responded, the node can use the information to finish autoconfiguration.

BOOTP and DHCP

BOOTP (first described in 1985 in RFC 951, *Bootstrap Protocol*) was initially designed to allow workstations to query a local server for their IP address, the address of a server host, and the name of a bootstrap executable file. While sufficient for some applications, as with diskless workstations that loaded all their software from network servers, BOOTP was inadequate for many other applications, such as connecting personal computers to an IPv4 network. The problem was that TCP/IP network software for PCs needed more information (such as host name, domain name, subnet mask, and DNS server addresses) than could be provided easily with BOOTP.

By 1993, RFC 1531, *Dynamic Host Configuration Protocol*, was published describing DHCP. Building on BOOTP's message structures, DHCP added mechanisms for transmitting all the IP configuration information necessary to get a host connected to an IPv4 network. Much of DHCP's function relates to the relative scarcity of IPv4 network addresses. For example, an organization assigned a Class C network address has a maximum of 254 addresses to allocate to its users. This is plenty for some applications; for example, a flower shop is unlikely to have more than a handful of networked computers. However, any business with a few hundred employees is likely to have a problem allocating addresses, particularly if there are more than 250 or so computers connected to the network.

DHCP added the ability to assign addresses to nodes for a limited period. This means that a Class C network can be sufficient to support up to 254 simultaneously connected nodes of a much larger network. ISPs like it, too, because it means they are not limited to serving as many subscribers as the number of IP addresses they control; if only a fraction of their customers are connected at any given time, the rest of their subscribers don't tie up extra, unused, IP addresses.

DHCPv6

Of course, like any protocol that deals directly with IP addresses, DHCP must be upgraded to support IPv6 addresses. DHCPv6 is in the works and goes beyond mere cosmetic updating to support longer addresses. Clearly, with the addition of stateless autoconfiguration to IPv6, it is beneficial for DHCPv6 to take advantage of this new capability.

With stateless autoconfiguration, nodes virtually automatically have at least local connectivity; DHCP is also no longer necessary to provide some of the other most basic configuration parameters. The default router is not part of the configuration, as any node can figure out its default routers by itself by listening for router advertisements (see Chapter 10).

The new DHCP will be able to support various new features. For example:

♦ The ability to configure dynamic updates to DNS, reflecting the current state of the network.

♦ Address deprecation, which is the state in which an address assignment is about to become invalid, can be used to do dynamic renumbering of networks (see next section).

Mobile Networking

Until relatively recently, almost all networked devices stayed put. Computers, even personal computers, were big, and they weren't moved too often. The past few years have seen the proliferation not only of notebook computers but more recently of handheld computers, personal digital assistants (PDAs), even cellular telephones and pagers that can support IP. The problem is that when devices move around, whether they normally connect to the network through wire or wireless transmission, it would be good if other devices could reach them at the same IP address no matter where the mobile node actually is.

This can be difficult, as the mobile node may have to connect to a different network using a different IP address when it moves. Mobile IP is described in RFC 2002, *IP Mobility Support*. A revision of this RFC, updating it for IPv6, is in the works. In any case, mobile IP is designed to support movement of nodes from one network to another, or macro-mobility, rather than the type of movement that would be described as micro-mobility, such as handing off of wireless connections from one cell to another (as is done with cellular telephones).

Mobile IP Under IPv4

As described in RFC 2002, mobile IP uses the concept of a mobility agents. A mobile host is assigned a home address, where it can always be reached. When the host is at its "normal" home, it connects to the local network using its home address, and everything works normally. A mobility agent, which is usually a regular router, can act as a foreign agent, to be used as a sort of poste restante when a mobile host is away from its home network; a mobility agent may also act as a home agent that handles transmissions intended for the mobile host.

When the mobile node is away from home, this is how it uses the mobile IP (as described for IPv4) to connect:

- ♦ Foreign and home agents periodically send out messages indicating that they are available; this information can be solicited by a mobile host. These advertisements are based on ICMP router advertisements and provide enough information for the mobile node to be able to figure out whether it is on its own home network or on some foreign network.
- ♦ If the mobile node determines that it is currently connected to its home network, it just works the way any nonmobile node would.
- ♦ However, if the node determines that it is on a foreign network, then it gets a care-of address on the foreign network. This is a sort of temporary address at which the mobile node can be reached while it is on the foreign network. The mobile node may use some external mechanism, like DHCP, to get assigned a valid address on the foreign network. Alternatively, it may use some address specified by the foreign agent, in which case it is called a foreign agent care-of address. In this case, the foreign agent uses the same inbound address for any mobile nodes that it is serving and forwards packets to the appropriate node as they come in.
- ♦ Once the mobile node has some kind of address at which it can be addressed on the foreign network, it then registers that address with its home agent by sending it a message saying, in effect: "If you get any packets intended for my home address, please forward them to *this* address for now."

♦ Now, once the home agent knows where to send the mobile node's packets, it intercepts them and encapsulates them in an IP tunnel directed to the care-of address provided by the mobile node. If the care-of address is a co-located care-of address, the foreign agent receives the encapsulating IP packets, unwraps the packets intended for the mobile node, and forwards them. If the care-of address is a separate IP address specifically assigned to the mobile node on the foreign network, then the mobile node receives the encapsulated packets and unwraps them itself.

When mobile nodes send packets while they are on the foreign network, nothing special needs to be done; they continue to use their home address as the source address of their packets, and there is no need for special handling for those packets.

Mobile IP Under IPv6

Mobile IPv6 will probably be considerably more convenient to implement and to use. For one thing, the process of getting a care-of address under IPv6 is much simpler with stateless autoconfiguration (or with stateful autoconfiguration using DHCPv6). Because of this, there are no foreign agent care-of addresses in IPv6, only co-located care-of addresses. For another, it should be possible to use various IPv6 features to improve the operation of mobile nodes. For example, the home agent can use neighbor discovery's proxy advertisements to intercept IPv6 packets intended for the mobile node. Nodes should also have some basic level of support for route optimization through destination options that can be used to bind address updates to the addresses.

Another new feature that may be included in mobile IPv6 is the ability for a mobile node to establish contact with its home network even if its regular home agent becomes unavailable. The mobile node can send an anycast packet to an address reserved for home agents on the home network, with the result that whatever home agent is available can notify the mobile node of its options.

12

IPv6 Transition Strategies

For IPv6 to work, it would seem, all hosts on a network must upgrade—a daunting challenge to network managers handling global corporate networks with thousands, or even tens of thousands, of hosts. However, this is very much not the case; people working on the IPv6 transition have worked very hard on designing IPv6 and its supporting protocols and mechanisms to allow a graceful and gradual upgrade. Updating existing networks to IPv6 will be possible with relatively low impact as long as the upgrade is done methodically and intelligently. This chapter discusses some of the strategies being proposed for a smooth transition.

Discussion of the IPv6 transition can be found in RFC 1933, *Transition Mechanisms for IPv6 Hosts and Routers*; RFC 2185, *Routing Aspects of IPv6 Transition*; RFC 2071, *Network Renumbering Overview: Why would I want it and what is it anyway?*; and RFC 2072, *Router Renumbering Guide*. There are also Internet drafts in progress on the IPv6 transition and the business case for upgrading to IPv6.

The IPv6 transition will by necessity be gradual. A massive, cutover-style upgrade would be unacceptable, considering the huge numbers of networks and nodes already connected to the Internet. It would require network administrators to find and install new versions of networking software for every host and router on the Internet—not easy, considering the number of different platforms running IPv4.

More likely, the IPv6 transition will continue to take place relatively slowly, as vendors and developers gradually introduce versions of IPv6 for different platforms and as network managers determine that they need the functions that IPv6 provides. It is expected that IPv4 and IPv6 will have to coexist for a long time, perhaps forever. Most strategies for the transition rely on the two-pronged approach of protocol tunneling, where IPv6 packets are encapsulated within IPv4 packets for transmission from IPv6 islands through IPv4 oceans. At least at first—after the early stages of the transition period—more and more of the IP population will be IPv6-capable. Even in the later stages of the transition, IPv6 encapsulation will continue to be useful for connectivity across IPv4-only backbones and other holdout networks. The other prong of the strategy is the dual-stack approach, in which hosts and routers run IPv4 and IPv6 stacks on the same network interfaces. This way, a dual-stack node can accept and transmit both IPv4 and IPv6 packets, so the two protocols can coexist on the same networks.

The IPv6 Protocol Tunneling Approach

This approach is useful for connecting isolated IPv6 islands that lie in the middle of IPv4 oceans, as Figure 12.1 shows. Tunneling requires that an IPv6 node at one end of the tunnel be capable of transmitting IPv4 packets (dual-stack node, see next section) and that there be another dual-stack node at the other end of the tunnel. Encapsulating IPv6 within IPv4 is a similar process to any other protocol encapsulation: A node at one end of the tunnel takes the IPv6 datagrams and treats them as payload data intended to be sent to the node at the other end of the tunnel. The result is a stream of

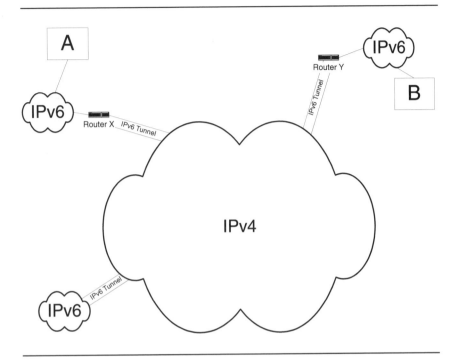

Figure 12.1. Isolated islands of IPv6 networks can be linked across the IPv4 ocean through tunneled connections between dual-stack IPv4/IPv6 routers.

IPv4 datagrams that contain IPv6 datagrams. As shown in Figure 12.1, node A and node B are both IPv6-only nodes. To get an IPv6 packet from A to B, node A simply addresses the packet to node B's IPv6 address and passes it to router X. This router encapsulates the IPv6 packet intended for node B and sends it to the IPv4 address of router Y. Router Y receives the IPv4 packet or packets and unwraps them. On finding the encapsulated IPv6 packet intended for node B, router Y forwards the packet appropriately.

IPv4-Compatible IPv6 Addresses

Back in Chapter 6, IPv6 addresses that contain IPv4 addresses were introduced. There are two types: the IPv4-compatible address and the IPv4-mapped addresses. IPv4-compatible addresses are simply

128-bit addresses, of which the highest-order 96 bits are set to zero and the last 32 bits contain an IPv4 address (refer back to Figure 6.4). These addresses are intended to be used by IPv4/IPv6 nodes capable of automatically tunneling IPv6 packets through IPv4 networks.

The dual-stack node then uses the "same" address for both IPv4 and IPv6 packets. IPv4-only nodes can send packets to the dual-stack node using its IPv4 address, while IPv6-only nodes can send packets to the IPv6 address (the IPv4 address padded out with zeros to make it 128 bits long). In general, this type of node would be a router linking IPv6 networks with automatic tunnels through IPv4 networks. The router would accept IPv6 packets from its local IPv6 networks and encapsulate them in IPv4 packets intended for another dual-stack router also using an IPv4-compatible address on the other side of the IPv4 network. The encapsulated packets are then forwarded through the IPv4 network cloud until they arrive at the dual-stack router at other end of the tunnel, where the IPv4 packets are unwrapped to reveal IPv6 packets that the router then forwards on its local IPv6 networks.

Configured Tunneling and Automatic Tunneling

The difference between configured tunneling and automatic tunneling lies largely in the fact that automatic tunneling is possible where the IPv6 addresses of the tunneling nodes are IPv4-compatible addresses. Automatic tunnels require no configuration to set up the IPv4 address of the tunneling nodes; configured tunneling requires that the tunnel end-point nodes acquire their IPv4 address through some other mechanism (for example, through DHCP, manual configuration, or any other IPv4 configuration mechanism).

IPv6 Tunnel Types

There are several different combination of node types that can be tunnel endpoints. Refer to Figure 12.2 to see how these different tunnels operate.

Figure 12.2 shows a generic internetwork with three network clouds, two routers, and two hosts. The following bullets describe

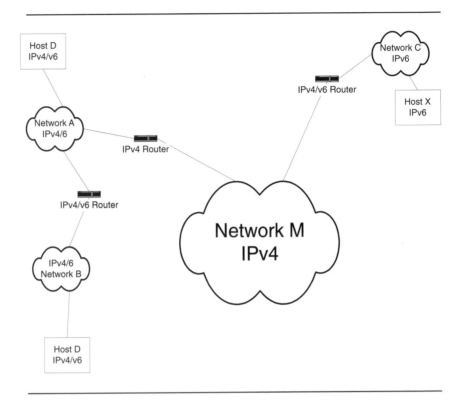

Figure 12.2. Different types of IPv6 tunnels.

the different types of tunnels using the internetwork pictured in Figure 12.2. However, to differentiate the different types of tunneling, the entities in the figure may be IPv4-only, IPv6-only, or IPv4/IPv6 dual-stack, depending on what type of tunneling is being demonstrated. The different types of tunnels are:

♦ *Router-to-router tunneling.* In Figure 12.2, router X and router Y tunnel IPv6 packets through network O, which is an IPv4-only network. Host A can send IPv6 packets to host B transparently; neither host needs to be concerned with the existence of an intervening IPv4 network (network O). In this case both host A and host B are IPv6-only nodes.

♦ *Router-to-host tunneling.* Look again at Figure 12.2. In this case, network N is an IPv4-only network, but host B runs IPv4 and IPv6; the rest of the network is IPv6-only. In this case, the tunneling takes place between router Y and host B. IPv6 packets flow freely along the rest of the network, but router Y must encapsulate them in IPv4 in order to deliver them across network N, which supports IPv4 only.

♦ *Host-to-host tunneling.* Consider Figure 12.2 again. This time, imagine that only host A and host B support IPv4 and IPv6; the rest of the entities in the diagram support only IPv4. In this case, the tunneling occurs from host A to host B; host A must encapsulate its IPv6 packet intended for host B in IPv4 packets for them to be carried through the IPv4-only routers.

♦ *Host-to-router tunneling.* Look at Figure 12.2 once more. Imagine now that host A and router X are dual-stack nodes, that network M is an IPv4-only network, and that the rest of the networks support IPv6 only. In this case, host A must tunnel its IPv6 packets only to router X; once past IPv4-only network M, router X can unwrap the tunneled packets and forward them normally across the IPv6 networks.

The IPv4/IPv6 Dual-Stack Approach

The tenacity of legacy systems, as demonstrated currently by the looming specter of year 2000 problems, should be underestimated at our peril. IPv4 will be with us for a long time, even as some or all of the rest of the networked world upgrades to IPv6. During that time, the upgraded systems will need to maintain interoperability with IPv4 systems; as time goes on, the burden of interoperability will be shifted from the early implementers to the maintainers of legacy systems. In any case, systems capable of supporting both IPv4 and IPv6 will be necessary.

The concept of dual-stack nodes is not new. Many, if not most, corporate hosts that support connectivity to the Internet as well as connectivity to corporate LANs using older versions of Novell's NetWare (in NetWare 5, IP replaces IPX as the native network layer protocol), for example, already support two disparate network

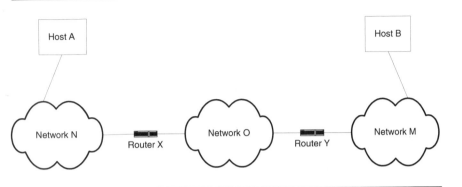

Figure 12.3. Dual-stack nodes, routers, and networks provide different degrees of interoperability depending on whether they can also tunnel IPv6 packets over IPv4 networks.

ldress Allocation

If you want an IPv4 network address, you normally must negotiate an arrangement with your Internet service provider, who is granted blocks of addresses in accordance with CIDR-style address aggregation. Assignment of IPv4 network addresses is ultimately controlled by the Internet Assigned Numbers Authority (IANA). However, if you want an IPv6 address, things are not so simple. As defined in RFC 1881, *IPv6 Address Allocation Management*, the IANA will assign chunks of IPv6 address space to regional or other types of registries. These registries will allocate smaller chunks of this address space to network service providers and other subregistries, which will in turn allocate them to businesses, organizations, and individuals requesting IPv6 addresses.

As of autumn 1998, however, these assignments had not yet been made; indeed, the precise format of IPv6 addresses is still pending. If you want officially assigned, globally unique IPv6 network addresses, you must wait until the IANA starts allocating the space. In the meantime, users have the option of running their own IPv6

stacks. Internet connectivity is provi
while the NetWare connectivity is pr
ments are received at the link layer
indicate whether the datagram is int
the IPX stack—and the packet is tl
stack for processing.

Dual-Stack Nodes

IPv4/IPv6 dual-stack nodes can wor
of multiple-stack nodes. As segment
they are unwrapped and the header
number of the IP packet (the first fie
four, then the packet is processed by
the packet is processed by the IPv6 s

The simplest dual-stack deploymen
IPv6 but without tunneling. This is
hosts, particularly if the Internet appl
has been updated to support both I]
applications can be used to access ser
as are used to access services on an
interoperate with any IPv4 node or IF
in what networks it has connectivity {
ple in which a dual-stack node D can
nodes on networks A and B, and all I
not with any nodes on network C, wh
IPv6 routing path from network A to
networks A and M supports IPv4 only
IPv6 packets to network C (via netwc

Dual-stack nodes that can perform tur
operate over IPv4 networks without
Tunneling IPv6 over IPv4 can change {
ure 12.3. For example, if node D is able
it can use its local IPv4 router to forwa
nodes both support automatic tunr
seamless; otherwise some configuratic

IPv6

stacks. Internet connectivity is provided through the TCP/IP stack, while the NetWare connectivity is provided by an IPX stack. As segments are received at the link layer and unwrapped, the headers indicate whether the datagram is intended for the TCP/IP stack or the IPX stack—and the packet is then passed to the appropriate stack for processing.

Dual-Stack Nodes

IPv4/IPv6 dual-stack nodes can work much the same as other type of multiple-stack nodes. As segments are received at the link layer, they are unwrapped and the headers are examined. If the version number of the IP packet (the first field in the IPv4/IPv6 header) is four, then the packet is processed by the IPv4 stack; if it is six, then the packet is processed by the IPv6 stack.

The simplest dual-stack deployment is to support both IPv4 and IPv6 but without tunneling. This is probably sufficient for most hosts, particularly if the Internet application software on those hosts has been updated to support both IPv4 and IPv6. Thus, the same applications can be used to access services on the local IPv6 network as are used to access services on an IPv4 network. The node can interoperate with any IPv4 node or IPv6 node, but it may be limited in what networks it has connectivity to. Figure 12.3 shows an example in which a dual-stack node D can interoperate with IPv4 or IPv6 nodes on networks A and B, and all IPv4 nodes on network M, but not with any nodes on network C, which is strictly IPv6—there is no IPv6 routing path from network A to network C. The router linking networks A and M supports IPv4 only and thus cannot forward any IPv6 packets to network C (via network M).

Dual-stack nodes that can perform tunneling add the ability to interoperate over IPv4 networks without any additional IPv6 routers. Tunneling IPv6 over IPv4 can change the connectivity picture in Figure 12.3. For example, if node D is able to tunnel IPv6 over IPv4, then it can use its local IPv4 router to forward packets to network C. If the nodes both support automatic tunneling, the interoperability is seamless; otherwise some configuration of the link may be necessary.

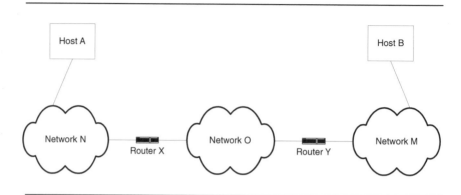

Figure 12.3. Dual-stack nodes, routers, and networks provide different degrees of interoperability depending on whether they can also tunnel IPv6 packets over IPv4 networks.

IPv6 Address Allocation

If you want an IPv4 network address, you normally must negotiate an arrangement with your Internet service provider, who is granted blocks of addresses in accordance with CIDR-style address aggregation. Assignment of IPv4 network addresses is ultimately controlled by the Internet Assigned Numbers Authority (IANA). However, if you want an IPv6 address, things are not so simple. As defined in RFC 1881, *IPv6 Address Allocation Management*, the IANA will assign chunks of IPv6 address space to regional or other types of registries. These registries will allocate smaller chunks of this address space to network service providers and other subregistries, which will in turn allocate them to businesses, organizations, and individuals requesting IPv6 addresses.

As of autumn 1998, however, these assignments had not yet been made; indeed, the precise format of IPv6 addresses is still pending. If you want officially assigned, globally unique IPv6 network addresses, you must wait until the IANA starts allocating the space. In the meantime, users have the option of running their own IPv6 networks in isolation from other networks, with their own internally assigned network addresses. With IPv6's support of stateless autoconfiguration, the chore of renumbering incorrectly numbered IPv6 networks is likely to be considerably less onerous than that of renumbering improperly numbered IPv4 networks—however, it will still require some effort to reconfigure routers, and some disruption will inevitably occur.

A single alternative is currently available. The 6BONE is a global IPv6 network for testing and preproduction deployment of IPv6 products, discussed in the next section.

The 6BONE

Starting in 1996, shortly after the first IPv6 standards had been accepted and published as RFCs, the 6BONE network was started. Any large internetwork needs to have a backbone structure to link disparate and widely distributed network, and the 6BONE serves as a virtual structure that is layered on top of the existing IPv4 infrastructure using tunnels to link participating networks.

By September 1998, the 6BONE had participants in 35 countries, with at least 200 sites connected. The 6BONE is intended for testing purposes or to gain exposure and experience with IPv6 prior to more general commercial rollout of IPv6 products.

To connect a site to the 6BONE, it is necessary to have:

   ♦ A router that supports IPv6 to connect to the 6BONE.
   ♦ One or more workstations that support IPv6 to build your own IPv6 network.
   ♦ Some way to connect to the 6BONE. This translates into finding some other organization connected to the 6BONE and setting up a connection to their site.
   ♦ A DNS server that supports IPv6 AAAA records.

Chapter 13 provides some guidance to vendors that are already implementing IPv6; however, the best way to get connected to the 6BONE is to start at the 6BONE web site at:

```
http://www.6bone.net
```

You can also subscribe to the 6BONE mailing list by sending a message to:

```
majordomo@isi.edu
```

The entire contents of the message should be:

```
subscribe 6bone
```

13

IPv6 Solutions

Networking products supporting IPv6 have slowly but surely been making their way to market. This chapter highlights some of the products currently or soon to be available that incorporate IPv6 support and explains how they are used and how they may be useful to network professionals.

What Products Need to Support IPv6

Any device that connects to an IPv6 network must support IPv6. This means that any IPv4 system to be used as an IPv6 system must be upgraded. Very simply, these devices fall into two broad categories: network hosts and network routers. A network host may be a personal computer used by a single user, or it may be a mainframe system; in all cases, at a minimum the IP stack must be upgraded to IPv6.

However, keeping in mind that IPv4 data can be routed through IPv6 networks with protocol tunneling, the upgrade of regular hosts can be deferred as long as users of those hosts don't require any IPv6-specific features. Routers, however, do have to be upgraded to IPv6. In particular, any router that links an IPv4 network with an IPv6 network must clearly implement IPv6.

Who Is Developing IPv6 Products?

Since the first IPv6 RFCs were published, the author has made a practice of informally asking network vendors about their IPv6 product plans. In most cases, the answer is, "We're working on it, but we have nothing ready for market yet." This response is perfectly adequate, considering that outside of test networks and research labs, there are very few places where you can use IPv6.

As for regular host IPv6 products, there are several to choose from, particularly for personal computers. FTP Software's Secure Client 3.0, a full TCP/IP stack that supports IPv6, was first made available in 1997; most vendors are still offering only beta or research versions of IPv6. For example, Microsoft has an experimental IPv6 stack available for the NT platform only. Sun; Berkeley Software Design, Inc. (BSDI); DEC; and others are all working on IPv6-enabled products. IBM offers a prototype version of IPv6 for its AIX 4.2 operating system. A version of IPv6 for the Linux operating system is also available, based on an implementation done by the U.S. Naval Research Lab (NRL).

Router vendors are doing a bit better. For example, Bay Networks' BayRS (Bay Routing Services) v. 12.0 routing product already supports IPv6; Hitachi Ltd. began selling an IPv6 router as early as June 1997 while Digital Equipment Corp. announced an IPv6 AlphaServer product in March 1997. On the other hand, not everyone is offering IPv6-enabled products yet. 3Com products are touted as being ready for upgrade to IPv6; Cisco is also putting considerable research effort into IPv6 projects but seems not to have incorporated IPv6 support into its current product line.

See Table 13.1 for pointers to these and other vendors' web sites relating to IPv6 products—and keep checking with your favorite vendors for updated information.

Another excellent URL for up-to-date information about products that support IPv6 is provided by Sun and can be found at:

```
http://playground.sun.com/pub/ipng/html/ipng
-implementations.html
```

Organization	Web Page	Description
3Com Corp.	http://www.3com.com/nsc/ipv6.html	3Com has been active in IPv6 research and development.
Bay Networks	http://www.baynetworks.com	Bay offers considerable IPv6 information, both in general and as it relates to the Bay product line. Bay is set to be acquired by Northern Telecom, as of mid-1998.
Berkeley Software Design, Inc.	http://www.bsdi.com	There are plans to support IPv6 in the 1998 upgrade to the BSDI Internet Server.
Cisco Systems	http://www.cisco.com/warp/public/732/ipv6/index.html	Cisco is another router vendor active in IPv6 research and development.
Digital Equipment Corp.	http://www.digital.com/info/ipv6/	This is 64-bit alpha-based server software.
FTP Software	http://www.ftp.com	NetManage, another TCP/IP product vendor, announced plans to purchase FTP Software in June 1998.
Hitachi Ltd.	http://www.hitachi.co.jp/Prod/comp/network/nr60e.htm	This page provides information about Hitachi's IPv6 router.
IBM	http://www.ibm.com	AIX 4.3 now supports IPv6.
Linux FAQ	http://www.bieringer.de/linux/IPv6/default.html	This URL points to a frequently updated Linux/IPv6 FAQ.
Mentat, Inc.	http://www.mentat.com/ipv6.html	Mentat TCP, licensed to Apple, Hewlett-Packard, Motorola, Stratus, and other hardware vendors, supports IPv6.
Novell	http://www.novell.com	NetWare 5.0 is designed to allow minimal-impact upgrade to IPv6.
Process Software Corp.	http://www.process.com/ipv6/	Process is developing IPv6 solutions for VMS operating system.
Sun Microsystems, Inc.	http://playground.sun.com/pub/solaris2-ipv6/html/solaris2-ipv6.html	Sun is one of the leading IPv6 vendors and provides a Solaris IPv6 prototype at this web page; Sun also hosts other IPv6 information pages (see text).

Table 13.1. Web references for IPv6 vendor information.

What Can We Expect?

In 1996, it seemed as though IPv6 was around the corner. Projections for depletion of the IPv4 address space were bleak, and there seemed to be a lot of enthusiasm from vendors—who probably imagined it would be an opportunity to cross-sell and upgrade all their existing customers as well as sell new products. By the middle of 1998, however, things were different. Many of the upbeat vendor predictions about IPv6 product availability are unfulfilled and embarassingly visible on vendors' web sites. Users still don't know and don't care about IPv6.

What about the network managers? Of course, they know about the problems with IPv4—but I suspect that the IP upgrade issues pale in comparison with the year 2000 issues facing most IT professionals. Worrying about upgrading IPv4 to IPv6 sometime during the next couple of years is not a high priority, particularly when there are so many problems to be solved—and on a much tighter schedule with no allowance for extensions—with year 2000 compliancy.

Consider: If you learned that a meteor the size of France would strike the earth on midnight, December 31, 1999, you would not worry too much about fixing a problem with traffic control signals expected to hit sometime in the next five or ten years, especially when the latter problem will inconvenience millions, as opposed to the meteor, which could kill billions.

IPv6 will probably happen, though it's unlikely to draw away any funds that might be needed to stem the year 2000 problem. Though IPv4 addresses are easily acquired in North America, network administrators in the rest of the world are suffering from significant address shortages. North American networking professionals familiar with IPv6 are so far not rushing to embrace it and many are hoping for something better, or at least different, to come along to replace IPv4. Autoconfiguration and user demand for IPv6 improvements are most likely to drive IPv6 deployment, but much still remains to be done before IPv6 is ready for large scale deployment. However, building a better understanding of the IP upgrade issues will help smooth the way to IPv6 in the next decade.

A

Index to IPv6-Related RFCs

Internet RFCs, or Requests for Comments, have been the traditional medium for publishing not only Internet standards but any document related to the Internet and its protocols. This appendix lists, in numerical order (which corresponds to date order as well), a selection of RFCs that directly or indirectly discuss issues related to the migration from IPv4 to IPv6. This list reflects all such RFCs published up to September 1998; the reader is urged to check for more recent RFCs at the an RFC online repository for more current listings. Appendix B includes several of the most important IPv6 and IPng-related RFCs in full.

RFC Number	RFC Title
1029	A MORE FAULT TOLERANT APPROACH TO ADDRESS RESOLUTION FOR A MULTI-LAN SYSTEM OF ETHERNETS
1287	Towards the Future Internet Architecture

RFC Number	RFC Title
1338	Supernetting: An Address Assignment and Aggregation Strategy
1366	Guidelines for Management of IP Address Space
1367	Schedule for IP Address Space Management Guidelines
1375	Suggestion for New Classes of IP Addresses
1454	Comparison of Proposals for Next Version of IP
1466	Guidelines for Management of IP Address Space
1467	Status of CIDR Deployment in the Internet
1519	Classless Inter-Domain Routing (CIDR): An Address Assignment and Aggregation Strategy
1550	IP: Next Generation (IPng) White Paper Solicitation
1560	The MultiProtocol Internet
1563	The text/enriched MIME Content-type
1629	Guidelines for OSI NSAP Allocation in the Internet
1667	Modeling and Simulation Requirements for IPng
1668	Unified Routing Requirements for IPng
1669	Market Viability as a IPng Criteria
1670	Input to IPng Engineering Considerations
1671	IPng White Paper on Transition and Other Considerations
1673	Electric Power Research Institute Comments on IPng
1674	A Cellular Industry View of IPng
1675	Security Concerns for IPng
1680	IPng Support for ATM Services
1683	Multiprotocol Interoperability In IPng
1686	IPng Requirements: A Cable Television Industry Viewpoint
1687	A Large Corporate User's View of IPng
1688	IPng Mobility Considerations
1700	ASSIGNED NUMBERS
1702	Generic Routing Encapsulation over IPv4 networks
1705	Six Virtual Inches to the Left: The Problem with IPng
1707	CATNIP: Common Architecture for the Internet
1715	The H Ratio for Address Assignment Efficiency
1719	A Direction for IPng
1726	Technical Criteria for Choosing IP The Next Generation (IPng)
1744	Observations on the Management of the Internet Address Space
1752	The Recommendation for the IP Next Generation Protocol

RFC Number	RFC Title
1768	Host Group Extensions for CLNP Multicasting
1770	IPv4 Option for Sender Directed Multi-Destination Delivery
1771	A Border Gateway Protocol 4 (BGP-4)
1809	Using the Flow Label Field in IPv6
1810	Report on MD5 Performance
1814	Unique Addresses are Good
1825	Security Architecture for the Internet Protocol
1826	IP Authentication Header
1827	IP Encapsulating Security Payload (ESP)
1860	Variable Length Subnet Table For IPv4
1878	Variable Length Subnet Table For IPv4
1881	IPv6 Address Allocation Management
1883	Internet Protocol, Version 6 (IPv6) Specification
1884	IP Version 6 Addressing Architecture
1885	Internet Control Message Protocol (ICMPv6) for the Internet Protocol Version 6 (IPv6) Specification
1886	DNS Extensions to support IP version 6
1887	An Architecture for IPv6 Unicast Address Allocation
1888	OSI NSAPs and IPv6
1897	IPv6 Testing Address Allocation
1917	An Appeal to the Internet Community to Return Unused IP Networks (Prefixes) to the IANA
1924	A Compact Representation of IPv6 Addresses
1933	Transition Mechanisms for IPv6 Hosts and Routers
1953	Ipsilon Flow Management Protocol Specification for IPv4 Version 1.0
1954	Transmission of Flow Labelled IPv4 on ATM Data Links Ipsilon Version 1.0
1955	New Scheme for Internet Routing and Addressing (ENCAPS) for IPNG
1970	Neighbor Discovery for IP Version 6 (IPv6)
1971	IPv6 Stateless Address Autoconfiguration
1972	A Method for the Transmission of IPv6 Packets over Ethernet Networks
1981	Path MTU Discovery for IP version 6
2002	IP Mobility Support
2019	A Method for the Transmission of IPv6 Packets over FDDI Networks
2022	Support for Multicast over UNI 3.0/3.1 based ATM Networks.
2023	IP Version 6 over PPP

RFC Number	RFC Title
2030	Simple Network Time Protocol (SNTP) Version 4 for IPv4, IPv6 and OSI
2036	Observations on the use of Components of the Class A Address Space within the Internet
2050	INTERNET REGISTRY IP ALLOCATION GUIDELINES
2071	Network Renumbering Overview: Why would I want it and what is it anyway?
2072	Router Renumbering Guide
2073	An IPv6 Provider-Based Unicast Address Format
2080	RIPng for IPv6
2081	RIPng Protocol Applicability Statement
2101	IPv4 Address Behaviour Today
2107	Ascend Tunnel Management Protocol - ATMP
2121	Issues affecting MARS Cluster Size
2126	ISO Transport Service on top of TCP (ITOT)
2133	Basic Socket Interface Extensions for IPv6
2147	TCP and UDP over IPv6 Jumbograms
2175	MAPOS 16—Multiple Access Protocol over SONET/SDH with 16 Bit Addressing
2176	IPv4 over MAPOS Version 1
2185	Routing Aspects Of IPv6 Transition
2202	Test Cases for HMAC-MD5 and HMAC-SHA-1
2205	Resource ReSerVation Protocol (RSVP)—Version 1 Functional Specification
2207	RSVP Extensions for IPSEC Data Flows
2236	Internet Group Management Protocol, Version 2
2240	A Legal Basis for Domain Name Allocation
2283	Multiprotocol Extensions for BGP-4
2292	Advanced Sockets API for IPv6
2300	INTERNET OFFICIAL PROTOCOL STANDARDS
2328	OSPF Version 2
2344	Reverse Tunneling for Mobile IP
2353	APPN/HPR in IP Networks APPN Implementers' Workshop Closed Pages Document
2365	Administratively Scoped IP Multicast
2373	IP Version 6 Addressing Architecture
2374	An IPv6 Aggregatable Global Unicast Address Format
2375	IPv6 Multicast Address Assignments

B

Selected RFCs

There are dozens of RFCs that relate to IPv6 in one form or another. Appendix A contains an index to such RFCs as were available at the time this book was written. This appendix presents a selection of RFCs that shed some light on the development of IPv6, from forging an understanding of the problems with IPv4 through examination of some of the possible solutions through the proposed standards themselves.

RFC 1287 was one of the earliest RFCs to plot a future for the Internet. Written in 1991 by some of the head honchos of the IETF and IAB, this document defines some of the issues and approaches to upgrading the Internet architecture. Some of the concepts introduced are so forward-looking that only recently are they coming into general currency. For example, the notion that "IP-based" networking defined the Internet was called old-fashioned and the authors suggest that the Internet can in the future be more profitably characterized as being "application based."

RFC 1454, written in 1993, compares the proposals then in hand for the next generation of the Internet Protocol. It is interesting to contrast the conclusions drawn in this document with the solutions ultimately put into the IPv6 standard. RFC 1671, written in 1994, provides a thoughtful consideration of the problems that the transition to a new version of IP would cause. RFC 1715, written by Christian Huitema, presents an interesting method for measuring the efficiency with which a network address architecture assigns addresses.

Also included here are RFCs 2373 and 2374, which are, respectively, the standards track specification for the IPv6 addressing architecture, and the standards track specification for the IPv6 aggregatable unicast address format. While I have attempted to present much of this information in context and explained clearly, that means some material may be simplified or skipped for clarity. Including these RFCs allows the reader to check out the details. It should be noted that a replacement RFC describing the IPv6 protocol specification will probably make RFC 1883 obsolete before the end of 1998. Rather than include an RFC that is about to become obsolete, I suggest that the reader find the most current Internet document (Internet draft or RFC) online.

Throughout the text of this book I've included the numbers of relevant RFCs where appropriate. Readers are urged to check out these documents themselves; there are a number of RFC repositories on the Internet, including these:

```
http://www.pmg.lcs.mit.edu/rfc.html
```

```
http://www.csl.sony.co.jp/rfc/
```

```
http://www.cis.ohio-state.edu/Excite/AT-rfcsquery.html
```

```
http://info.internet.isi.edu/1s/in-notes/rfc/files
```

```
http://www.nexor.com/public/rfc/index/rfc.html
```

Readers are urged to use their favorite search engine if these sites are unavailable or if they are not easy to use.

Network Working Group   D. Clark
Request for Comments: 1287   MIT
                                                           L. Chapin
                                                                 BBN
                                                             V. Cerf
                                                                CNRI
                                                           R. Braden
                                                                 ISI
                                                            R. Hobby
                                                            UC Davis
                                                       December 1991

Towards the Future Internet Architecture

Status of this Memo

This informational RFC discusses important directions for possible
future evolution of the Internet architecture, and suggests steps
towards the desired goals. It is offered to the Internet community
for discussion and comment. This memo provides information for the
Internet community. It does not specify an Internet standard.
Distribution of this memo is unlimited.

Table of Contents

RFC 1287   Future of Internet Architecture   December 1991

1. INTRODUCTION

1.1 The Internet Architecture

The Internet architecture, the grand plan behind the TCP/IP
protocol suite, was developed and tested in the late 1970s by a
small group of network researchers [1-4]. Several important
features were added to the architecture during the early 1980's --
subnetting, autonomous systems, and the domain name system [5,6].
More recently, IP multicasting has been added [7].

Within this architectural framework, the Internet Engineering Task
Force (IETF) has been working with great energy and effectiveness
to engineer, define, extend, test, and standardize protocols for
the Internet. Three areas of particular importance have been
routing protocols, TCP performance, and network management.
Meanwhile, the Internet infrastructure has continued to grow at an
astonishing rate. Since January 1983 when the ARPANET first
switched from NCP to TCP/IP, the vendors, managers, wizards, and
researchers of the Internet have all been laboring mightily to
survive their success.

A set of the researchers who had defined the Internet architecture
formed the original membership of the Internet Activities Board
(IAB). The IAB evolved from a technical advisory group set up in
1981 by DARPA to become the general technical and policy oversight
body for the Internet. IAB membership has changed over the years
to better represent the changing needs and issues in the Internet
community, and more recently, to reflect the internationalization
of the Internet, but it has retained an institutional concern for
the protocol architecture.

The IAB created the Internet Engineering Task Force (IETF) to
carry out protocol development and engineering for the Internet.
To manage the burgeoning IETF activities, the IETF chair set up
the Internet Engineering Steering Group (IESG) within the IETF.
The IAB and IESG work closely together in ratifying protocol
standards developed within the IETF.

Over the past few years, there have been increasing signs of
strains on the fundamental architecture, mostly stemming from
continued Internet growth. Discussions of these problems
reverberate constantly on many of the major mailing lists.

1.2 Assumptions

The priority for solving the problems with the current Internet
architecture depends upon one's view of the future relevance of

RFC 1287   Future of Internet Architecture   December 1991

TCP/IP with respect to the OSI protocol suite. One view has been
that we should just let the TCP/IP suite strangle in its success,
and switch to OSI protocols. However, many of those who have
worked hard and successfully on Internet protocols, products, and
service are anxious to try to solve the new problems within the
existing framework. Furthermore, some believe that OSI protocols
will suffer from versions of many of the same problems.

To begin to attack these issues, the IAB and the IESG held a one-
day joint discussion of Internet architectural issues in January
1991. The framework for this meeting was set by Dave Clark (see
Appendix A for his slides). The discussion was spirited,
provocative, and at times controversial, with a lot of soul-
searching over questions of relevance and future direction. The
major result was to reach a consensus on the following four basic
assumptions regarding the networking world of the next 5-10 years.

(1)   The TCP/IP and OSI suites will coexist for a long time.

       There are powerful political and market forces as well as
       some technical advantages behind the introduction of the OSI
       suite. However, the entrenched market position of the TCP/IP
       protocols means they are very likely to continue in service
       for the foreseeable future.

(2)   The Internet will continue to include diverse networks and
       services, and will never be comprised of a single network
       technology.

       Indeed, the range of network technologies and characteristics
       that are connected into the Internet will increase over the
       next decade.

(3)   Commercial and private networks will be incorporated, but we
       cannot expect the common carriers to provide the entire
       service. There will be mix of public and private networks,
       common carriers and private lines.

(4)   The Internet architecture needs to be able to scale to $10^{**}9$
       networks.

       The historic exponential growth in the size of the Internet
       will presumably saturate some time in the future, but
       forecasting when is about as easy as forecasting the future
       economy. In any case, responsible engineering requires an
       architecture that is CAPABLE of expanding to a worst-case
       size. The exponent "9" is rather fuzzy; estimates have
       varied from 7 to 10.

RFC 1287   Future of Internet Architecture   December 1991

1.3 Beginning a Planning Process

Another result of the IAB and IESG meeting was the following list
of the five most important areas for architectural evolution:

(1)   Routing and Addressing

       This is the most urgent architectural problem, as it is
       directly involved in the ability of the Internet to continue
       to grow successfully.

(2)   Multi-Protocol Architecture

       The Internet is moving towards widespread support of both the
       TCP/IP and the OSI protocol suites. Supporting both suites
       raises difficult technical issues, and a plan -- i.e., an
       architecture -- is required to increase the chances of
       success. This area was facetiously dubbed "making the
       problem harder for the good of mankind."

       Clark had observed that translation gateways (e.g., mail
       gateways) are very much a fact of life in Internet operation
       but are not part of the architecture or planning. The group
       discussed the possibility of building the architecture around
       the partial connectivity that such gateways imply.

(3)   Security Architecture

       Although military security was considered when the Internet
       architecture was designed, the modern security issues are
       much broader, encompassing commercial requirements as well.
       Furthermore, experience has shown that it is difficult to add
       security to a protocol suite unless it is built into the
       architecture from the beginning.

(4)   Traffic Control and State

       The Internet should be extended to support "real-time"
       applications like voice and video. This will require new
       packet queueing mechanisms in gateways -- "traffic control"
       -- and additional gateway state.

(5)   Advanced Applications

       As the underlying Internet communication mechanism matures,
       there is an increasing need for innovation and
       standardization in building new kinds of applications.

The IAB and IESG met again in June 1991 at SDSC and devoted three full days to a discussion of these five topics. This meeting, which was called somewhat perversely the "Architecture Retreat", was convened with a strong resolve to take initial steps towards planning evolution of the architecture. Besides the IAB and IESG, the group of 32 people included the members of the Research Steering Group (IRSG) and a few special guests. On the second day, the Retreat broke into groups, one for each of the five areas. The group membership is listed in Appendix B.

This document was assembled from the reports by the chairs of these groups. This material was presented at the Atlanta IETF meeting, and appears in the minutes of that meeting [8].

2. ROUTING AND ADDRESSING

Changes are required in the addressing and routing structure of IP to deal with the anticipated growth and functional evolution of the Internet. We expect that:

o   The Internet will run out of certain classes of IP network addresses, e.g., B addresses.

o   The Internet will run out of the 32-bit IP address space altogether, as the space is currently subdivided and managed.

o   The total number of IP network numbers will grow to the point where reasonable routing algorithms will not be able to perform routing based upon network numbers.

o   There will be a need for more than one route from a source to a destination, to permit variation in TOS and policy conformance. This need will be driven both by new applications and by diverse transit services. The source, or an agent acting for the source, must control the selection of the route options.

2.1 Suggested Approach

There is general agreement on the approach needed to deal with these facts.

(a)   We must move to an addressing scheme in which network numbers are aggregated into larger units as the basis for routing. An example of an aggregate is the Autonomous System, or the Administrative Domain (AD).

Aggregation will accomplish several goals: define regions where policy is applied, control the number of routing

elements, and provide elements for network management. Some
believe that it must be possible to further combine
aggregates, as in a nesting of ADs.

(b)   We must provide some efficient means to compute common
         routes, and some general means to compute "special" routes.

         The general approach to special routes will be some form of
         route setup specified by a "source route".

There is not full agreement on how ADs may be expected to be
aggregated, or how routing protocols should be organized to deal
with the aggregation boundaries.A very general scheme may be
used [ref. Chiappa], but some prefer a scheme that more restricts
and defines the expected network model.

To deal with the address space exhaustion, we must either expand
the address space or else reuse the 32 bit field ("32bf") in
different parts of the net. There are several possible address
formats that might make sense, as described in the next section.

Perhaps more important is the question of how to migrate to the
new scheme. All migration plans will require that some routers
(or other components inside the Internet) be able to rewrite
headers to accommodate hosts that handle only the old or format or
only the new format. Unless the need for such format conversion
can be inferred algorithmically, migration by itself will require
some sort of setup of state in the conversion element.

We should not plan a series of "small" changes to the
architecture. We should embark now on a plan that will take us
past the exhaustion of the address space. This is a more long-
range act of planning than the Internet community has undertaken
recently, but the problems of migration will require a long lead
time, and it is hard to see an effective way of dealing with some
of the more immediate problems, such as class B exhaustion, in a
way that does not by itself take a long time. So, once we embark
on a plan of change, it should take us all the way to replacing
the current 32-bit global address space. (This conclusion is
subject to revision if, as is always possible, some very clever
idea surfaces that is quick to deploy and gives us some breathing
room. We do not mean to discourage creative thinking about
short-term actions. We just want to point out that even small
changes take a long time to deploy.)

Conversion of the address space by itself is not enough. We must
at the same time provide a more scalable routing architecture, and
tools to better manage the Internet. The proposed approach is to

ADs as the unit of aggregation for routing. We already have
partial means to do this. IDPR does this. The OSI version of BGP
(IDRP) does this. BGP could evolve to do this. The additional
facility needed is a global table that maps network numbers to
ADs.

For several reasons (special routes and address conversion, as
well as accounting and resource allocation), we are moving from a
"stateless" gateway model, where only precomputed routes are
stored in the gateway, to a model where at least some of the
gateways have per-connection state.

2.2 Extended IP Address Formats

There are three reasonable choices for the extended IP address
format.

A   Replace the 32 bit field (32bf) with a field of the same size
        but with different meaning. Instead of being globally
        unique, it would now be unique only within some smaller
        region (an AD or an aggregate of ADs). Gateways on the
        boundary would rewrite the address as the packet crossed the
        boundary.

        Issues: (1) addresses in the body of packets must be found
        and rewritten; (2) the host software need not be changed; (3)
        some method (perhaps a hack to the DNS) must set up the
        address mappings.

        This scheme is due to Van Jacobson. See also the work by
        Paul Tsuchiya on NAT.

B)   Expand the 32bf to a 64 bit field (or some other new size),
        and use the field to hold a global host address and an AD for
        that host.

        This choice would provide a trivial mapping from the host to
        the value (the AD) that is the basis of routing. Common
        routes (those selected on the basis of destination address
        without taking into account the source address as well) can
        be selected directly from the packet address, as is done
        today, without any prior setup.

3)   Expand the 32bf to a 64 bit field (or some other new size),
        and use the field as a "flat" host identifier. Use
        connection setup to provide routers with the mapping from
        host id to AD, as needed.

RFC 1287   Future of Internet Architecture   December 1991

> The 64 bits can now be used to simplify the problem of
> allocating host ids, as in Ethernet addresses.

Each of these choices would require an address re-writing module
as a part of migration. The second and third require a change to
the IP header, so host software must change.

2.3 Proposed Actions

The following actions are proposed:

A)   Time Line

      Construct a specific set of estimates for the time at which
      the various problems above will arise, and construct a
      corresponding time-line for development and deployment of a
      new addressing/routing architecture. Use this time line as a
      basis for evaluating specific proposals for changes. This is
      a matter for the IETF.

B)   New Address Format

      Explore the options for a next generation address format and
      develop a plan for migration. Specifically, construct a
      prototype gateway that does address mapping. Understand the
      complexity of this task, to guide our thinking about
      migration options.

C)   Routing on ADs

      Take steps to make network aggregates (ADs) the basis of
      routing. In particular, explore the several options for a
      global table that maps network numbers to ADs. This is a
      matter for the IETF.

D)   Policy-Based Routing

      Continue the current work on policy based routing. There are
      several specific objectives.

      -     Seek ways to control the complexity of setting policy
            (this is a human interface issue, not an algorithm
            complexity issue).

      -     Understand better the issues of maintaining connection
            state in gateways.

      -     Understand better the issues of connection state setup.

E)   Research on Further Aggregation

       Explore, as a research activity, how ADs should be aggregated
       into still larger routing elements.

       -     Consider whether the architecture should define the
             "role" of an AD or an aggregate.

       -     Consider whether one universal routing method or
             distinct methods should be used inside and outside ADs
             and aggregates.

Existing projects planned for DARTnet will help resolve several of
these issues: state in gateways, state setup, address mapping,
accounting and so on. Other experiments in the R&D community also
bear on this area.

3. MULTI-PROTOCOL ARCHITECTURE

Changing the Internet to support multiple protocol suites leads to
three specific architectural questions:

o   How exactly will we define "the Internet"?

o   How would we architect an Internet with n>1 protocol suites,
       regardless of what the suites are?

o   Should we architect for partial or filtered connectivity?

o   How to add explicit support for application gateways into the
       architecture?

3.1 What is the "Internet"?

It is very difficult to deal constructively with the issue of "the
multi-protocol Internet" without first determining what we believe
"the Internet" is (or should be).We distinguish "the Internet",
a set of communicating systems, from "the Internet community", a
set of people and organizations. Most people would accept a loose
definition of the latter as "the set of people who believe
themselves to be part of the Internet community". However, no
such "sociological" definition of the Internet itself is likely to
be useful.

Not too long ago, the Internet was defined by IP connectivity (IP
and ICMP were - and still are - the only "required" Internet
protocols). If I could PING you, and you could PING me, then we
were both on the Internet, and a satisfying working definition of

the Internet could be constructed as a roughly transitive closure of IP-speaking systems. This model of the Internet was simple, uniform, and - perhaps most important - testable. The IP-connectivity model clearly distinguished systems that were "on the Internet" from those that were not.

As the Internet has grown and the technology on which it is based has gained widespread commercial acceptance, the sense of what it means for a system to be "on the Internet" has changed, to include:

*   Any system that has partial IP connectivity, restricted by
        policy filters.

*   Any system that runs the TCP/IP protocol suite, whether or
        not it is actually accessible from other parts of the
        Internet.

*   Any system that can exchange RFC-822 mail, without the
        intervention of mail gateways or the transformation of mail
        objects.

*   Any system with e-mail connectivity to the Internet, whether
        or not a mail gateway or mail object transformation is
        required.

These definitions of "the Internet", are still based on the original concept of connectivity, just "moving up the stack".

We propose instead a new definition of the Internet, based on a different unifying concept:

*   "Old" Internet concept: IP-based.
        The organizing principle is the IP address, i.e., a common
        network address space.

*   "New" Internet concept: Application-based.
        The organizing principle is the domain name system and
        directories, i.e., a common - albeit necessarily multiform -
        application name space.

This suggests that the idea of "connected status", which has traditionally been tied to the IP address(via network numbers, should instead be coupled to the names and related identifying information contained in the distributed Internet directory.

RFC 1287   Future of Internet Architecture   December 1991

A naming-based definition of "the Internet" implies a much larger
Internet community, and a much more dynamic (and unpredictable)
operational Internet. This argues for an Internet architecture
based on adaptability (to a broad spectrum of possible future
developments) rather than anticipation.

3.2 A Process-Based Model of the Multiprotocol Internet

Rather than specify a particular "multi-protocol Internet",
embracing a pre-determined number of specific protocol
architectures, we propose instead a process-oriented model of the
Internet, which accommodates different protocol architectures
according to the traditional "things that work" principle.

A process-oriented Internet model includes, as a basic postulate,
the assertion that there is no *steady-state* "multi-protocol
Internet". The most basic forces driving the evolution of the
Internet are pushing it not toward multi-protocol diversity, but
toward the original state of protocol-stack uniformity (although
it is unlikely that it will ever actually get there). We may
represent this tendency of the Internet to evolve towards
homogeneity as the most "thermodynamically stable" state by
describing four components of a new process-based Internet
architecture:

Part 1: The core Internet architecture

        This is the traditional TCP/IP-based architecture. It is the
        "magnetic center" of Internet evolution, recognizing that (a)
        homogeneity is still the best way to deal with diversity in
        an internetwork, and (b) IP connectivity is still the best
        basic model of the Internet (whether or not the actual state
        of IP ubiquity can be achieved in practice in a global
        operational Internet).

"In the beginning", the Internet architecture consisted only of
this first part. The success of the Internet, however, has
carried it beyond its uniform origins; ubiquity and uniformity
have been sacrificed in order to greatly enrich the Internet "gene
pool".

Two additional parts of the new Internet architecture express the
ways in which the scope and extent of the Internet have been
expanded.

Part 2: Link sharing

        Here physical resources -- transmission media, network

interfaces, perhaps some low-level (link) protocols -- are
shared by multiple, non-interacting protocol suites. This
part of the architecture recognizes the necessity and
convenience of coexistence, but is not concerned with
interoperability; it has been called "ships in the night" or
"S.I.N.".

Coexisting protocol suites are not, of course, genuinely
isolated in practice; the ships passing in the night raise
issues of management, non-interference, coordination, and
fairness in real Internet systems.

Part 3: Application interoperability

Absent ubiquity of interconnection (i.e., interoperability of
the "underlying stacks"), it is still possible to achieve
ubiquitous application functionality by arranging for the
essential semantics of applications to be conveyed among
disjoint communities of Internet systems. This can be
accomplished by application relays, or by user agents that
present a uniform virtual access method to different
application services by expressing only the shared semantics.

This part of the architecture emphasizes the ultimate role of
the Internet as a basis for communication among applications,
rather than as an end in itself. To the extent that it
enables a population of applications and their users to move
from one underlying protocol suite to another without
unacceptable loss of functionality, it is also a "transition
enabler".

Adding parts 2 and 3 to the original Internet architecture is at
best a mixed blessing. Although they greatly increase the scope
of the Internet and the size of the Internet community, they also
introduce significant problems of complexity, cost, and
management, and they usually represent a loss of functionality
(particularly with respect to part 3). Parts 2 and 3 represent
unavoidable, but essentially undesirable, departures from the
homogeneity represented by part 1. Some functionality is lost,
and additional system complexity and cost is endured, in order to
expand the scope of the Internet. In a perfect world, however,
the Internet would evolve and expand without these penalties.

There is a tendency, therefore, for the Internet to evolve in
favor of the homogeneous architecture represented by part 1, and
away from the compromised architectures of parts 2 and 3. Part 4
expresses this tendency.

RFC 1287   Future of Internet Architecture   December 1991

Part 4: Hybridization/Integration.

> Part 4 recognizes the desirability of integrating similar
> elements from different Internet protocol architectures to
> form hybrids that reduce the variability and complexity of
> the Internet system. It also recognizes the desirability of
> leveraging the existing Internet infrastructure to facilitate
> the absorption of "new stuff" into the Internet, applying to
> "new stuff" the established Internet practice of test,
> evaluate, adopt.

> This part expresses the tendency of the Internet, as a
> system, to attempt to return to the original "state of grace"
> represented by the uniform architecture of part 1. It is a
> force acting on the evolution of the Internet, although the
> Internet will never actually return to a uniform state at any
> point in the future.

According to this dynamic process model, running X.400 mail over
RFC 1006 on a TCP/IP stack, integrated IS-IS routing, transport
gateways, and the development of a single common successor to the
IP and CLNP protocols are all examples of "good things". They
represent movement away from the non-uniformity of parts 2 and 3
towards greater homogeneity, under the influence of the "magnetic
field" asserted by part 1, following the hybridization dynamic of
part 4.

4. SECURITY ARCHITECTURE

4.1 Philosophical Guidelines

The principal themes for development of an Internet security
architecture are simplicity, testability, trust, technology and
security perimeter identification.

*   There is more to security than protocols and cryptographic
         methods.

*   The security architecture and policies should be simple
         enough to be readily understood. Complexity breeds
         misunderstanding and poor implementation.

*   The implementations should be testable to determine if the
         policies are met.

*   We are forced to trust hardware, software and people to make
         any security architecture function. We assume that the
         technical instruments of security policy enforcement are at

Clark, Chapin, Cerf, Braden, & Hobby   [Page 13]

RFC 1287   Future of Internet Architecture   December 1991

least as powerful as modern personal computers and work
stations; we do not require less capable components to be
self-protecting (but might apply external remedies such as
link level encryption devices).

*   Finally, it is essential to identify security perimeters at
        which protection is to be effective.

4.2 Security Perimeters

There were four possible security perimeters: link level,
net/subnet level, host level, and process/application level. Each
imposes different requirements, can admit different techniques,
and makes different assumptions about what components of the
system must be trusted to be effective.

Privacy Enhanced Mail is an example of a process level security
system; providing authentication and confidentiality for SNMP is
another example. Host level security typically means applying an
external security mechanism on the communication ports of a host
computer. Network or subnetwork security means applying the
external security capability at the gateway/router(s) leading from
the subnetwork to the "outside". Link-level security is the
traditional point-to-point or media-level (e.g., Ethernet)
encryption mechanism.

There are many open questions about network/subnetwork security
protection, not the least of which is a potential mismatch between
host level (end/end) security methods and methods at the
network/subnetwork level. Moreover, network level protection does
not deal with threats arising within the security perimeter.

Applying protection at the process level assumes that the
underlying scheduling and operating system mechanisms can be
trusted not to prevent the application from applying security when
appropriate. As the security perimeter moves downward in the
system architecture towards the link level, one must make many
assumptions about the security threat to make an argument that
enforcement at a particular perimeter is effective. For example,
if only link-level encryption is used, one must assume that
attacks come only from the outside via communications lines, that
hosts, switches and gateways are physically protected, and the
people and software in all these components are to be trusted.

4.3 Desired Security Services

We need authenticatable distinguished names if we are to implement
discretionary and non-discretionary access control at application

RFC 1287   Future of Internet Architecture   December 1991

and lower levels in the system. In addition, we need enforcement
for integrity (anti-modification, anti-spoof and anti-replay
defenses), confidentiality, and prevention of denial-of-service.
For some situations, we may also need to prevent repudiation of
message transmission or to prevent covert channels.

We have some building blocks with which to build the Internet
security system. Cryptographic algorithms are available (e.g.,
Data Encryption Standard, RSA, El Gamal, and possibly other public
key and symmetric key algorithms), as are hash functions such as
MD2 and MD5.

We need Distinguished Names (in the OSI sense) and are very much
in need of an infrastructure for the assignment of such
identifiers, together with widespread directory services for
making them known. Certificate concepts binding distinguished
names to public keys and binding distinguished names to
capabilities and permissions may be applied to good advantage.

At the router/gateway level, we can apply address and protocol
filters and other configuration controls to help fashion a
security system. The proposed OSI Security Protocol 3 (SP3) and
Security Protocol 4 (SP4) should be given serious consideration as
possible elements of an Internet security architecture.

Finally, it must be observed that we have no good solutions to
safely storing secret information (such as the secret component of
a public key pair) on systems like PCs or laptop computers that
are not designed to enforce secure storage.

4.4 Proposed Actions

The following actions are proposed.

A   Security Reference Model

       A Security Reference Model for the Internet is needed, and it
       should be developed expeditiously. This model should
       establish the target perimeters and document the objectives
       of the security architecture.

B)   Privacy-Enhanced Mail (PEM)

       For Privacy Enhanced Mail, the most critical steps seem to be
       the installation of (1) a certificate generation and
       management infrastructure, and (2) X.500 directory services
       to provide access to public keys via distinguished names.
       Serious attention also needs to be placed on any limitations

RFC 1287   Future of Internet Architecture   December 1991

   imposed by patent and export restrictions on the deployment
   of this system.

C)   Distributed System Security

   We should examine security methods for distributed systems
   applications, in both simple (client/server) and complex
   (distributed computing environment) cases. For example, the
   utility of certificates granting permissions/capabilities to
   objects bound to distinguished names should be examined.

D)   Host-Level Security

   SP4 should be evaluated for host-oriented security, but SP3
   should also be considered for this purpose.

E)   Application-Level Security

   We should implement application-level security services, both
   for their immediate utility (e.g., PEM, SNMP authentication)
   and also to gain valuable practical experience that can
   inform the refinement of the Internet security architecture.

5. TRAFFIC CONTROL AND STATE

In the present Internet, all IP datagrams are treated equally. Each
datagram is forwarded independently, regardless of any relationship
it has to other packets for the same connection, for the same
application, for the same class of applications, or for the same user
class. Although Type-of-Service and Precedence bits are defined in
the IP header, these are not generally implemented, and in fact it is
not clear how to implement them.

It is now widely accepted that the future Internet will need to
support important applications for which best-effort is not
sufficient -- e.g., packet video and voice for teleconferencing.
This will require some "traffic control" mechanism in routers,
controlled by additional state, to handle "real-time" traffic.

5.1 Assumptions and Principles

o   ASSUMPTION: The Internet will need to support performance
      guarantees for particular subsets of the traffic.

Unfortunately, we are far from being able to give precise meanings
to the terms "performance", "guarantees", or "subsets" in this
statement. Research is still needed to answer these questions.

RFC 1287   Future of Internet Architecture   December 1991

o   The default service will continue to be the current "best-
      effort" datagram delivery, with no service guarantees.

o   The mechanism of a router can be separated into (1) the
      forwarding path and (2) the control computations (e.g.,
      routing) which take place in the background.

      The forwarding path must be highly optimized, sometimes with
      hardware-assist, and it is therefore relatively costly and
      difficult to change. The traffic control mechanism operates
      in the forwarding path, under the control of state created by
      routing and resource control computations that take place in
      background. We will have at most one shot at changing the
      forwarding paths of routers, so we had better get it right
      the first time.

o   The new extensions must operate in a highly heterogeneous
      environment, in which some parts will never support
      guarantees. For some hops of a path (e.g., a high-speed
      LAN), "over-provisioning" (i.e., excess capacity) will allow
      adequate service for real-time traffic, even when explicit
      resource reservation is unavailable.

o   Multicast distribution is probably essential.

5.2 Technical Issues

There are a number of technical issues to be resolved, including:

o   Resource Setup

      To support real-time traffic, resources need to be reserved
      in each router along the path from source to destination.
      Should this new router state be "hard" (as in connections) or
      "soft" (i.e., cached state)?

o   Resource binding vs. route binding

      Choosing a path from source to destination is traditionally
      performed using a dynamic routing protocol. The resource
      binding and the routing might be folded into a single complex
      process, or they might be performed essentially
      independently. There is a tradeoff between complexity and
      efficiency.

o   Alternative multicast models

      IP multicasting uses a model of logical addressing in which

RFC 1287   Future of Internet Architecture   December 1991

   targets attach themselves to a group. In ST-2, each host in
   a multicast session includes in its setup packet an explicit
   list of target addresses. Each of these approaches has
   advantages and drawbacks; it is not currently clear which
   will prevail for n-way teleconferences.

o   Resource Setup vs. Inter-AD routing

   Resource guarantees of whatever flavor must hold across an
   arbitrary end-to-end path, including multiple ADs. Hence,
   any resource setup mechanism needs to mesh smoothly with the
   path setup mechanism incorporated into IDPR.

o   Accounting

   The resource guarantee subsets ("classes") may be natural
   units for accounting.

5.3 Proposed Actions

The actions called for here are further research on the technical
issues listed above, followed by development and standardization
of appropriate protocols. DARTnet, the DARPA Research Testbed
network, will play an important role in this research.

6. ADVANCED APPLICATIONS

One may ask: "What network-based applications do we want, and why
don't we have them now?" It is easy to develop a large list of
potential applications, many of which would be based on a
client/server model. However, the more interesting part of the
question is: "Why haven't people done them already?" We believe the
answer to be that the tools to make application writing easy just do
not exist.

To begin, we need a set of common interchange formats for a number of
data items that will be used across the network. Once these common
data formats have been defined, we need to develop tools that the
applications can use to move the data easily.

6.1 Common Interchange Formats

The applications have to know the format of information that they
are exchanging, for the information to have any meaning.The
following format types are to concern:

(1)   Text - Of the formats in this list, text is the most stable,
      but today's international Internet has to address the needs

of character sets other than USASCII.

(2)   Image - As we enter the "Multimedia Age", images will become
         increasingly important, but we need to agree on how to
         represent them in packets.

(3)   Graphics - Like images, vector graphic information needs a
         common definition. With such a format we could exchange
         things like architectural blueprints.

(4)   Video - Before we can have a video window running on our
         workstation, we need to know the format of that video
         information coming over the network.

(5)   Audio/Analog - Of course, we also need the audio to go with
         the video, but such a format would be used for representation
         of all types of analog signals.

(6)   Display - Now that we are opening windows on our workstation,
         we want to open a window on another person's workstation to
         show her some data pertinent to the research project, so now
         we need a common window display format.

(7)   Data Objects - For inter-process communications we need to
         agree on the formats of things like integers, reals, strings,
         etc.

Many of these formats are being defined by other, often several
other, standards organizations. We need to agree on one format
per category for the Internet.

6.2 Data Exchange Methods

Applications will require the following methods of data exchange.

(1)   Store and Forward

         Not everyone is on the network all the time. We need a
         standard means of providing an information flow to
         sometimes-connected hosts, i.e., we need a common store-and-
         forward service. Multicasting should be included in such a
         service.

(2)   Global File Systems

         Much of the data access over the network can be broken down
         to simple file access. If you had a real global file system
         where you access any file on the Internet (assuming you have

RFC 1287   Future of Internet Architecture   December 1991

permission), would you ever need FTP?

(3)   Inter-process Communications

For a true distributed computing environment, we need the
means to allow processes to exchange data in a standard
method over the network. This requirement encompasses RPC,
APIs, etc.

(4)   Data Broadcast

Many applications need to send the same information to many
other hosts. A standard and efficient method is needed to
accomplish this.

(5)   Database Access

For good information exchange, we need to have a standard
means for accessing databases. The Global File System can get
you to the data, but the database access methods will tell
you about its structure and content.

Many of these items are being addressed by other organizations,
but for Internet interoperability, we need to agree on the methods
for the Internet.

Finally, advanced applications need solutions to the problems of
two earlier areas in this document. From the Traffic Control and
State area, applications need the ability to transmit real-time
data. This means some sort of expectation level for data delivery
within a certain time frame. Applications also require global
authentication and access control systems from the Security area.
Much of the usefulness of today's Internet applications is lost
due to the lack of trust and security. This needs to be solved
for tomorrow's applications.

RFC 1287   Future of Internet Architecture   December 1991

7. REFERENCES

[1]   Cerf, V. and R. Kahn, "A Protocol for Packet Network
       Intercommunication," IEEE Transactions on Communication, May
       1974.

[2]   Postel, J., Sunshine, C., and D. Cohen, "The ARPA Internet
       Protocol," Computer Networks, Vol. 5, No. 4, July 1981.

[3]   Leiner, B., Postel, J., Cole, R., and D. Mills, "The DARPA
       Internet Protocol Suite," Proceedings INFOCOM 85, IEEE,
       Washington DC, March 1985. Also in: IEEE Communications
       Magazine, March 1985.

[4]   Clark, D., "The Design Philosophy of the DARPA Internet
       Protocols", Proceedings ACM SIGCOMM '88, Stanford, California,
       August 1988.

[5]   Mogul, J., and J. Postel, "Internet Standard Subnetting
       Procedure", RFC 950, USC/Information Sciences Institute, August
       1985.

[6]   Mockapetris, P., "Domain Names - Concepts and Facilities", RFC
       1034, USC/Information Sciences Institute, November 1987.

[7]   Deering, S., "Host Extensions for IP Multicasting", RFC 1112,
       Stanford University, August 1989.

[8]   "Proceedings of the Twenty-First Internet Engineering Task
       Force", Bell-South, Atlanta, July 29 - August 2, 1991.

RFC 1287   Future of Internet Architecture   December 1991

APPENDIX A: Setting the Stage

     Slide 1

WHITHER THE INTERNET?
OPTIONS FOR ARCHITECTURE

IAB/IESG -- Jan 1990

David D. Clark

Slide 2

SETTING THE TOPIC OF DISCUSSION

Goals:
- o   Establish a common frame of understanding for
      IAB, IESG and the Internet community.
- o   Understand the set of problems to be solved.
- o   Understand the range of solutions open to us.
- o   Draw some conclusions, or else
      "meta-conclusions".

RFC 1287   Future of Internet Architecture   December 1991

Slide 3

SOME CLAIMS -- MY POSITION

We have two different goals:
    o   Make it possible to build "The Internet"
    o   Define a protocol suite called Internet

Claim: These goals have very different implications.
       The protocols are but a means, though a powerful one.

Claim: If "The Internet" is to succeed and grow, it will
       require specific design efforts. This need will continue
       for at least another 10 years.

Claim: Uncontrolled growth could lead to chaos.

Claim: A grass-roots solution seems to be the only
       means to success. Top-down mandates are powerless.

Slide 4

OUTLINE OF PRESENTATION

1) The problem space and the solution space.

2) A set of specific questions -- discussion.

3) Return to top-level questions -- discussion.

4) Plan for action -- meta discussion.

Try to separate functional requirements from technical approach.

Understand how we are bounded by our problem space and our
solution space.

Is architecture anything but protocols?

RFC 1287   Future of Internet Architecture   December 1991

Slide 5

WHAT IS THE PROBLEM SPACE?

Routing and addressing:
     How big, what topology, and what routing model?

Getting big:
     User services, what technology for host and nets?

Divestiture of the Internet:
     Accounting, controlling usage and fixing faults.

New services:
     Video? Transactions? Distributed computing?

Security:
     End node or network? Routers or relays?

Slide 6

BOUNDING THE SOLUTION SPACE

How far can we migrate from the current state?
     o   Can we change the IP header (except to OSI)?
     o   Can we change host requirements in mandatory ways?
     o   Can we manage a long-term migration objective?
         - Consistent direction vs. diverse goals, funding.

Can we assume network-level connectivity?
     o   Relays are the wave of the future (?)
     o   Security a key issue; along with conversion.
     o   Do we need a new "relay-based" architecture?

How "managed" can/must "The Internet" be?
     o   Can we manage or constrain connectivity?

What protocols are we working with? One or many?

Slide 7

THE MULTI-PROTOCOL INTERNET

"Making the problem harder for the good of mankind."

Are we migrating, interoperating, or tolerating multiple protocols?
- o   Not all protocol suites will have same range of functionality
     at the same time.
- o   "The Internet" will require specific functions.

Claim: Fundamental conflict (not religion or spite):
- o   Meeting aggressive requirements for the Internet
- o   Dealing with OSI migration.

Conclusion: One protocol must "lead", and the others must follow.
     When do we "switch" to OSI?

Consider every following slide in this context.

Slide 8

ROUTING and ADDRESSING

What is the target size of "The Internet"?
- o   How do addresses and routes relate?
- o   What is the model of topology?
- o   What solutions are possible?

What range of policy routing is required?
- o   BGP and IDRP are two answers. What is the question?
- o   Fixed classes, or variable paths?
- o   Source controlled routing is a minimum.

How seamless is the needed support for mobile hosts?
- o   New address class, rebind to local address, use DNS?

Shall we push for Internet multicast?

Slide 9

GETTING BIG -- AN OLD TITLE

(Addressing and routing was on previous slide...)

What user services will be needed in the next 10 years?
  o   Can we construct a plan?
  o   Do we need architectural changes?

Is there a requirement for dealing better with ranges in
      speed, packet sizes, etc.
  o   Policy to phase out fragmentation?

What range of hosts (things != Unix) will we support?

Slide 10

DEALING WITH DIVESTITURE

The Internet is composed of parts separately managed and
controlled.

What support is needed for network charging?
  o   No architecture implies bulk charges and re-billing, pay
      for lost packets.
  o   Do we need controls to supply billing id or routing?

Requirement: we must support links with controlled sharing.
      (Simple form is classes based on link id.)
  o   How general?

Is there an increased need for fault isolation? (I vote yes!)
  o   How can we find managers to talk to?
  o   Do we need services in hosts?

RFC 1287   Future of Internet Architecture   December 1991

Slide 11

NEW SERVICES

Shall we support video and audio? Real time? What %?
- o   Need to plan for input from research. What quality?
- o   Target date for heads-up to vendors.

Shall we "better" support transactions?
- o   Will TCP do? VMTP? Presentation? Locking?

What application support veneers are coming?
- o   Distributed computing -- will it actually happen?
- o   Information networking?

Slide 12

SECURITY

Can we persist in claiming the end-node is the only line of defense?
- o   What can we do inside the network?
- o   What can ask the host to do?

Do we tolerate relays, or architect them?
Can find a better way to construct security boundaries?

Do we need global authentication?

Do we need new host requirements:
- o   Logging.
- o   Authentication.
- o   Management interfaces.
- - Phone number or point of reference.

RFC 1287   Future of Internet Architecture   December 1991

APPENDIX B: Group Membership

    Group 1: ROUTING AND ADDRESSING

        Dave Clark, MIT [Chair]
        Hans-Werner Braun, SDSC
        Noel Chiappa, Consultant
        Deborah Estrin, USC
        Phill Gross, CNRI
        Bob Hinden, BBN
        Van Jacobson, LBL
        Tony Lauck, DEC.

    Group 2: MULTI-PROTOCOL ARCHITECTURE

        Lyman Chapin, BBN [Chair]
        Ross Callon, DEC
        Dave Crocker, DEC
        Christian Huitema, INRIA
        Barry Leiner,
        Jon Postel, ISI

    Group 3: SECURITY ARCHITECTURE

        Vint Cerf, CNRI [Chair]
        Steve Crocker, TIS
        Steve Kent, BBN
        Paul Mockapetris, DARPA

    Group 4: TRAFFIC CONTROL AND STATE

        Robert Braden, ISI [Chair]
        Chuck Davin, MIT
        Dave Mills, University of Delaware
        Claudio Topolcic, CNRI

    Group 5: ADVANCED APPLICATIONS

        Russ Hobby, UCDavis [Chair]
        Dave Borman, Cray Research
        Cliff Lynch, University of California
        Joyce K. Reynolds, ISI
        Bruce Schatz, University of Arizona
        Mike Schwartz, University of Colorado
        Greg Vaudreuil, CNRI.

RFC 1287   Future of Internet Architecture   December 1991

Security Considerations
Security issues are discussed in Section 4.

Authors' Addresses

        David D. Clark
        Massachusetts Institute of Technology
        Laboratory for Computer Science
        545 Main Street
        Cambridge, MA 02139

        Phone: (617) 253-6003
        EMail: ddc@LCS.MIT.EDU

        Vinton G. Cerf
        Corporation for National Research Initiatives
        1895 Preston White Drive, Suite 100
        Reston, VA 22091

        Phone: (703) 620-8990
        EMail: vcerf@nri.reston.va.us

        Lyman A. Chapin
        Bolt, Beranek & Newman
        Mail Stop 20/5b
        150 Cambridge Park Drive
        Cambridge, MA 02140

        Phone: (617) 873-3133
        EMail: lyman@BBN.COM

        Robert Braden
        USC/Information Sciences Institute
        4676 Admiralty Way
        Marina del Rey, CA 90292

        Phone: (310) 822-1511
        EMail: braden@isi.edu

        Russell Hobby
        University of California
        Computing Services
        Davis, CA 95616

        Phone: (916) 752-0236
        EMail: rdhobby@ucdavis.edu

Network Working Group   T. Dixon
Request for Comments: 1454   RARE
                                                        May 1993

            Comparison of Proposals for Next Version of IP

Status of this Memo

This memo provides information for the Internet community. It does
not specify an Internet standard. Distribution of this memo is
unlimited.

Abstract

This is a slightly edited reprint of RARE Technical Report
(RTC(93)004).

The following is a brief summary of the characteristics of the three
main proposals for replacing the current Internet Protocol. It is not
intended to be exhaustive or definitive (a brief bibliography at the
end points to sources of more information), but to serve as input to
the European discussions on these proposals, to be co-ordinated by
RARE and RIPE. It should be recognised that the proposals are
themselves "moving targets", and in so far as this paper is accurate
at all, it reflects the position at the 25th IETF meeting in
Washington, DC. Comments from Ross Callon and Paul Tsuchiya on the
original draft have been incorporated. Note that for a time the term
"IPv7" was use to mean the eventual next version of IP, but that the
same term was closely associated with a particilar proposal, so the
term "IPng" is now used to identify the eventual next generation of
IP.

The paper begins with a "generic" discussion of the mechanisms for
solving problems and achieving particular goals, before discussing
the proposals invidually.

1. WHY IS THE CURRENT IP INADEQUATE?

The problem has been investigated and formulated by the ROAD group,
but briefly reduces to the following:

        - Exhaustion of IP Class B Address Space.

        - Exhaustion of IP Address Space in General.

        - Non-hierarchical nature of address allocation leading to flat
          routing space.

RFC 1454   Comparison of Next Version IP Proposals   May 1993

Although the IESG requirements for a new Internet Protocol go further than simply routing and addressing issues, it is these issues that make extension of the current protocol an impractical option. Consequently, most of the discussion and development of the various proposed protocols has concentrated on these specific problems.

Near term remedies for these problems include the CIDR proposals (which permit the aggregation of Class C networks for routing purposes) and assignment policies which will allocate Class C network numbers in a fashion which CIDR can take advantage of. Routing protocols supporting CIDR are OSPF and BGP4. None of these are pre-requisites for the new IP (IPng), but are necessary to prolong the life of the current Internet long enough to work on longer-term solutions. Ross Callon points out that there are other options for prolonging the life of IP and that some ideas have been distributed on the TUBA list.

Longer term proposals are being sought which ultimately allow for further growth of the Internet. The timescale for considering these proposals is as follows:

        - Dec 15 Issue selection criteria as RFC.

        - Feb 12 Two interoperable implementations available.

        - Feb 26 Second draft of proposal documents available.

The (ambitious) target is for a decision to be made at the 26th IETF (Columbus, Ohio in March 1993) on which proposals to pursue.

The current likely candidates for selection are:

        - PIP ('P' Internet Protocol - an entirely new protocol).

        - TUBA (TCP/UDP with Big Addresses - uses ISO CLNP).

        - SIP (Simple IP - IP with larger addresses and fewer options).

There is a further proposal from Robert Ullman of which I don't claim to have much knowledge. Associated with each of the candidates are transition plans, but these are largely independent of the protocol itself and contain elements which could be adopted separately, even with IP v4, to further extend the life of current implementations and systems.

2. WHAT THE PROPOSALS HAVE IN COMMON

2.1 Larger Addresses

All the proposals (of course) make provision for larger address
fields which not only increase the number of addressable systems, but
also permit the hierarchical allocation of addresses to facilitate
route aggregation.

2.2 Philosophy

The proposals also originate from a "routing implementation" view of
the world - that is to say they focus on the internals of routing
within the network and do not primarily look at the network service
seen by the end-user, or by applications. This is perhaps inevitable,
especially given the tight time constraints for producing
interoperable implementations. However, the (few) representatives of
real users at the 25th IETF, the people whose support is ultimately
necessary to deploy new host implementations, were distinctly
unhappy.

There is an inbuilt assumption in the proposals that IPng is
intended to be a universal protocol: that is, that the same network-
layer protocol will be used between hosts on the same LAN, between
hosts and routers, between routers in the same domain, and between
routers in different domains. There are some advantages in defining
separate "access" and "long-haul" protocols, and this is not
precluded by the requirements. However, despite the few opportunities
for major change of this sort within the Internet, the need for speed
of development and low risk have led to the proposals being
incremental, rather than radical, changes to well-proven existing
technology.

There is a further unstated assumption that the architecture is
targeted at the singly-connected host. It is currently difficult to
design IPv4 networks which permit hosts with more than one interface
to benefit from increased bandwidth and reliability compared with
singly-connected hosts (a consequence of the address belonging to the
interface and not the host). It would be preferable if topological
constraints such as these were documented. It has been asserted that
this is not necessarily a constraint of either the PIP or TUBA
proposals, but I believe it is an issue that has not emerged so far
amongst the comparative criteria.

RFC 1454   Comparison of Next Version IP Proposals   May 1993

2.3 Source Routing

The existing IPv4 has provision for source-specified routes, though
this is little used [would someone like to contradict me here?],
partly because it requires knowledge of the internal structure of the
network down to the router level. Source routes are usually required
by users when there are policy requirements which make it preferable
or imperative that traffic between a source and destination should
pass through particular administrative domains. Source routes can
also be used by routers within administrative domains to route via
particular logical topologies. Source-specified routing requires a
number of distinct components:

>   a. The specification by the source of the policy by which the
>   route should be selected.
>
>   b. The selection of a route appropriate to the policy.
>
>   c. Marking traffic with the identified route.
>
>   d. Routing marked traffic accordingly.

These steps are not wholly independent. The way in which routes are
identified in step (c) may constrain the kinds of route which can be
selected in previous steps. The destination, inevitably, participates
in the specification of source routes either by advertising the
policies it is prepared to accept or, conceivably, by a negotiation
process.

All of the proposals mark source routes by adding a chain of (perhaps
partially-specified) intermediate addresses to each packet. None
specifies the process by which a host might acquire the information
needed to specify these intermediate addresses [not entirely
unreasonably at this stage, but further information is expected]. The
negative consequences of these decisions are:

>   - Packet headers can become quite long, depending on the number of
>   intermediate addresses that must be specified (although there are
>   mechanisms which are currently specified or which can be imagined
>   to specify only the significant portions of intermediate addresses).
>
>   - The source route may have to be re-specified periodically if
>   particular intermediate addresses are no longer reachable.

The positive consequences are:

>   - Inter-domain routers do not have to understand policies, they
>   simply have to mechanically follow the source route.

Dixon   [Page 4]

RFC 1454   Comparison of Next Version IP Proposals   May 1993

- Routers do not have to store context identifying routes, since the information is specified in each packet header.

- Route servers can be located anywhere in the network, provided the hosts know how to find them.

2.4 Encapsulation

Encapsulation is the ability to enclose a network-layer packet within another one so that the actual packet can be directed via a path it would not otherwise take to a router that can remove the outermost packet and direct the resultant packet to its destination. Encapsulation requires:

    a. An indication in the packet that it contains another packet.

    b. A function in routers which, on receiving such a packet, removes the encapsulation and re-enters the forwarding process.

All the proposals support encapsulation. Note that it is possible to achieve the effect of source routing by suitable encapsulation by the source.

2.5 Multicast

The specification of addresses to permit multicast with various scopes can be accomodated by all the proposals. Internet-wide multicast is, of course, for further study!

2.6 Fragmentation

All the proposals support the fragmentation of packets by intermediate routers, though there has been some recent discussion of removing this mechanism from some of the proposals and requiring the use of an MTU-discovery process to avoid the need for fragmentation. Such a decision would effectively preclude the use of transport protocols which use message-count sequence numbering (such as OSI Transport) over the network, as only protocols with byte-count acknowledgement (such as TCP) can deal with MTU reductions during the lifetime of a connection. OSI Transport may not be particularly relevant to the IP community (though it may be of relevance to commercial suppliers providing multiprotocol services), however the consequences for the types of services which may be supported over IPng should be noted.

RFC 1454   Comparison of Next Version IP Proposals   May 1993

2.7 The End of Lifetime as We Know It

The old IPv4 "Time to Live" field has been recast in every case as a simple hop count, largely on grounds of implementation convenience. Although the old TTL was largely implemented in this fashion anyway, it did serve an architectural purpose in putting an upper bound on the lifetime of a packet in the network. If this field is recast as a hop-count, there must be some other specification of the maximum lifetime of a packet in the network so that a source host can ensure that network-layer fragment ids and transport-layer sequence numbers are never in danger of re-use whilst there is a danger of confusion. There are, in fact, three separate issues here:

1. Terminating routing loops (solved by hop count).

2. Bounding lifetime of network-layer packets (a necessity, unspecified so far) to support assumptions by the transport layer.

3. Permitting the source to place further restrictions on packet lifetime (for example so that "old" real-time traffic can be discarded in favour of new traffic in the case of congestion (an optional feature, unspecified so far).

3. WHAT THE PROPOSALS ONLY HINT AT

3.1 Resource Reservation

Increasingly, applications require a certain bandwidth or transit delay if they are to be at all useful (for example, real-time video and audio transport). Such applications need procedures to indicate their requirements to the network and to have the required resources reserved. This process is in some ways analogous to the selection of a source route:

a. The specification by the source of its requirements.

b. The confirmation that the requirements can be met.

c. Marking traffic with the requirement.

d. Routing marked traffic accordingly.

Traffic which is routed according to the same set of resource requirements is sometimes called a "flow". The identification of flows requires a setup process, and it is tempting to suppose that the same process might also be used to set up source routes, however, there are a number of differences:

   - All the routers on a path must participate in resource
     reservation and agree to it.

   - Consequently, it is relatively straightforward to maintain
     context in each router and the identification for flows can be
     short.

   - The network can choose to reroute on failure.

By various means, each proposal could carry flow-identification,
though this is very much "for future study" at present. No setup
mechansisms are defined. The process for actually reserving the
resources is a higher-order problem. The interaction between source-
routing and resource reservation needs further investigation:
although the two are distinct and have different implementation
constraints, the consequence of having two different mechanisms could
be that it becomes difficult to select routes which meet both policy
and performance goals.

3.2 Address-Assignment Policies

In IPv4, addresses were bound to systems on a long-term basis and in
many cases could be used interchangeably with DNS names. It is
tacitly accepted that the association of an address with a particular
system may be more volatile in IPng. Indeed, one of the proposals,
PIP, makes a distinction between the identification of a system (a
fixed quantity) and its address, and permits the binding to be
altered on the fly. None of the proposals defines bounds for the
lifetime of addresses, and the manner in which addresses are assigned
is not necessarily bound to a particular proposal. For example,
within the larger address space to be provided by IPng, there is a
choice to be made of assigning the "higher order" part of the
hierarchical address in a geographically-related fashion or by
reference to service provider. Geographically-based addresses can be
constant and easy to assign, but represent a renewed danger of
degeneration to "flat" addresses within the region of assignment,
unless certain topological restrictions are assumed. Provider-based
address assignment results in a change of address (if providers are
changed) or multiple addresses (if multiple providers are used).
Mobile hosts (depending on the underlying technology) can present
problems in both geographic and provider-based schemes.

Without firm proposals for address-assignment schemes and the
consequences for likely address lifetimes, it is impossible to assume
that the existing DNS model by which name-to-address bindings can be
discovered remains valid.

RFC 1454   Comparison of Next Version IP Proposals   May 1993

Note that there is an interaction between the mechanism for
assignment of addresses and way in which automatic configuration may
be deployed.

3.3 Automatic Configuration

Amongst the biggest (user) bugbears of current IP services is the
administrative effort of maintaining basic configuration information,
such as assigning names and addresses to hosts, ensuring these are
refelected in the DNS, and keeping this information correct. Part of
this results from poor implementation (or the blind belief that vi
and awk are network management tools). However, a lot of the problems
could be alleviated by making this process more automatic. Some of
the possibilities (some mutually-exlusive) are:

  - Assigning host addresses from some (relative) invariant, such
    as a LAN address.

  - Defining a protocol for dynamic assignment of addresses within a
    subnetwork.

  - Defining "generic addresses" by which hosts can without
    preconfiguration reach necessary local servers (DNS, route
    servers, etc.).

  - Have hosts determine their name by DNS lookup.

  - Have hosts update their name/address bindings when their
    configuration changes.

Whilst a number of the proposals make mention of some of these
possibilities, the choice of appropriate solutions depends to some
extent on address-assignment policies. Also, dynamic configuration
results in some difficult philosopical and practical issues (what
exactly is the role of an address?, In what sense is a host "the same
host" when its address changes?, How do you handle dynamic changes to
DNS mappings and how do you authenticate them?).

The groups involved in the proposals would, I think, see most of
these questions outside their scope. It would seem to be a failure in
the process of defining and selecting candidates for IPng that
"systemness" issues like these will probably not be much discussed.
This is recognised by the participants, and it is likely that, even
when a decision is made, some of these ideas will be revisited by a
wider audience.

It is, however, unlikely that IP will make an impact on proprietary
networking systems for the non-technical environment (e.g., Netware,

RFC 1454   Comparison of Next Version IP Proposals   May 1993

Appletalk), without automatic configuration being taken seriously
either in the architecture, or by suppliers. I believe that there are
ideas on people's heads of how to address these issues - they simply
have not made it onto paper yet.

3.4 Application Interface/Application Protocol Changes

A number of common application protocols (FTP, RPC, etc.) have been
identified which specifically transfer 32-bit IPv4 addresses, and
there are doubtless others, both standard and proprietary. There are
also many applications which treat IPv4 addresses as simple 32-bit
integers. Even applications which use BSD sockets and try to handle
addresses opaquely will not understand how to parse or print longer
addresses (even if the socket structure is big enough to accommodate
them).

Each proposal, therefore, needs to specify mechanisms to permit
existing applications and interfaces to operate in the new
environment whilst conversion takes place. It would be useful also,
to have (one) specification of a reference programming interface for
(TCP and) IPng (which would also operate on IPv4), to allow
developers to begin changing applications now. All the proposals
specify transition mechansisms from which existing application-
compatibility can be inferred. There is no sign yet of a new
interface specification independent of chosen protocol.

3.5 DNS Changes

It is obvious that there has to be a name to address mapping service
which supports the new, longer, addresses. All the proposals assume
that this service will be provided by DNS, with some suitably-defined
new resource record. There is some discussion ongoing about the
appropriateness of returning this information along with "A" record
information in response to certain enquiries, and which information
should be requested first. There is a potential tradeoff between the
number of queries needed to establish the correct address to use and
the potential for breaking existing implementations by returning
information that they do not expect.

There has been heat, but not light, generated by discussion of the
use of DNS for auto-configuration and the scaling (or otherwise) of
reverse translations for certain addressing schemes.

RFC 1454   Comparison of Next Version IP Proposals   May 1993

4. WHAT THE PROPOSALS DON'T REALLY MENTION

4.1 Congestion Avoidance

IPv4 offers "Source Quench" control messages which may be used by
routers to indicate to a source that it is congested and has or may
shortly drop packets. TUBA/PIP have a "congestion encountered" bit
which provides similar information to the destination. None of these
specifications offers detailed instructions on how to use these
facilities. However, there has been a substantial body of analysis
over recent years that suggests that such facilities can be used (by
providing information to the transport protocol) not only to signal
congestion, but also to minimise delay through the network layer.
Each proposal can offer some form of congestion signalling, but none
specifies a mechanism for its use (or an analysis of whether the
mechanism is in fact useful).

As a user of a network service which currently has a discard rate of
around 30% and a round-trip-time of up to 2 seconds for a distance of
only 500 miles I would be most interested in some proposals for a
more graceful degradation of the network service under excess load.

4.2 Mobile Hosts

A characteristic of mobile hosts is that they (relatively) rapidly
move their physical location and point of attachment to the network
topology. This obviously has signficance for addressing (whether
geographical or topological) and routing. There seems to be an
understanding of the problem, but so far no detailed specification of
a solution.

4.3 Accounting

The IESG selection criteria require only that proposals do not have
the effect of preventing the collection of information that may be of
interest for audit or billing purposes. Consequently, none of the
proposals consider potential accounting mechanisms.

4.4 Security

"Network Layer Security Issues are For Further Study". Or secret.
However, it would be useful to have it demonstrated that each
candidate could be extended to provide a level of security, for
example against address-spoofing. This will be particularly
important if resource-allocation features will permit certain hosts
to claim large chunks of available bandwidth for specialised
applications.

RFC 1454   Comparison of Next Version IP Proposals   May 1993

Note that providing some level of security implies manual
configuration of security information within the network and must be
considered in relationship to auto-configuration goals.

5. WHAT MAKES THE PROPOSALS DIFFERENT?

Each proposal is about as different to the others as it is to IPv4 -
that is the differences are small in principle, but may have
significant effects (extending the size of addresses is only a small
difference in principle!). The main distinct characteristics are:

PIP:

        PIP has an innovative header format that facilitates hierarchical,
        policy and virtual-circuit routing. It also has "opaque" fields in
        the header whose semantics can be defined differently in different
        administrative domains and whose use and translation can be
        negotiated across domain boundaries. No control protocol is yet
        specified.

SIP:

        SIP offers a "minimalist" approach - removing all little-used
        fields from the IPv4 header and extending the size of addresses to
        (only) 64 bits. The control protocol is based on modifications to
        ICMP. This proposal has the advantages of processing efficiency
        and familiarity.

TUBA:

        TUBA is based on CLNP (ISO 8473) and the ES-IS (ISO 9542) control
        protocol. TUBA provides for the operation of TCP transport and UDP
        over a CLNP network. The main arguments in favour of TUBA are that
        routers already exist which can handle the network-layer protocol,
        that the extensible addresses offer a wide margin of "future-
        proofing" and that there is an opportunity for convergence of
        standards and products.

5.1 PIP

PIP packet headers contain a set of instructions to the router's
forwarding processor to perform certain actions on the packet. In
traditional protocols, the contents of certain fields imply certain
actions; PIP gives the source the flexibility to write small
"programs" which direct the routing of packets through the network.

PIP addresses have an effectively unlimited length: each level in the
topological hierarchy of the network contributes part of the address

RFC 1454   Comparison of Next Version IP Proposals   May 1993

and addresses change as the network topology changes. In a completely
hierarchical network topology, the amount of routing information
required at each level could be very small. However, in practice,
levels of hierarchy will be determined more by commercial and
practical factors than by the constraints of any particular routing
protocol. A greater advantage is that higher-order parts of the
address may be omitted in local exchanges and that lower-order parts
may be omitted in source routes, reducing the amount of topological
information that host systems are required to know.

There is an assumption that PIP addresses are liable to change, so a
further quantity, the PIP ID, is assigned to systems for the purposes
of identification. It isn't clear that this quantity has any purpose
which could not equally be served by a DNS name [it is more compact,
but equally it does not need to be carried in every packet and
requires an additional lookup]. However, the problem does arise of
how two potentially-communicating host systems find the correct
addresses to use.

The most complex part of PIP is that the meaning of some of the
header fields is determined by mutual agreement within a particular
domain. The semantics of specific processing facilities (for example,
queuing priority) are registered globally, but the actual use and
encoding of requests for these facilities in the packet header can be
different in different domains. Border routers between two domains
which use different encodings must map from one encoding to another.
Since routers may not only be adjacent physically to other domains,
but also via "tunnels", the number of different encoding rules a
router may need to understand is potentially quite large. Although
there is a saving in header space by using such a scheme as opposed
to the more familiar "options", the cost in the complexity of
negotiating the use and encoding of these facilities, together with
re-coding the packets at each domain border, is a subject of some
concern. Although it may be possible for hosts to "precompile" the
encoding rules for their local domain, there are many potential
implementaion difficulties.

Although PIP offers the most flexibility of the three proposals, more
work needs to be done on "likely use" scenarios which make the
potential advantages and disadvantages more concrete.

5.2 SIP

SIP is simply IP with larger addresses and fewer options. Its main
advantage is that it is even simpler that IPv4 to process. Its main
disadvantages are:

RFC 1454   Comparison of Next Version IP Proposals   May 1993

  - It is far from clear that, if 32 bits of address are
  insufficient, 64 will be enough for the forseeable future;

  - although there are a few "reserved" bits in the header, the
  extension of SIP to support new features is not obvious.
  There's really very little else to say!

5.3 TUBA

The characteristics of ISO CLNS are reasonably well known: the
protocol bears a strong cultural resemblance to IPv4, though with
20-byte network-layer addressing. Apart from a spurious "Not Invented
Here" prejudice, the main argument againt TUBA is that it is rather
too like IPv4, offering nothing other than larger, more flexible,
addresses. There is proof-by-example that routers are capable of
handling the (very) long addresses efficiently, rather less that the
longer headers do not adversely impact network bandwidth.

There are a number of objections to the proposed control protocol
(ISO 9542):

  - My early experience is that the process by which routers
  discover hosts is inefficient and resource consuming for
  routers - and requires quite fine timer resolution on hosts -
  if large LANs are to be accomodated reasonably. Proponents of
  TUBA suggest that recent experience suggests that ARP is no
  better, but I think this issue needs examination.

  - The "redirect" mechanism is based on (effectively) LAN
  addresses and not network addresses, meaning that local routers
  can only "hand-off" complex routing decisions to other routers
  on the same LAN. Equally, redirection schemes (such as that of
  IPv4) which redirect to network addresses can result in
  unnecessary extra hops. Analysis of which solution is better
  is rather dependent on the scenarios which are constructed.
  To be fair, however, the part of the protocol which provides for
  router-discovery provides a mechanism, absent from other proposals,
  by which hosts can locate nearby gateways and potentially
  automatically configure their addresses.

6. Transition Plans

It should be obvious that a transition which permits "old" hosts to
talk to "new" hosts requires:

Dixon   [Page 13]

RFC 1454   Comparison of Next Version IP Proposals   May 1993

Either:

     (a) That IPng hosts can also use IPv4 or

     (b) There is translation by an intermediate system

and either:

     (c) The infrastructure between systems is capable of carrying both IPng and IPv4 or (d) Tunneling or translation is used to carry one protocol within another in parts of the network

The transition plans espoused by the various proposals are simply different combinations of the above. Experience would tend to show that all these things will in fact happen, regardless of which protocol is chosen.

One problem of the tunneling/translation process is that there is additional information (the extra address parts) which must be carried across IPv4 tunnels in the network. This can either be carried by adding an extra "header" to the data before encapsulation in the IPv4 packet, or by encoding the information as new IPv4 option types. In the former case, it may be difficult to map error messages correctly, since the original packet is truncated before return; in the latter case there is a danger of the packet being discarded (IPv4 options are not self-describing and new ones may not pass through IPv4 routers). There is thus the possibility of having to introduce a "new" version of IPv4 in order to support IPng tunneling.

The alternative (in which IPng hosts have two stacks and the infrastructure may or may not support IPng or IPv4) of course requires a mechanism for resolving which protocols to try.

7. Random Comments

This is the first fundamental change in the Internet protocols that has occurred since the Internet was manageable as an entity and its development was tied to US government contracts. It was perhaps inevitable that the IETF/IESG/IAB structure would not have evolved to manage a change of this magnitude and it is to be hoped that the new structures that are proposed will be more successful in promoting a (useful) consensus. It is interesting to see that many of the perceived problems of the OSI process (slow progress, factional infighting over trivia, convergence on the lowest-common denominator solution, lack of consideration for the end-user) are in danger of attaching themselves to IPng and it will be interesting to see to what extent these difficulties are an inevitable consequence of wide representation and participation in network design.

RFC 1454   Comparison of Next Version IP Proposals   May 1993

It could be regarded either as a sign of success or failure of the
competitive process for the selection of IPng that the three main
proposals have few really significant differences. In this respect,
the result of the selection process is not of particular
significance, but the process itself is perhaps necessary to repair
the social and technical cohesion of the Internet Engineering
process.

8. Further Information

The main discussion lists for the proposals listed are:

            TUBA: tuba@lanl.gov
            PIP: pip@thumper.bellcore.com
            SIP: sip@caldera.usc.edu
            General: big-internet@munnari.oz.au

            (Requests to: <list name>-request@<host>)

Internet-Drafts and RFCs for the various proposals can be found in
the usual places.

Security Considerations

Security issues are not discussed in this memo.

Author's Address

Tim Dixon
RARE Secretariat
Singel 466-468
NL-1017AW Amsterdam
(Netherlands)

Phone: +31 20 639 1131 or + 44 91 232 0936
EMail: dixon@rare.nl or Tim.Dixon@newcastle.ac.uk

Network Working Group   B. Carpenter
Request for Comments: 1671   CERN
Category: Informational   August 1994

         IPng White Paper on Transition and Other Considerations

Status of this Memo

This memo provides information for the Internet community. This memo
does not specify an Internet standard of any kind. Distribution of
this memo is unlimited.

Abstract

This document was submitted to the IETF IPng area in response to RFC
1550. Publication of this document does not imply acceptance by the
IPng area of any ideas expressed within. Comments should be
submitted to the big-internet@munnari.oz.au mailing list.

Summary

This white paper outlines some general requirements for IPng in
selected areas. It identifies the following requirements for stepwise
transition:

A) Interworking at every stage and every layer.
B) Header translation considered harmful
C) Coexistence.
D) IPv4 to IPng address mapping.
E) Dual stack hosts.
F) DNS.
G) Smart dual-stack code.
H) Smart management tools.

Some remarks about phsysical and logical multicast follow, and it is
suggested that a model of how IPng will run over ATM is needed.
Finally, the paper suggests that the requirements for policy routing,
accounting, and security firewalls will in turn require all IPng
packets to carry a trace of the type of transaction involved as well
as of their source and destination.

Transition and deployment

It is clear that the transition will take years and that every site
will have to decide its own staged transition plan. Only the very
smallest sites could envisage a single step ("flag day") transition,

RFC 1671   IPng White Paper on Transition, etc.   August 1994

presumably under pressure from their Internet service providers.
Furthermore, once the IPng decision is taken, the next decade (or
more) of activity in the Internet and in all private networks using
the Internet suite will be strongly affected by the process of IPng
deployment. User sites will look at the decision whether to change
from IPv4 in the same way as they have looked in the past at changes
of programming language or operating system. It may not be a foregone
conclusion that what they change to is IPng. Their main concern will
be to minimise the cost of the change and the risk of lost
production.

This concern immediately defines strong constraints on the model for
transition and deployment of IPng. Some of these constraints are
listed below, with a short explanation of each one.

Terminology: an "IPv4 host" is a host that runs exactly what it runs
today, with no maintenance releases and no configuration changes. An
"IPng host" is a host that has a new version of IP, and has been
reconfigured. Similarly for routers.

A) Interworking at every stage and every layer.

This is the major constraint. Vendors of computer systems, routers,
and applications software will certainly not coordinate their product
release dates. Users will go on running their old equipment and
software. Therefore, any combination of IPv4 and IPng hosts and
routers must be able to interwork (i.e., participate in UDP and TCP
sessions). An IPv4 packet must be able to find its way from any IPv4
host, to any other IPv4 or IPng host, or vice versa, through a
mixture of IPv4 and IPng routers, with no (zero, null) modifications
to the IPv4 hosts. IPv4 routers must need no modifications to
interwork with IPng routers. Additionally, an application package
which is "aware" of IPv4 but still "unaware" of IPng must be able to
run on a computer system which is running IPv4, but communicating
with an IPng host. For example an old PC in Europe should be able to
access a NIC server in the USA, even if the NIC server is running
IPng and the transatlantic routing mechanisms are only partly
converted. Or a Class C network in one department of a company
should retain full access to corporate servers which are running
IPng, even though nothing whatever has been changed inside the Class
C network.

(This does NOT require an IPv4-only application to run on an IPng
host; thus we accept that some hosts cannot be upgraded until all
their applications are IPng-compatible. In other words we accept that
the API may change to some extent. However, even this relaxation is
debatable and some vendors may want to strictly preserve the IPv4 API
on an IPng host.)

Carpenter   [Page 2]

RFC 1671   IPng White Paper on Transition, etc.   August 1994

B) Header translation considered harmful.

This author believes that any transition scenario which REQUIRES
dynamic header translation between IPv4 and IPng packets will create
almost insurmountable practical difficulties:

B1) It is taken for granted for the purposes of this paper that
     IPng functionality will be a superset of IPv4 functionality.
     However, successful translation between protocols requires
     that the functionalities of the two protocols which are to be
     translated are effectively identical. To achieve this,
     applications will need to know when they are interworking,
     via the IPng API and a translator somewhere in the network,
     with an IPv4 host, so as to use only IPv4 functionality. This
     is an unrealistic constraint.

B2) Administration of translators will be quite impracticable for
     large sites, unless the translation mechanism is completely
     blind and automatic. Specifically, any translation mechanism
     that requires special tags to be maintained manually for each
     host in tables (such as DNS tables or router tables) to
     indicate the need for translation will be impossible to
     administer. On a site with thousands of hosts running many
     versions and releases of several operating systems, hosts
     move forwards and even backwards between software releases in
     such a way that continuously tracking the required state of
     such tags will be impossible. Multiplied across the whole
     Internet, this will lead to chaos, complex failure modes, and
     difficult diagnosis. In particular, it will make the
     constraint of paragraph B1) impossible to respect.

In practice, the knowledge that translation is needed should
never leak out of the site concerned if chaos is to be
avoided, and yet without such knowledge applications cannot
limit themselves to IPv4 functionality when necessary.

To avoid confusion, note that header translation, as discussed here,
is not the same thing as address translation (NAT). This paper does
not discuss NAT.

This paper does not tackle performance issues in detail, but clearly
another disadvantage of translation is the consequent overhead.

C) Coexistence.

The Internet infrastructure (whether global or private) must allow
coexistence of IPv4 and IPng in the same routers and on the same

RFC 1671   IPng White Paper on Transition, etc.   August 1994

physical paths.

This is a necessity, in order that the network infrastructure can be updated to IPng without requiring hosts to be updated in lock step and without requiring translators.

Note that this requirement does NOT impose a decision about a common or separate (ships-in-the-night) approach to routing. Nor does it exclude encapsulation as a coexistence mechanism.

D) IPv4 to IPng address mapping.

Human beings will have to understand what is happening during transition. Although auto-configuration of IPng addresses may be a desirable end point, management of the transition will be greatly simplified if there is an optional simple mapping, on a given site, between IPv4 and IPng addresses.

Therefore, the IPng address space should include a mapping for IPv4 addresses, such that (if a site or service provider wants to do this) the IPv4 address of a system can be transformed mechanically into its IPng address, most likely by adding a prefix. The prefix does not have to be the same for every site; it is likely to be at least service-provider specific.

This does not imply that such address mapping will be used for dynamic translation (although it could be) or to embed IPv4 routing within IPng routing (although it could be). Its main purpose is to simplify transition planning for network operators.

By the way, this requirement does not actually assume that IPv4 addresses are globally unique.
Neither does it help much in setting up the relationship, if any, between IPv4 and IPng routing domains and hierarchies. There is no reason to suppose these will be in 1:1 correspondence.

E) Dual stack hosts.

Stepwise transition without translation is hard to imagine unless a large proportion of hosts are simultaneously capable of running IPng and IPv4. If A needs to talk to B (an IPng host) and to C (an IPv4 host) then either A or B must be able to run both IPv4 and IPng. In other words, all hosts running IPng must still be able to run IPv4. IPng-only hosts are not allowed during transition.

This requirement does not imply that IPng hosts really have two completely separate IP implementations (dual stacks and dual APIs),

RFC 1671   IPng White Paper on Transition, etc.   August 1994

but just that they behave as if they did. It is compatible with
encapsulation (i.e., one of the two stacks encapsulates packets for
the other).

Obviously, management of dual stack hosts will be simplified by the
address mapping just mentioned. Only the site prefix has to be
configured (manually or dynamically) in addition to the IPv4 address.

In a dual stack host the IPng API and the IPv4 API will be logically
distinguishable even if they are implemented as a single entity.
Applications will know from the API whether they are using IPng or
IPv4.

F) DNS.

The dual stack requirement implies that DNS has to reply with both an
IPv4 and IPng address for IPng hosts, or with a single reply that
encodes both.

If a host is attributed an IPng address in DNS, but is not actually
running IPng yet, it will appear as a black hole in IPng space - see
the next point.

G) Smart dual-stack code.

The dual-stack code may get two addresses back from DNS; which does
it use? During the many years of transition the Internet will
contain black holes. For example, somewhere on the way from IPng host
A to IPng host B there will sometimes (unpredictably) be IPv4-only
routers which discard IPng packets. Also, the state of the DNS does
not necessarily correspond to reality. A host for which DNS claims to
know an IPng address may in fact not be running IPng at a particular
moment; thus an IPng packet to that host will be discarded on
delivery. Knowing that a host has both IPv4 and IPng addresses gives
no information about black holes. A solution to this must be proposed
and it must not depend on manually maintained information. (If this
is not solved, the dual stack approach is no better than the packet
translation approach.)

H) Smart management tools.

A whole set of management tools is going to be needed during the
transition. Why is my IPng route different from my IPv4 route? If
there is translation, where does it happen? Where are the black
holes? (Cosmologists would like the same tool :-) Is that host REALLY
IPng-capable today?...

RFC 1671   IPng White Paper on Transition, etc.   August 1994

Multicasts high and low

It is taken for granted that multicast applications must be supported
by IPng. One obvious architectural rule is that no multicast packet
should ever travel twice over the same wire, whether it is a LAN or
WAN wire. Failure to observe this would mean that the maximum number
of simultaneous multicast transactions would be halved.

A negative feature of IPv4 on LANs is the cavalier use of physical
broadcast packets by protcols such as ARP (and various non-IETF
copycats). On large LANs this leads to a number of undesirable
consequences (often caused by poor products or poor users, not by the
protcol design itself). The obvious architectural rule is that
physical broadcast should be replaced by unicast (or at worst,
multicast) whenever possible.

ATM

The networking industry is investing heavily in ATM. No IPng proposal
will be plausible (in the sense of gaining management approval)
unless it is "ATM compatible", i.e., there is a clear model of how it
will run over an ATM network. Although a fully detailed document such
as RFC 1577 is not needed immediately, it must be shown that the
basic model works.

Similar remarks could be made about X.25, Frame Relay, SMDS etc. but
ATM is the case with the highest management hype ratio today.

Policy routing and accounting

Unfortunately, this cannot be ignored, however much one would like
to. Funding agencies want traffic to flow over the lines funded to
carry it, and they want to know afterwards how much traffic there
was. Accounting information can also be used for network planning
and for back-charging.

It is therefore necessary that IPng and its routing procedures allow
traffic to be routed in a way that depends on its source and
destination in detail. (As an example, traffic from the Physics
department of MIT might be required to travel a different route to
CERN than traffic from any other department.)

A simple approach to this requirement is to insist that IPng must
support provider-based addressing and routing.

Accounting of traffic is required at the same level of detail (or
more, for example how much of the traffic is ftp and how much is
www?).

RFC 1671   IPng White Paper on Transition, etc.   August 1994

Both of these requirements will cost time or money and may impact
more than just the IP layer, but IPng should not duck them.

Security Considerations

Corporate network operators, and campus network operators who have
been hacked a few times, take this more seriously than many protocol
experts. Indeed many corporate network operators would see improved
security as a more compelling argument for transition to IPng than
anything else.

Since IPng will presumably be a datagram protocol, limiting what can
be done in terms of end-to-end security, IPng must allow more
effective firewalls in routers than IPv4. In particular efficient
traffic barring based on source and destination addresses and types
of transaction is needed.

It seems likely that the same features needed to allow policy routing
and detailed accounting would be needed for improved firewall
security. It is outside the scope of this document to discuss these
features in detail, but it seems unlikely that they are limited to
implementation details in the border routers. Packets will have to
carry some authenticated trace of the (source, destination,
transaction) triplet in order to check for unwanted traffic, to allow
policy-based source routing, and/or to allow detailed accounting.
Presumably any IPng will carry source and destination identifiers in
some format in every packet, but identifying the type of transaction,
or even the individual transaction, is an extra requirement.

Disclaimer and Acknowledgements

This is a personal view and does not necessarily represent that of my
employer.

CERN has been through three network transitions in recent years (IPv4
renumbering managed by John Gamble, AppleTalk Phase I to Phase II
transition managed by Mike Gerard, and DECnet Phase IV to DECnet/OSI
routing transition managed by Denise Heagerty). I could not have
written this document without having learnt from them. I have also
benefitted greatly from discussions with or the writings of many
people, especially various members of the IPng Directorate. Several
Directorate members gave comments that helped clarify this paper, as
did Bruce L Hutfless of Boeing. However the opinions are mine and
are not shared by all Directorate members.

RFC 1671   IPng White Paper on Transition, etc.   August 1994

Author's Address

Brian E. Carpenter
Group Leader, Communications Systems
Computing and Networks Division
CERN
European Laboratory for Particle Physics
1211 Geneva 23, Switzerland

Phone: +41 22 767-4967
Fax:+41 22 767-7155
Telex: 419000 cer ch
EMail: brian@dxcoms.cern.ch

Network Working Group   C. Huitema
Request for Comments: 1715   INRIA
Category: Informational   November 1994

          The H Ratio for Address Assignment Efficiency

Status of this Memo

This memo provides information for the Internet community. This memo
does not specify an Internet standard of any kind. Distribution of
this memo is unlimited.

Abstract

This document was submitted to the IETF IPng area in response to RFC
1550. Publication of this document does not imply acceptance by the
IPng area of any ideas expressed within. Comments should be
submitted to the author and/or the sipp@sunroof.eng.sun.com mailing
list.

Table of Contents

1. Efficiency of address assignment

A substantial part of the "IPng" debate was devoted to the choice of
an address size. A recurring concept was that of "assignment
efficiency", which most people involved in the discussion expressed
as a the ratio of the effective number of systems in the network over
the theoretical maximum. For example, the 32 bits IP addressing plan
could in theory number over 7 billions of systems; as of today, we
have about 3.5 millions of addresses reported in the DNS, which would
translate in an efficiency of 0.05%.

RFC 1715   H Ratio   November 1994

But this classic evaluation is misleading, as it does not take into account the number of hierarchical elements. IP addresses, for example, have at least three degrees of hierarchy: network, subnet and host. In order to remove these dependencies, I propose to use a logarithmic scale for the efficiency ratio:

$$H = \frac{\log \text{(number of objects)}}{\text{available bits}}$$

The ratio H is not too dependent of the number of hierarchical levels. Suppose for example that we have the choice between two levels, encoded on 8 bits each, and one single level, encoded in 16 bits. We will obtain the same efficiency if we allocate in average 100 elements at each 8 bits level, or simply 10000 elements in the single 16 bits level.

Note that I use base 10 logs in what follows, because they are easier to compute mentally. When it comes to large numbers, people tend to use "powers of 10", as in "IPng should be capable of numbering 1 E+15 systems". It follows from this choice of units that H varies between 0 and a theoretical maximum of 0.30103 (log base 10 of 2).

2. Estimating reasonable values for the ratio H:

Indeed, we don't expect to achieve a ratio of 0.3 in practice, and the interesting question is to assert the values which can be reasonably expected. We can try to evaluate them from existing numbering plans. What is especially interesting is to consider the moment where the plans broke, i.e. when people were forced to add digits to phone number, or to add bits to computer addresses. I have

a number of such figures handy, e.g.:

* Adding one digit to all French telephone numbers, moving from 8 digits to 9, when the number of phones reached a threshold of 1.0 E+7. The log value is 7, the number of bits was about 27 (1 decimal digit is about 3.3 bits). The ratio is thus 0.26

* Expending the number of areas in the US telephone system, making it effectively 10 digits long, for about 1.0 E+8 subscribers. The log value is 8, the number of bits is 33, the ratio is about 0.24

* Expending the size of the Internet addresses, from 32 bits to something else. There are currently about 3 million hosts on the net, for 32 bits. The log of 3.E6 is about 6.5; this gives a ratio of 0.20. Indeed, we believe that 32 bits will still be enough for some years, e.g. to multiply the number of hosts by 10, in which case the ratio would climb to 0.23

Huitema   [Page 2]

RFC 1715   H Ratio   November 1994

* Expending the size of the SITA 7 characters address. According to
their documentation, they have about 64000 addressed points in
their network, scattered in 1200 cities, 180 countries. An upper
case character provides about 5 bits of addressing, which results
in an efficiency of 0.14. This is an extreme case, as SITA uses
fixed length tokens in its hierarchy.

* The globally-connected physics/space science DECnet (Phase IV)
stopped growing at about 15K nodes (i.e. new nodes were hidden)
which in a 16 bit space gives a ratio of 0.26

* There are about 200 million IEEE 802 nodes in a 46 bit space, which
gives a ratio of 0.18. That number space, however, is not
saturated.

From these examples, we can assert that the efficiency ratio usually
lies between 0.14 and 0.26.

3. Evaluating proposed address plans

Using a reverse computation, we get the following population counts
in the network:

	Pessimistic (0.14)	Optimistic (0.26)
32 bits	3 E+4 (!)	2 E+8
64 bits	9 E+84	E+16
80 bits	1.6 E+11	2.6 E+27
128 bits	8 E+17	2 E+33

I guess that the figure explains well why some feel that 64 bits is
"not enough" while other feel it is "sufficient by a large margin":
depending of the assignment efficiency, we are either well below the
target or well above. But there is no question, in my view, that 128
bits is "more than enough". Even if we presume the lowest efficiency,
we are still way above the hyperbolic estimate of 1.E+15 Internet
hosts.

It is also interesting to note that if we devote 80 bits to the
"network" and use 48 bits for "server less autoconfiguration", we can
number more that E.11 networks in the pessimistic case - it would
only take an efficiency of 0.15 to reach the E+12 networks hyperbole.

I guess this explains well why I feel that 128 bits is entirely safe
for the next 30 year. The level of constraints that we will have to
incorporate in the address assignment appears very much in line with
what we know how to do, today.

RFC 1715   H Ratio   November 1994

4. Security Considerations

    Security issues are not discussed in this memo.

5. Author's Address

        Christian Huitema
        INRIA, Sophia-Antipolis
        2004 Route des Lucioles
        BP 109
        F-06561 Valbonne Cedex
        France

        Phone: +33 93 65 77 15
        EMail: Christian.Huitema@MIRSA.INRIA.FR

Network Working Group   R. Hinden
Request for Comments: 2373   Nokia
Obsoletes: 1884   S. Deering
Category: Standards Track   Cisco Systems

                  IP Version 6 Addressing Architecture

Status of this Memo

This document specifies an Internet standards track protocol for the
Internet community, and requests discussion and suggestions for
improvements. Please refer to the current edition of the "Internet
Official Protocol Standards" (STD 1) for the standardization state
and status of this protocol. Distribution of this memo is unlimited.

Copyright Notice

Abstract

This specification defines the addressing architecture of the IP
Version 6 protocol [IPV6]. The document includes the IPv6 addressing
model, text representations of IPv6 addresses, definition of IPv6
unicast addresses, anycast addresses, and multicast addresses, and an
IPv6 node's required addresses.

Table of Contents

RFC 2373   IPv6 Addressing Architecture   July 1998

1.0 INTRODUCTION

This specification defines the addressing architecture of the IP
Version 6 protocol. It includes a detailed description of the
currently defined address formats for IPv6 [IPV6].
The authors would like to acknowledge the contributions of Paul
Francis, Scott Bradner, Jim Bound, Brian Carpenter, Matt Crawford,
Deborah Estrin, Roger Fajman, Bob Fink, Peter Ford, Bob Gilligan,
Dimitry Haskin, Tom Harsch, Christian Huitema, Tony Li, Greg
Minshall, Thomas Narten, Erik Nordmark, Yakov Rekhter, Bill Simpson,
and Sue Thomson.

The key words "MUST", "MUST NOT", "REQUIRED", "SHALL", "SHALL NOT",
"SHOULD", "SHOULD NOT", "RECOMMENDED", "MAY", and "OPTIONAL" in this
document are to be interpreted as described in [RFC 2119].

2.0 IPv6 ADDRESSING

IPv6 addresses are 128-bit identifiers for interfaces and sets of
interfaces. There are three types of addresses:

Unicast: An identifier for a single interface. A packet sent to
            a unicast address is delivered to the interface
            identified by that address.

Anycast: An identifier for a set of interfaces (typically
            belonging to different nodes). A packet sent to an
            anycast address is delivered to one of the interfaces
            identified by that address (the "nearest" one, according
            to the routing protocols' measure of distance).

Multicast: An identifier for a set of interfaces (typically
            belonging to different nodes). A packet sent to a
            multicast address is delivered to all interfaces
            identified by that address.

RFC 2373   IPv6 Addressing Architecture   July 1998

There are no broadcast addresses in IPv6, their function being
superseded by multicast addresses.

In this document, fields in addresses are given a specific name, for
example "subscriber". When this name is used with the term "ID" for
identifier after the name (e.g., "subscriber ID"), it refers to the
contents of the named field. When it is used with the term "prefix"
(e.g. "subscriber prefix") it refers to all of the address up to and
including this field.

In IPv6, all zeros and all ones are legal values for any field,
unless specifically excluded. Specifically, prefixes may contain
zero-valued fields or end in zeros.

2.1 Addressing Model

IPv6 addresses of all types are assigned to interfaces, not nodes.
An IPv6 unicast address refers to a single interface. Since each
interface belongs to a single node, any of that node's interfaces'
unicast addresses may be used as an identifier for the node.
All interfaces are required to have at least one link-local unicast
address (see section 2.8 for additional required addresses). A
single interface may also be assigned multiple IPv6 addresses of any
type (unicast, anycast, and multicast) or scope. Unicast addresses
with scope greater than link-scope are not needed for interfaces that
are not used as the origin or destination of any IPv6 packets to or
from non-neighbors. This is sometimes convenient for point-to-point
interfaces. There is one exception to this addressing model:

> An unicast address or a set of unicast addresses may be assigned to
> multiple physical interfaces if the implementation treats the
> multiple physical interfaces as one interface when presenting it to
> the internet layer. This is useful for load-sharing over multiple
> physical interfaces.

Currently IPv6 continues the IPv4 model that a subnet prefix is
associated with one link. Multiple subnet prefixes may be assigned
to the same link.

2.2 Text Representation of Addresses

There are three conventional forms for representing IPv6 addresses as
text strings:

1. The preferred form is x:x:x:x:x:x:x:x, where the 'x's are the
hexadecimal values of the eight 16-bit pieces of the address.
Examples:

```
        FEDC:BA98:7654:3210:FEDC:BA98:7654:3210
        1080:0:0:0:8:800:200C:417A
```

Note that it is not necessary to write the leading zeros in an individual field, but there must be at least one numeral in every field (except for the case described in 2.).

2. Due to some methods of allocating certain styles of IPv6 addresses, it will be common for addresses to contain long strings of zero bits. In order to make writing addresses containing zero bits easier a special syntax is available to compress the zeros. The use of "::" indicates multiple groups of 16-bits of zeros. The "::" can only appear once in an address. The "::" can also be used to compress the leading and/or trailing zeros in an address.

For example the following addresses:

```
        1080:0:0:0:8:800:200C:417A        a unicast address
        FF01:0:0:0:0:0:0:101              a multicast address
        0:0:0:0:0:0:0:1                   the loopback address
        0:0:0:0:0:0:0:0                   the unspecified addresses
```

may be represented as:

```
        1080::8:800:200C:417A             a unicast address
        FF01::101                         a multicast address
        ::1                               the loopback address
        ::                                the unspecified addresses
```

3. An alternative form that is sometimes more convenient when dealing with a mixed environment of IPv4 and IPv6 nodes is x:x:x:x:x:x:d.d.d.d, where the 'x's are the hexadecimal values of the six high-order 16-bit pieces of the address, and the 'd's are the decimal values of the four low-order 8-bit pieces of the address (standard IPv4 representation). Examples:

```
        0:0:0:0:0:0:13.1.68.3

        0:0:0:0:0:FFFF:129.144.52.38
```

or in compressed form:

```
        ::13.1.68.3

        ::FFFF:129.144.52.38
```

RFC 2373   IPv6 Addressing Architecture   July 1998

2.3 Text Representation of Address Prefixes

The text representation of IPv6 address prefixes is similar to the
way IPv4 addresses prefixes are written in CIDR notation. An IPv6
address prefix is represented by the notation:

> ipv6-address/prefix-length

where

> ipv6-address   is an IPv6 address in any of the notations listed
> in section 2.2.

> prefix-length   is a decimal value specifying how many of the
> leftmost contiguous bits of the address comprise
> the prefix.

For example, the following are legal representations of the 60-bit
prefix 12AB00000000CD3 (hexadecimal):

> 12AB:0000:0000:CD30:0000:0000:0000:0000/60
> 12AB::CD30:0:0:0:0/60
> 12AB:0:0:CD30::/60

The following are NOT legal representations of the above prefix:

> 12AB:0:0:CD3/60   may drop leading zeros, but not trailing zeros,
> within any 16-bit chunk of the address

> 12AB::CD30/60   address to left of "/" expands to
> 12AB:0000:0000:0000:0000:000:0000:CD30

> 12AB::CD3/60   address to left of "/" expands to
> 12AB:0000:0000:0000:0000:000:0000:0CD3

When writing both a node address and a prefix of that node address
(e.g., the node's subnet prefix), the two can combined as follows:

> the node address   12AB:0:0:CD30:123:4567:89AB:CDEF
> and its subnet number   12AB:0:0:CD30::/60

> can be abbreviated as   12AB:0:0:CD30:123:4567:89AB:CDEF/60

RFC 2373   IPv6 Addressing Architecture   July 1998

2.4 Address Type Representation

The specific type of an IPv6 address is indicated by the leading bits
in the address. The variable-length field comprising these leading
bits is called the Format Prefix (FP). The initial allocation of
these prefixes is as follows:

Allocation	Prefix (binary)	Fraction of Address Space
Reserved	0000 0000	1/256
Unassigned	0000 000	11/256
Reserved for NSAP Allocation	0000 001	1/128
Reserved for IPX Allocation	0000 010	1/128
Unassigned	0000 011	1/128
Unassigned	0000	11/32
Unassigned	0001	1/16
Aggregatable Global Unicast Addresses	001	1/8
Unassigned	010	1/8
Unassigned	011	1/8
Unassigned	100	1/8
Unassigned	101	1/8
Unassigned	110	1/8
Unassigned	1110	1/16
Unassigned	1111 0	1/32
Unassigned	1111 10	1/64
Unassigned	1111 110	1/128
Unassigned	1111 1110 0	1/512
Link-Local Unicast Addresses	1111 1110 10	1/1024
Site-Local Unicast Addresses	1111 1110 11	1/1024
Multicast Addresses	1111 1111	1/256

Notes:

(1)   The "unspecified address" (see section 2.5.2), the loopback
       address (see section 2.5.3), and the IPv6 Addresses with
       Embedded IPv4 Addresses (see section 2.5.4), are assigned out
       of the 0000 0000 format prefix space.

(2)   The format prefixes 001 through 111, except for Multicast
       Addresses (1111 1111), are all required to have to have 64-bit
       interface identifiers in EUI-64 format. See section 2.5.1 for
       definitions.

This allocation supports the direct allocation of aggregation
addresses, local use addresses, and multicast addresses. Space is
reserved for NSAP addresses and IPX addresses. The remainder of the
address space is unassigned for future use. This can be used for
expansion of existing use (e.g., additional aggregatable addresses,
etc.) or new uses (e.g., separate locators and identifiers). Fifteen
percent of the address space is initially allocated. The remaining
85% is reserved for future use.

Unicast addresses are distinguished from multicast addresses by the
value of the high-order octet of the addresses: a value of FF
(11111111) identifies an address as a multicast address; any other
value identifies an address as a unicast address. Anycast addresses
are taken from the unicast address space, and are not syntactically
distinguishable from unicast addresses.

2.5 Unicast Addresses

IPv6 unicast addresses are aggregatable with contiguous bit-wise
masks similar to IPv4 addresses under Class-less Interdomain Routing
[CIDR].

There are several forms of unicast address assignment in IPv6,
including the global aggregatable global unicast address, the NSAP
address, the IPX hierarchical address, the site-local address, the
link-local address, and the IPv4-capable host address. Additional
address types can be defined in the future.

IPv6 nodes may have considerable or little knowledge of the internal
structure of the IPv6 address, depending on the role the node plays
(for instance, host versus router). At a minimum, a node may
consider that unicast addresses (including its own) have no internal
structure:

```
                          |128 bits|
+------------------------------------------------------------------+
                        | node address|
+------------------------------------------------------------------+
```

A slightly sophisticated host (but still rather simple) may
additionally be aware of subnet prefix(es) for the link(s) it is
attached to, where different addresses may have different values for
n:

```
|                    n bits                  |   128-n bits   |
+--------------------------------------------+----------------+
|                  subnet prefix             |  interface ID  |
+--------------------------------------------+----------------+
```

Still more sophisticated hosts may be aware of other hierarchical
boundaries in the unicast address. Though a very simple router may
have no knowledge of the internal structure of IPv6 unicast
addresses, routers will more generally have knowledge of one or more
of the hierarchical boundaries for the operation of routing
protocols. The known boundaries will differ from router to router,
depending on what positions the router holds in the routing
hierarchy.

2.5.1 Interface Identifiers

Interface identifiers in IPv6 unicast addresses are used to identify
interfaces on a link. They are required to be unique on that link.
They may also be unique over a broader scope. In many cases an
interface's identifier will be the same as that interface's link-
layer address. The same interface identifier may be used on multiple
interfaces on a single node.

Note that the use of the same interface identifier on multiple
interfaces of a single node does not affect the interface
identifier's global uniqueness or each IPv6 addresses global
uniqueness created using that interface identifier.

In a number of the format prefixes (see section 2.4) Interface IDs
are required to be 64 bits long and to be constructed in IEEE EUI-64
format [EUI64]. EUI-64 based Interface identifiers may have global
scope when a global token is available (e.g., IEEE 48bit MAC) or may
have local scope where a global token is not available (e.g., serial
links, tunnel end-points, etc.). It is required that the "u" bit
(universal/local bit in IEEE EUI-64 terminology) be inverted when
forming the interface identifier from the EUI-64. The "u" bit is set
to one (1) to indicate global scope, and it is set to zero (0) to
indicate local scope. The first three octets in binary of an EUI-64
identifier are as follows:

```
   0        0 0      1 1      2
   |0       7 8      5 6      3|
   +----+----+----+----+----+----+
   |cccc|ccug|cccc|cccc|cccc|cccc|
   +----+----+----+----+----+----+
```

written in Internet standard bit-order , where "u" is the
universal/local bit, "g" is the individual/group bit, and "c" are the
bits of the company_id. Appendix A: "Creating EUI-64 based Interface
Identifiers" provides examples on the creation of different EUI-64
based interface identifiers.

The motivation for inverting the "u" bit when forming the interface
identifier is to make it easy for system administrators to hand
configure local scope identifiers when hardware tokens are not
available. This is expected to be case for serial links, tunnel end-
points, etc. The alternative would have been for these to be of the
form 0200:0:0:1, 0200:0:0:2, etc., instead of the much simpler ::1,
::2, etc.

The use of the universal/local bit in the IEEE EUI-64 identifier is
to allow development of future technology that can take advantage of
interface identifiers with global scope.

The details of forming interface identifiers are defined in the
appropriate "IPv6 over <link>" specification such as "IPv6 over
Ethernet" [ETHER], "IPv6 over FDDI" [FDDI], etc.

2.5.2 The Unspecified Address

The address 0:0:0:0:0:0:0:0 is called the unspecified address. It
must never be assigned to any node. It indicates the absence of an
address. One example of its use is in the Source Address field of
any IPv6 packets sent by an initializing host before it has learned
its own address.

The unspecified address must not be used as the destination address
of IPv6 packets or in IPv6 Routing Headers.

2.5.3 The Loopback Address

The unicast address 0:0:0:0:0:0:0:1 is called the loopback address.
It may be used by a node to send an IPv6 packet to itself. It may
never be assigned to any physical interface. It may be thought of as
being associated with a virtual interface (e.g., the loopback
interface).

The loopback address must not be used as the source address in IPv6
packets that are sent outside of a single node. An IPv6 packet with
a destination address of loopback must never be sent outside of a
single node and must never be forwarded by an IPv6 router.

2.5.4 IPv6 Addresses with Embedded IPv4 Addresses

The IPv6 transition mechanisms [TRAN] include a technique for hosts
and routers to dynamically tunnel IPv6 packets over IPv4 routing
infrastructure. IPv6 nodes that utilize this technique are assigned
special IPv6 unicast addresses that carry an IPv4 address in the low-
order 32-bits. This type of address is termed an "IPv4-compatible
IPv6 address" and has the format:

```
|                80 bits               | 16 |      32 bits        |
+--------------------------------------+--------------------------+
|0000..............................0000|0000|    IPv4 address     |
+--------------------------------------+----+--------------------+
```

A second type of IPv6 address which holds an embedded IPv4 address is
also defined. This address is used to represent the addresses of
IPv4-only nodes (those that *do not* support IPv6) as IPv6 addresses.
This type of address is termed an "IPv4-mapped IPv6 address" and has
the format:

```
|                80 bits               | 16 |      32 bits        |
+--------------------------------------+--------------------------+
|0000..............................0000|FFFF|    IPv4 address     |
+--------------------------------------+----+--------------------+
```

2.5.5 NSAP Addresses

This mapping of NSAP address into IPv6 addresses is defined in
[NSAP]. This document recommends that network implementors who have
planned or deployed an OSI NSAP addressing plan, and who wish to
deploy or transition to IPv6, should redesign a native IPv6
addressing plan to meet their needs. However, it also defines a set
of mechanisms for the support of OSI NSAP addressing in an IPv6
network. These mechanisms are the ones that must be used if such
support is required. This document also defines a mapping of IPv6
addresses within the OSI address format, should this be required.

2.5.6 IPX Addresses

This mapping of IPX address into IPv6 addresses is as follows:

```
|   7   |                      121 bits                           |
+-------+---------------------------------------------------------+
|0000010|                    to be defined                        |
+-------+---------------------------------------------------------+
```

The draft definition, motivation, and usage are under study.

RFC 2373   IPv6 Addressing Architecture   July 1998

2.5.7 Aggregatable Global Unicast Addresses

The global aggregatable global unicast address is defined in [AGGR].
This address format is designed to support both the current provider
based aggregation and a new type of aggregation called exchanges.
The combination will allow efficient routing aggregation for both
sites which connect directly to providers and who connect to
exchanges. Sites will have the choice to connect to either type of
aggregation point.

The IPv6 aggregatable global unicast address format is as follows:

```
| 3| 13  | 8 |   24   |   16   |            64 bits              |
+--+-----+---+--------+--------+--------------------------------+
|FP| TLA |RES|  NLA   |  SLA   |          Interface ID          |
|  | ID  |   |  ID    |  ID    |                                |
+--+-----+---+--------+--------+--------------------------------+
```

Where

```
        001             Format Prefix (3 bit) for Aggregatable Global
                        Unicast Addresses
        TLA ID          Top-Level Aggregation Identifier
        RES             Reserved for future use
        NLA ID          Next-Level Aggregation Identifier
        SLA ID          Site-Level Aggregation Identifier
        INTERFACE ID    Interface Identifier
```

The contents, field sizes, and assignment rules are defined in
[AGGR].

2.5.8 Local-Use IPv6 Unicast Addresses

There are two types of local-use unicast addresses defined. These
are Link-Local and Site-Local. The Link-Local is for use on a single
link and the Site-Local is for use in a single site. Link-Local
addresses have the following format:

```
|    10    |
|   bits   |         54 bits         |           64 bits          |
+----------+-------------------------+----------------------------+
|1111111010|            0            |        interface ID        |
+----------+-------------------------+----------------------------+
```

Link-Local addresses are designed to be used for addressing on a
single link for purposes such as auto-address configuration, neighbor
discovery, or when no routers are present.

RFC 2373   IPv6 Addressing Architecture   July 1998

Routers must not forward any packets with link-local source or
destination addresses to other links.

Site-Local addresses have the following format:

```
|    10   |
|   bits  |  38 bits   |  16 bits  |              64 bits             |
+---------+------------+-----------+----------------------------------+
|1111111011|     0     | subnet ID |            interface ID          |
+---------+------------+-----------+----------------------------------+
```

Site-Local addresses are designed to be used for addressing inside of
a site without the need for a global prefix.

Routers must not forward any packets with site-local source or
destination addresses outside of the site.

2.6 Anycast Addresses

An IPv6 anycast address is an address that is assigned to more than
one interface (typically belonging to different nodes), with the
property that a packet sent to an anycast address is routed to the
"nearest" interface having that address, according to the routing
protocols' measure of distance.

Anycast addresses are allocated from the unicast address space, using
any of the defined unicast address formats. Thus, anycast addresses
are syntactically indistinguishable from unicast addresses. When a
unicast address is assigned to more than one interface, thus turning
it into an anycast address, the nodes to which the address is
assigned must be explicitly configured to know that it is an anycast
address.

For any assigned anycast address, there is a longest address prefix P
that identifies the topological region in which all interfaces
belonging to that anycast address reside. Within the region
identified by P, each member of the anycast set must be advertised as
a separate entry in the routing system (commonly referred to as a
"host route"); outside the region identified by P, the anycast
address may be aggregated into the routing advertisement for prefix
P.

Note that in, the worst case, the prefix P of an anycast set may be
the null prefix, i.e., the members of the set may have no topological
locality. In that case, the anycast address must be advertised as a
separate routing entry throughout the entire internet, which presents

a severe scaling limit on how many such "global" anycast sets may be supported. Therefore, it is expected that support for global anycast sets may be unavailable or very restricted.

One expected use of anycast addresses is to identify the set of routers belonging to an organization providing internet service. Such addresses could be used as intermediate addresses in an IPv6 Routing header, to cause a packet to be delivered via a particular aggregation or sequence of aggregations. Some other possible uses are to identify the set of routers attached to a particular subnet, or the set of routers providing entry into a particular routing domain.

There is little experience with widespread, arbitrary use of internet anycast addresses, and some known complications and hazards when using them in their full generality [ANYCST]. Until more experience has been gained and solutions agreed upon for those problems, the following restrictions are imposed on IPv6 anycast addresses:

 o An anycast address must not be used as the source address of an
   IPv6 packet.

 o An anycast address must not be assigned to an IPv6 host, that
   is, it may be assigned to an IPv6 router only.

2.6.1 Required Anycast Address

The Subnet-Router anycast address is predefined. Its format is as follows:

```
|                    n bits                    |   128-n bits   |
+----------------------------------------------+----------------+
|                 subnet prefix                | 00000000000000 |
+----------------------------------------------+----------------+
```

The "subnet prefix" in an anycast address is the prefix which identifies a specific link. This anycast address is syntactically the same as a unicast address for an interface on the link with the interface identifier set to zero.

Packets sent to the Subnet-Router anycast address will be delivered to one router on the subnet. All routers are required to support the Subnet-Router anycast addresses for the subnets which they have interfaces.

The subnet-router anycast address is intended to be used for
applications where a node needs to communicate with one of a set of
routers on a remote subnet. For example when a mobile host needs to
communicate with one of the mobile agents on its "home" subnet.

2.7 Multicast Addresses

An IPv6 multicast address is an identifier for a group of nodes. A
node may belong to any number of multicast groups. Multicast
addresses have the following format:

```
|   8    |  4 |  4 |                  112 bits                     |
+------- -+----+----+-----------------------------------------------+
|11111111|flgs|scop|                 group ID                      |
+--------+----+----+-----------------------------------------------+
```

11111111 at the start of the address identifies the address as
being a multicast address.

```
                              +-+-+-+-+
flgs is a set of 4 flags:     |0|0|0|T|
                              +-+-+-+-+
```

    The high-order 3 flags are reserved, and must be initialized to
0.

    T = 0 indicates a permanently-assigned ("well-known") multicast
address, assigned by the global internet numbering authority.

    T = 1 indicates a non-permanently-assigned ("transient")
multicast address.

scop is a 4-bit multicast scope value used to limit the scope of
the multicast group. The values are:

    0 reserved
    1 node-local scope
    2 link-local scope
    3 (unassigned)
    4 (unassigned)
    5 site-local scope
    6 (unassigned)
    7 (unassigned)
    8 organization-local scope
    9 (unassigned)
    A (unassigned)
    B (unassigned)
    C (unassigned)

RFC 2373   IPv6 Addressing Architecture   July 1998

    D (unassigned)
    E global scope
    F reserved

group ID identifies the multicast group, either permanent or
transient, within the given scope.

The "meaning" of a permanently-assigned multicast address is
independent of the scope value. For example, if the "NTP servers
group" is assigned a permanent multicast address with a group ID of
101 (hex), then:

    FF01:0:0:0:0:0:0:101 means all NTP servers on the same node as the
    sender.

    FF02:0:0:0:0:0:0:101 means all NTP servers on the same link as the
    sender.

    FF05:0:0:0:0:0:0:101 means all NTP servers at the same site as the
    sender.

    FF0E:0:0:0:0:0:0:101 means all NTP servers in the internet.

Non-permanently-assigned multicast addresses are meaningful only
within a given scope. For example, a group identified by the non-
permanent, site-local multicast address FF15:0:0:0:0:0:0:101 at one
site bears no relationship to a group using the same address at a
different site, nor to a non-permanent group using the same group ID
with different scope, nor to a permanent group with the same group
ID.

Multicast addresses must not be used as source addresses in IPv6
packets or appear in any routing header.

2.7.1 Pre-Defined Multicast Addresses

The following well-known multicast addresses are pre-defined:

Reserved Multicast Addresses: FF00:0:0:0:0:0:0:0
                                     FF01:0:0:0:0:0:0:0
                                     FF02:0:0:0:0:0:0:0
                                     FF03:0:0:0:0:0:0:0
                                     FF04:0:0:0:0:0:0:0
                                     FF05:0:0:0:0:0:0:0
                                     FF06:0:0:0:0:0:0:0
                                     FF07:0:0:0:0:0:0:0
                                     FF08:0:0:0:0:0:0:0
                                     FF09:0:0:0:0:0:0:0

RFC 2373   IPv6 Addressing Architecture   July 1998

                            FF0A:0:0:0:0:0:0:0
                            FF0B:0:0:0:0:0:0:0
                            FF0C:0:0:0:0:0:0:0
                            FF0D:0:0:0:0:0:0:0
                            FF0E:0:0:0:0:0:0:0
                            FF0F:0:0:0:0:0:0:0

The above multicast addresses are reserved and shall never be
assigned to any multicast group.

        All Nodes Addresses   FF01:0:0:0:0:0:0:1
                                   FF02:0:0:0:0:0:0:1

The above multicast addresses identify the group of all IPv6 nodes,
within scope 1 (node-local) or 2 (link-local).

        All Routers Addresses: FF01:0:0:0:0:0:0:2
                                   FF02:0:0:0:0:0:0:2
                                   FF05:0:0:0:0:0:0:2

The above multicast addresses identify the group of all IPv6 routers,
within scope 1 (node-local), 2 (link-local), or 5 (site-local).

        Solicited-Node Address: FF02:0:0:0:0:1:FFXX:XXXX

The above multicast address is computed as a function of a node's
unicast and anycast addresses. The solicited-node multicast address
is formed by taking the low-order 24 bits of the address (unicast or
anycast) and appending those bits to the prefix
FF02:0:0:0:0:1:FF00::/104 resulting in a multicast address in the
range

        FF02:0:0:0:0:1:FF00:0000

to

        FF02:0:0:0:0:1:FFFF:FFFF

For example, the solicited node multicast address corresponding to
the IPv6 address 4037::01:800:200E:8C6C is FF02::1:FF0E:8C6C. IPv6
addresses that differ only in the high-order bits, e.g. due to
multiple high-order prefixes associated with different aggregations,
will map to the same solicited-node address thereby reducing the
number of multicast addresses a node must join.

A node is required to compute and join the associated Solicited-Node
multicast addresses for every unicast and anycast address it is
assigned.

2.7.2 Assignment of New IPv6 Multicast Addresses

The current approach [ETHER] to map IPv6 multicast addresses into
IEEE 802 MAC addresses takes the low order 32 bits of the IPv6
multicast address and uses it to create a MAC address. Note that
Token Ring networks are handled differently. This is defined in
[TOKEN]. Group ID's less than or equal to 32 bits will generate
unique MAC addresses. Due to this new IPv6 multicast addresses
should be assigned so that the group identifier is always in the low
order 32 bits as shown in the following:

```
|   8    |  4 |  4 |              80 bits            |    32 bits   |
+------- -+----+----+--------------------------------+--------------+
|11111111|flgs|scop|    reserved must be zero        |   group ID   |
+--------+----+----+--------------------------------+--------------+
```

While this limits the number of permanent IPv6 multicast groups to
2^32 this is unlikely to be a limitation in the future. If it
becomes necessary to exceed this limit in the future multicast will
still work but the processing will be sightly slower.

Additional IPv6 multicast addresses are defined and registered by the
IANA [MASGN].

2.8 A Node's Required Addresses

A host is required to recognize the following addresses as
identifying itself:

>   o Its Link-Local Address for each interface
>   o Assigned Unicast Addresses
>   o Loopback Address
>   o All-Nodes Multicast Addresses
>   o Solicited-Node Multicast Address for each of its assigned
>   unicast and anycast addresses
>   o Multicast Addresses of all other groups to which the host
>   belongs.

A router is required to recognize all addresses that a host is
required to recognize, plus the following addresses as identifying
itself:

>   o The Subnet-Router anycast addresses for the interfaces it is
>   configured to act as a router on.
>   o All other Anycast addresses with which the router has been
>   configured.
>   o All-Routers Multicast Addresses

RFC 2373   IPv6 Addressing Architecture   July 1998

   o Multicast Addresses of all other groups to which the router
     belongs.

The only address prefixes which should be predefined in an
implementation are the:

   o Unspecified Address
   o Loopback Address
   o Multicast Prefix (FF)
   o Local-Use Prefixes (Link-Local and Site-Local)
   o Pre-Defined Multicast Addresses
   o IPv4-Compatible Prefixes

Implementations should assume all other addresses are unicast unless
specifically configured (e.g., anycast addresses).

3. Security Considerations

IPv6 addressing documents do not have any direct impact on Internet
infrastructure security. Authentication of IPv6 packets is defined
in [AUTH].

RFC 2373   IPv6 Addressing Architecture   July 1998

APPENDIX A : Creating EUI-64 based Interface Identifiers

Depending on the characteristics of a specific link or node there are
a number of approaches for creating EUI-64 based interface
identifiers. This appendix describes some of these approaches.

Links or Nodes with EUI-64 Identifiers

The only change needed to transform an EUI-64 identifier to an
interface identifier is to invert the "u" (universal/local) bit. For
example, a globally unique EUI-64 identifier of the form:

```
|0              1|1              3|3              4|4              6|
|0              5|6              1|2              7|8              3|
+----------------+----------------+----------------+----------------+
|cccccc0gcccccccc|ccccccccmmmmmmmm|mmmmmmmmmmmmmmmm|mmmmmmmmmmmmmmmm|
+----------------+----------------+----------------+----------------+
```

where "c" are the bits of the assigned company_id, "0" is the value
of the universal/local bit to indicate global scope, "g" is
individual/group bit, and "m" are the bits of the manufacturer-
selected extension identifier. The IPv6 interface identifier would
be of the form:

```
|0              1|1              3|3              4|4              6|
|0              5|6              1|2              7|8              3|
+----------------+----------------+----------------+----------------+
|cccccc0gcccccccc|ccccccccmmmmmmmm|mmmmmmmmmmmmmmmm|mmmmmmmmmmmmmmmm|
+----------------+----------------+----------------+----------------+
```

The only change is inverting the value of the universal/local bit.

Links or Nodes with IEEE 802 48 bit MAC's

[EUI64] defines a method to create a EUI-64 identifier from an IEEE
48bit MAC identifier. This is to insert two octets, with hexadecimal
values of 0xFF and 0xFE, in the middle of the 48 bit MAC (between the
company_id and vendor supplied id). For example the 48 bit MAC with
global scope:

```
|0              1|1              3|3              4|
|0              5|6              1|2              7|
+----------------+----------------+----------------+
|cccccc0gcccccccc|ccccccccmmmmmmmm|mmmmmmmmmmmmmmmm|
+----------------+----------------+----------------+
```

RFC 2373   IPv6 Addressing Architecture   July 1998

where "c" are the bits of the assigned company_id, "0" is the value
of the universal/local bit to indicate global scope, "g" is
individual/group bit, and "m" are the bits of the manufacturer-
selected extension identifier. The interface identifier would be of
the form:

```
|0               1|1             3|3             4|4             6|
|0               5|6             1|2             7|8             3|
+----------------+---------------+---------------+---------------+
| cccccc1gcccccccc |cccccccc11111111|11111110mmmmmmmm| mmmmmmmmmmmmmmmm|
+----------------+---------------+---------------+---------------+
```

When IEEE 802 48bit MAC addresses are available (on an interface or a
node), an implementation should use them to create interface
identifiers due to their availability and uniqueness properties.

Links with Non-Global Identifiers

There are a number of types of links that, while multi-access, do not
have globally unique link identifiers. Examples include LocalTalk
and Arcnet. The method to create an EUI-64 formatted identifier is
to take the link identifier (e.g., the LocalTalk 8 bit node
identifier) and zero fill it to the left. For example a LocalTalk 8
bit node identifier of hexadecimal value 0x4F results in the
following interface identifier:

```
|0               1|1             3|3             4|4             6|
|0               5|6             1|2             7|8             3|
+----------------+---------------+---------------+---------------+
| 0000000000000000 |0000000000000000|0000000000000000| 0000000001001111 |
+----------------+---------------+---------------+---------------+
```

Note that this results in the universal/local bit set to "0" to
indicate local scope.

Links without Identifiers

There are a number of links that do not have any type of built-in
identifier. The most common of these are serial links and configured
tunnels. Interface identifiers must be chosen that are unique for
the link.

When no built-in identifier is available on a link the preferred
approach is to use a global interface identifier from another
interface or one which is assigned to the node itself. To use this
approach no other interface connecting the same node to the same link
may use the same identifier.

If there is no global interface identifier available for use on the
link the implementation needs to create a local scope interface
identifier. The only requirement is that it be unique on the link.
There are many possible approaches to select a link-unique interface
identifier. They include:

>   Manual Configuration
>   Generated Random Number
>   Node Serial Number (or other node-specific token)

The link-unique interface identifier should be generated in a manner
that it does not change after a reboot of a node or if interfaces are
added or deleted from the node.

The selection of the appropriate algorithm is link and implementation
dependent. The details on forming interface identifiers are defined
in the appropriate "IPv6 over <link>" specification. It is strongly
recommended that a collision detection algorithm be implemented as
part of any automatic algorithm.

RFC 2373   IPv6 Addressing Architecture   July 1998

APPENDIX B: ABNF Description of Text Representations

This appendix defines the text representation of IPv6 addresses and
prefixes in Augmented BNF [ABNF] for reference purposes.

```
        IPv6address = hexpart [ ":" IPv4address ]
        IPv4address = 1*3DIGIT "." 1*3DIGIT "." 1*3DIGIT "." 1*3DIGIT

        IPv6prefix = hexpart "/" 1*2DIGIT

        hexpart = hexseq | hexseq "::" [ hexseq ] | "::" [ hexseq ]
        hexseq = hex4 *( ":" hex4)
        hex4= 1*4HEXDIG
```

RFC 2373   IPv6 Addressing Architecture   July 1998

APPENDIX C: CHANGES FROM RFC-1884

The following changes were made from RFC-1884 "IP Version 6
Addressing Architecture":

- Added an appendix providing a ABNF description of text
  representations.
- Clarification that link unique identifiers not change after
  reboot or other interface reconfigurations.
- Clarification of Address Model based on comments.
- Changed aggregation format terminology to be consistent with
  aggregation draft.
- Added text to allow interface identifier to be used on more than
  one interface on same node.
- Added rules for defining new multicast addresses.
- Added appendix describing procedures for creating EUI-64 based
  interface ID's.
- Added notation for defining IPv6 prefixes.
- Changed solicited node multicast definition to use a longer
  prefix.
- Added site scope all routers multicast address.
- Defined Aggregatable Global Unicast Addresses to use "001" Format
  Prefix.
- Changed "010" (Provider-Based Unicast) and "100" (Reserved for
  Geographic) Format Prefixes to Unassigned.
- Added section on Interface ID definition for unicast addresses.
  Requires use of EUI-64 in range of format prefixes and rules for
  setting global/local scope bit in EUI-64.
- Updated NSAP text to reflect working in RFC1888.
- Removed protocol specific IPv6 multicast addresses (e.g., DHCP)
  and referenced the IANA definitions.
- Removed section "Unicast Address Example". Had become OBE.
- Added new and updated references.
- Minor text clarifications and improvements.

RFC 2373   IPv6 Addressing Architecture   July 1998

REFERENCES

    [ABNF]   Crocker, D., and P. Overell, "Augmented BNF for
               Syntax Specifications: ABNF", RFC 2234, November 1997.

    [AGGR]   Hinden, R., O'Dell, M., and S. Deering, "An
               Aggregatable Global Unicast Address Format", RFC 2374, July
               1998.

    [AUTH]   Atkinson, R., "IP Authentication Header", RFC 1826, August
               1995.

    [ANYCST]   Partridge, C., Mendez, T., and W. Milliken, "Host
               Anycasting Service", RFC 1546, November 1993.

    [CIDR]   Fuller, V., Li, T., Yu, J., and K. Varadhan, "Classless
               Inter-Domain Routing (CIDR): An Address Assignment and
               Aggregation Strategy", RFC 1519, September 1993.

    [ETHER]   Crawford, M., "Transmission of IPv6 Pacekts over Ethernet
               Networks", Work in Progress.

    [EUI64]   IEEE, "Guidelines for 64-bit Global Identifier (EUI-64)
               Registration Authority",
               http://standards.ieee.org/db/oui/tutorials/EUI64.html,
               March 1997.

    [FDDI]   Crawford, M., "Transmission of IPv6 Packets over FDDI
               Networks", Work in Progress.

    [IPV6]   Deering, S., and R. Hinden, Editors, "Internet Protocol,
               Version 6 (IPv6) Specification", RFC 1883, December 1995.

    [MASGN]   Hinden, R., and S. Deering, "IPv6 Multicast Address
               Assignments", RFC 2375, July 1998.

    [NSAP]   Bound, J., Carpenter, B., Harrington, D., Houldsworth, J.,
               and A. Lloyd, "OSI NSAPs and IPv6", RFC 1888, August 1996.

    [RFC2119] Bradner, S., "Key words for use in RFCs to Indicate
               Requirement Levels", BCP 14, RFC 2119, March 1997.

    [TOKEN]   Thomas, S., "Transmission of IPv6 Packets over Token Ring
               Networks", Work in Progress.

    [TRAN]   Gilligan, R., and E. Nordmark, "Transition Mechanisms for
               IPv6 Hosts and Routers", RFC 1993, April 1996.

RFC 2373   IPv6 Addressing Architecture   July 1998

AUTHORS' ADDRESSES

Robert M. Hinden
Nokia
232 Java Drive
Sunnyvale, CA 94089
USA

Phone: +1 408 990-2004
Fax:+1 408 743-5677
EMail: hinden@iprg.nokia.com

Stephen E. Deering
Cisco Systems, Inc.
170 West Tasman Drive
San Jose, CA 95134-1706
USA

Phone: +1 408 527-8213
Fax:+1 408 527-8254
EMail: deering@cisco.com

RFC 2373   IPv6 Addressing Architecture   July 1998

Full Copyright Statement

   Copyright (C) The Internet Society (1998). All Rights Reserved.

   This document and translations of it may be copied and furnished to
   others, and derivative works that comment on or otherwise explain it
   or assist in its implementation may be prepared, copied, published
   and distributed, in whole or in part, without restriction of any
   kind, provided that the above copyright notice and this paragraph are
   included on all such copies and derivative works. However, this
   document itself may not be modified in any way, such as by removing
   the copyright notice or references to the Internet Society or other
   Internet organizations, except as needed for the purpose of
   developing Internet standards in which case the procedures for
   copyrights defined in the Internet Standards process must be
   followed, or as required to translate it into languages other than
   English.

   The limited permissions granted above are perpetual and will not be
   revoked by the Internet Society or its successors or assigns.

   This document and the information contained herein is provided on an
   "AS IS" basis and THE INTERNET SOCIETY AND THE INTERNET ENGINEERING
   TASK FORCE DISCLAIMS ALL WARRANTIES, EXPRESS OR IMPLIED, INCLUDING
   BUT NOT LIMITED TO ANY WARRANTY THAT THE USE OF THE INFORMATION
   HEREIN WILL NOT INFRINGE ANY RIGHTS OR ANY IMPLIED WARRANTIES OF
   MERCHANTABILITY OR FITNESS FOR A PARTICULAR PURPOSE.

Network Working Group   R. Hinden
Request for Comments: 2374   Nokia
Obsoletes: 2073   M. O'Dell
Category: Standards Track   UUNET
                                                               S. Deering
                                                                    Cisco
                                                                July 1998

             An IPv6 Aggregatable Global Unicast Address Format

Status of this Memo

This document specifies an Internet standards track protocol for the
Internet community, and requests discussion and suggestions for
improvements. Please refer to the current edition of the "Internet
Official Protocol Standards" (STD 1) for the standardization state
and status of this protocol. Distribution of this memo is unlimited.

Copyright Notice

1.0 Introduction

This document defines an IPv6 aggregatable global unicast address
format for use in the Internet. The address format defined in this
document is consistent with the IPv6 Protocol [IPV6] and the "IPv6
Addressing Architecture" [ARCH]. It is designed to facilitate
scalable Internet routing.

This documented replaces RFC 2073, "An IPv6 Provider-Based Unicast
Address Format". RFC 2073 will become historic. The Aggregatable
Global Unicast Address Format is an improvement over RFC 2073 in a
number of areas. The major changes include removal of the registry
bits because they are not needed for route aggregation, support of
EUI-64 based interface identifiers, support of provider and exchange
based aggregation, separation of public and site topology, and new
aggregation based terminology.

The key words "MUST", "MUST NOT", "REQUIRED", "SHALL", "SHALL NOT",
"SHOULD", "SHOULD NOT", "RECOMMENDED", "MAY", and "OPTIONAL" in this
document are to be interpreted as described in [RFC 2119].

RFC 2374   IPv6 Global Unicast Address Format   July 1998

2.0 Overview of the IPv6 Address

IPv6 addresses are 128-bit identifiers for interfaces and sets of interfaces. There are three types of addresses: Unicast, Anycast, and Multicast. This document defines a specific type of Unicast address.

In this document, fields in addresses are given specific names, for example "subnet". When this name is used with the term "ID" (for "identifier") after the name (e.g., "subnet ID"), it refers to the contents of the named field. When it is used with the term "prefix" (e.g. "subnet prefix") it refers to all of the addressing bits to the left of and including this field.

IPv6 unicast addresses are designed assuming that the Internet routing system makes forwarding decisions based on a "longest prefix match" algorithm on arbitrary bit boundaries and does not have any knowledge of the internal structure of IPv6 addresses. The structure in IPv6 addresses is for assignment and allocation. The only exception to this is the distinction made between unicast and multicast addresses.

The specific type of an IPv6 address is indicated by the leading bits in the address. The variable-length field comprising these leading bits is called the Format Prefix (FP).

This document defines an address format for the 001 (binary) Format Prefix for Aggregatable Global Unicast addresses. The same address format could be used for other Format Prefixes, as long as these Format Prefixes also identify IPv6 unicast addresses. Only the "001" Format Prefix is defined here.

3.0 IPv6 Aggregatable Global Unicast Address Format

This document defines an address format for the IPv6 aggregatable global unicast address assignment. The authors believe that this address format will be widely used for IPv6 nodes connected to the Internet. This address format is designed to support both the current provider-based aggregation and a new type of exchange-based aggregation. The combination will allow efficient routing aggregation for sites that connect directly to providers and for sites that connect to exchanges. Sites will have the choice to connect to either type of aggregation entity.

RFC 2374   IPv6 Global Unicast Address Format   July 1998

While this address format is designed to support exchange-based
aggregation (in addition to current provider-based aggregation) it is
not dependent on exchanges for it's overall route aggregation
properties. It will provide efficient route aggregation with only
provider-based aggregation.

Aggregatable addresses are organized into a three level hierarchy:

- Public Topology
- Site Topology
- Interface Identifier

Public topology is the collection of providers and exchanges who
provide public Internet transit services. Site topology is local to
a specific site or organization which does not provide public transit
service to nodes outside of the site. Interface identifiers identify
interfaces on links.

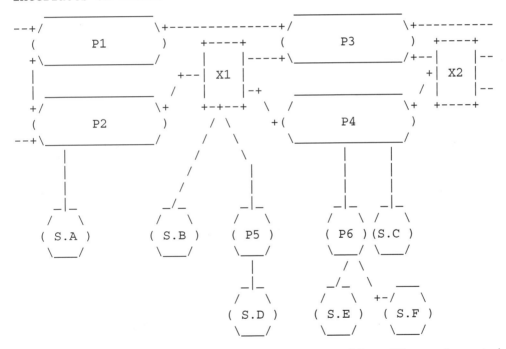

As shown in the figure above, the aggregatable address format is
designed to support long-haul providers (shown as P1, P2, P3, and
P4), exchanges (shown as X1 and X2), multiple levels of providers
(shown at P5 and P6), and subscribers (shown as S.x) Exchanges
(unlike current NAPs, FIXes, etc.) will allocate IPv6 addresses.
Organizations who connect to these exchanges will also subscribe
(directly, indirectly via the exchange, etc.) for long-haul service
from one or more long-haul providers. Doing so, they will achieve

addressing independence from long-haul transit providers. They will
be able to change long-haul providers without having to renumber
their organization. They can also be multihomed via the exchange to
more than one long-haul provider without having to have address
prefixes from each long-haul provider. Note that the mechanisms used
for this type of provider selection and portability are not discussed
in the document.

3.1 Aggregatable Global Unicast Address Structure

The aggregatable global unicast address format is as follows:

```
| 3|  13 | 8 |   24   |   16   |             64 bits             |
+--+-----+---+--------+--------+--------------------------------+
|FP| TLA |RES|  NLA   |  SLA   |          Interface ID          |
|  | ID  |   |  ID    |  ID    |                                |
+--+-----+---+--------+--------+--------------------------------+

<--Public Topology--->Site
<-------->
Topology
<------Interface Identifier----->
```

Where

```
        FP              Format Prefix (001)
        TLA ID          Top-Level Aggregation Identifier
        RES             Reserved for future use
        NLA ID          Next-Level Aggregation Identifier
        SLA ID          Site-Level Aggregation Identifier
        INTERFACE ID    Interface Identifier
```

The following sections specify each part of the IPv6 Aggregatable
Global Unicast address format.

3.2 Top-Level Aggregation ID

Top-Level Aggregation Identifiers (TLA ID) are the top level in the
routing hierarchy. Default-free routers must have a routing table
entry for every active TLA ID and will probably have additional
entries providing routing information for the TLA ID in which they
are located. They may have additional entries in order to optimize
routing for their specific topology, but the routing topology at all
levels must be designed to minimize the number of additional entries
fed into the default free routing tables.

RFC 2374   IPv6 Global Unicast Address Format   July 1998

This addressing format supports 8,192 (2^13) TLA ID's. Additional TLA ID's may be added by either growing the TLA field to the right into the reserved field or by using this format for additional format prefixes.

The issues relating to TLA ID assignment are beyond the scope of this document. They will be described in a document under preparation.

3.3 Reserved

The Reserved field is reserved for future use and must be set to zero.

The Reserved field allows for future growth of the TLA and NLA fields as appropriate. See section 4.0 for a discussion.

3.4 Next-Level Aggregation Identifier

Next-Level Aggregation Identifier's are used by organizations assigned a TLA ID to create an addressing hierarchy and to identify sites. The organization can assign the top part of the NLA ID in a manner to create an addressing hierarchy appropriate to its network. It can use the remainder of the bits in the field to identify sites it wishes to serve. This is shown as follows:

```
| n |     24-n bits      |   16   |     64 bits     |
+-----+--------------------+--------+-----------------+
|NLA1 |      Site ID       | SLA ID |  Interface ID   |
+-----+--------------------+--------+-----------------+
```

Each organization assigned a TLA ID receives 24 bits of NLA ID space. This NLA ID space allows each organization to provide service to approximately as many organizations as the current IPv4 Internet can support total networks.

Organizations assigned TLA ID's may also support NLA ID's in their own Site ID space. This allows the organization assigned a TLA ID to provide service to organizations providing public transit service and to organizations who do not provide public transit service. These organizations receiving an NLA ID may also choose to use their Site ID space to support other NLA ID's. This is shown as follows:

RFC 2374   IPv6 Global Unicast Address Format   July 1998

```
  | n |     24-n bits      |   16   |     64 bits     |
  +-----+-------------------+--------+-----------------+
  |NLA1 |      Site ID      | SLA ID |  Interface ID   |
  +-----+-------------------+--------+-----------------+

        | m |    24-n-m     |   16   |     64 bits     |
        +-----+-------------+--------+-----------------+
        |NLA2 |   Site ID   | SLA ID |  Interface ID   |
        +-----+-------------+--------+-----------------+

              | o |24-n-m-o|   16   |     64 bits     |
              +-----+--------+--------+-----------------+
              |NLA3 | Site ID| SLA ID |  Interface ID   |
              +-----+--------+--------+-----------------+
```

The design of the bit layout of the NLA ID space for a specific TLA
ID is left to the organization responsible for that TLA ID. Likewise
the design of the bit layout of the next level NLA ID is the
responsibility of the previous level NLA ID. It is recommended that
organizations assigning NLA address space use "slow start" allocation
procedures similar to [RFC2050].

The design of an NLA ID allocation plan is a tradeoff between routing
aggregation efficiency and flexibility. Creating hierarchies allows
for greater amount of aggregation and results in smaller routing
tables. Flat NLA ID assignment provides for easier allocation and
attachment flexibility, but results in larger routing tables.

3.5 Site-Level Aggregation Identifier

The SLA ID field is used by an individual organization to create its
own local addressing hierarchy and to identify subnets. This is
analogous to subnets in IPv4 except that each organization has a much
greater number of subnets. The 16 bit SLA ID field support 65,535
individual subnets.

Organizations may choose to either route their SLA ID "flat" (e.g.,
not create any logical relationship between the SLA identifiers that
results in larger routing tables), or to create a two or more level
hierarchy (that results in smaller routing tables) in the SLA ID
field. The latter is shown as follows:

```
| n |   16-n    |              64 bits                 |
+-----+-----------+-------------------------------------+
|SLA1 |  Subnet   |           Interface ID              |
+-----+-----------+-------------------------------------+

      | m  |16-n-m |              64 bits                 |
      +----+-------+-------------------------------------+
      |SLA2|Subnet |           Interface ID              |
      +----+-------+-------------------------------------+
```

The approach chosen for structuring an SLA ID field is the
responsibility of the individual organization.
The number of subnets supported in this address format should be
sufficient for all but the largest of organizations. Organizations
which need additional subnets can arrange with the organization they
are obtaining Internet service from to obtain additional site
identifiers and use this to create additional subnets.

3.6 Interface ID

Interface identifiers are used to identify interfaces on a link.
They are required to be unique on that link. They may also be unique
over a broader scope. In many cases an interfaces identifier will be
the same or be based on the interface's link-layer address.
Interface IDs used in the aggregatable global unicast address format
are required to be 64 bits long and to be constructed in IEEE EUI-64
format [EUI-64]. These identifiers may have global scope when a
global token (e.g., IEEE 48bit MAC) is available or may have local
scope where a global token is not available (e.g., serial links,
tunnel end-points, etc.). The "u" bit (universal/local bit in IEEE
EUI-64 terminology) in the EUI-64 identifier must be set correctly,
as defined in [ARCH], to indicate global or local scope.

The procedures for creating EUI-64 based Interface Identifiers is
defined in [ARCH]. The details on forming interface identifiers is
defined in the appropriate "IPv6 over <link>" specification such as
"IPv6 over Ethernet" [ETHER], "IPv6 over FDDI" [FDDI], etc.

4.0 Technical Motivation

The design choices for the size of the fields in the aggregatable
address format were based on the need to meet a number of technical
requirements. These are described in the following paragraphs.

The size of the Top-Level Aggregation Identifier is 13 bits. This
allows for 8,192 TLA ID's. This size was chosen to insure that the
default-free routing table in top level routers in the Internet is

RFC 2374   IPv6 Global Unicast Address Format   July 1998

kept within the limits, with a reasonable margin, of the current
routing technology. The margin is important because default-free
routers will also carry a significant number of longer (i.e., more-
specific) prefixes for optimizing paths internal to a TLA and between
TLAs.

The important issue is not only the size of the default-free routing
table, but the complexity of the topology that determines the number
of copies of the default-free routes that a router must examine while
computing a forwarding table. Current practice with IPv4 it is
common to see a prefix announced fifteen times via different paths.

The complexity of Internet topology is very likely to increase in the
future. It is important that IPv6 default-free routing support
additional complexity as well as a considerably larger internet.

It should be noted for comparison that at the time of this writing
(spring, 1998) the IPv4 default-free routing table contains
approximately 50,000 prefixes. While this shows that it is possible
to support more routes than 8,192 it is matter of debate if the
number of prefixes supported today in IPv4 is already too high for
current routing technology. There are serious issues of route
stability as well as cases of providers not supporting all top level
prefixes. The technical requirement was to pick a TLA ID size that
was below, with a reasonable margin, what was being done with IPv4.

The choice of 13 bits for the TLA field was an engineering
compromise. Fewer bits would have been too small by not supporting
enough top level organizations. More bits would have exceeded what
can be reasonably accommodated, with a reasonable margin, with
current routing technology in order to deal with the issues described
in the previous paragraphs.

If in the future, routing technology improves to support a larger
number of top level routes in the default-free routing tables there
are two choices on how to increase the number TLA identifiers. The
first is to expand the TLA ID field into the reserved field. This
would increase the number of TLA ID's to approximately 2 million.
The second approach is to allocate another format prefix (FP) for use
with this address format. Either or a combination of these
approaches allows the number of TLA ID's to increase significantly.

The size of the Reserved field is 8 bits. This size was chosen to
allow significant growth of either the TLA ID and/or the NLA ID
fields.

The size of the Next-Level Aggregation Identifier field is 24 bits.

RFC 2374   IPv6 Global Unicast Address Format   July 1998

This allows for approximately sixteen million NLA ID's if used in a
flat manner. Used hierarchically it allows for a complexity roughly
equivalent to the IPv4 address space (assuming an average network
size of 254 interfaces). If in the future additional room for
complexity is needed in the NLA ID, this may be accommodated by
extending the NLA ID into the Reserved field.

The size of the Site-Level Aggregation Identifier field is 16 bits.
This supports 65,535 individual subnets per site. The design goal
for the size of this field was to be sufficient for all but the
largest of organizations. Organizations which need additional
subnets can arrange with the organization they are obtaining Internet
service from to obtain additional site identifiers and use this to
create additional subnets.

The Site-Level Aggregation Identifier field was given a fixed size in
order to force the length of all prefixes identifying a particular
site to be the same length (i.e., 48 bits). This facilitates
movement of sites in the topology (e.g., changing service providers
and multi-homing to multiple service providers).

The Interface ID Interface Identifier field is 64 bits. This size
was chosen to meet the requirement specified in [ARCH] to support
EUI-64 based Interface Identifiers.

5.0 Acknowledgments

The authors would like to express our thanks to Thomas Narten, Bob
Fink, Matt Crawford, Allison Mankin, Jim Bound, Christian Huitema,
Scott Bradner, Brian Carpenter, John Stewart, and Daniel Karrenberg
for their review and constructive comments.

6.0 References

[ALLOC]   IAB and IESG, "IPv6 Address Allocation Management",
          RFC 1881, December 1995.

[ARCH]   Hinden, R., "IP Version 6 Addressing Architecture",
          RFC 2373, July 1998.

[AUTH]   Atkinson, R., "IP Authentication Header", RFC 1826, August
          1995.

[AUTO]   Thompson, S., and T. Narten., "IPv6 Stateless Address
          Autoconfiguration", RFC 1971, August 1996.

[ETHER]   Crawford, M., "Transmission of IPv6 Packets over Ethernet
          Networks", Work in Progress.

RFC 2374   IPv6 Global Unicast Address Format   July 1998

[EUI64]   IEEE, "Guidelines for 64-bit Global Identifier (EUI-64)
           Registration Authority",
           http://standards.ieee.org/db/oui/tutorials/EUI64.html,
           March 1997.

[FDDI]   Crawford, M., "Transmission of IPv6 Packets over FDDI
           Networks", Work in Progress.

[IPV6]   Deering, S., and R. Hinden, "Internet Protocol, Version 6
           (IPv6) Specification", RFC 1883, December 1995.

[RFC2050] Hubbard, K., Kosters, M., Conrad, D., Karrenberg, D.,
           and J. Postel, "Internet Registry IP Allocation
           Guidelines", BCP 12, RFC 1466, November 1996.

[RFC2119] Bradner, S., "Key words for use in RFCs to Indicate
           Requirement Levels", BCP 14, RFC 2119, March 1997.

7.0 Security Considerations

IPv6 addressing documents do not have any direct impact on Internet
infrastructure security. Authentication of IPv6 packets is defined
in [AUTH].

8.0 Authors' Addresses

Robert M. Hinden
Nokia
232 Java Drive
Sunnyvale, CA 94089
USA

Phone: 1 408 990-2004
EMail: hinden@iprg.nokia.com

Mike O'Dell
UUNET Technologies, Inc.
3060 Williams Drive
Fairfax, VA 22030
USA

Phone: 1 703 206-5890
EMail: mo@uunet.uu.net

Stephen E. Deering
Cisco Systems, Inc.
170 West Tasman Drive
San Jose, CA 95134-1706
USA

Phone: 1 408 527-8213
EMail: deering@cisco.com

RFC 2374   IPv6 Global Unicast Address Format   July 1998

9.0 Full Copyright Statement

Index